Western Japaneseness
Intercultural Translations of Japan in Western Media

Edited by

Frank Jacob
Nord University, Norway

and

Bruno Surace
Università degli Studi di Torino, Italy

Series in Critical Media Studies

VERNON PRESS

www.vernonpress.com

In the Americas:	In the rest of the world:
Vernon Press	Vernon Press
1000 N West Street, Suite 1200	C/Sancti Espiritu 17,
Wilmington, Delaware, 19801	Malaga, 29006
United States	Spain

Series in Critical Media Studies

Library of Congress Control Number: 2020946404

ISBN: 978-1-64889-216-5

Also available: 978-1-64889-115-1 [Hardback]; 978-1-64889-154-0 [PDF, E-Book]

Cover design by Vernon Press using elements designed by Freepik.

Table of Contents

Western Japaneseness:
An Introduction

Frank Jacob

Nord University

and

Bruno Surace

Università degli Studi di Torino, Italy

Do you remember *The Simpsons* episode in which Japanese yakuza are shown interfering in a local conflict between Marge and her former associates about the selling of pretzels in Springfield?[1] They were introduced as "the poison fists of the Pacific Rim"[2] and nothing much else needed to be said, as the audience immediately realized that it was yakuza that were being shown in this scene. Homer had previously hired the Italian mob to secure Marge's business, but the response by her former business associates was not a retreat from but an internationalization of the involvement of organized crime. This little episode already shows that references to Japanese (popular) culture are often easily integrated into Western popular media and do not need a lot of introduction. Very often, the common stereotypes refer to sushi, *manga*, Ghibli *anime*,[3] the

---

[1] The Simpsons, season 8, episode 11, "The Twisted World of Marge Simpson," directed by Chuck Sheetz, written by Jennifer Crittenden, aired January 19, 1997.

[2] Hugo Dobson, "Mister Sparkle Meets the Yakuza: Depictions of Japan in The Simpsons," The Journal of Popular Culture 39, no. 1 (2006): 44-68.

[3] After the success of Miyazaki Hayao's Kaze no Tani no Naushika (Nausicaä of the Valley of the Wind) in 1984, the studio was founded one year later and has created tremendously popular animantion films (anime) ever since, including Sen to Chihiro no kamikakushi (Spirited Away, 2001) that received an Academy Award for Best Animated Feature. On the success story of anime in Japan in general, see Ian Condry, The Soul of Anime: Collaborative Creativity and Japan's Media Success Story (Durham, NC: Duke University Press, 2013). On the visual practices manga and anime refer to within the context of Japanese narrative traditions, see Stephan Köhn, Traditionen visuellen Erzählens in Japan: Eine paradigmatische Untersuchung der Entwicklungslinien vom Faltschirmbild zum narrativen Manga (Wiesbaden: Harrassowitz, 2005).

yakuza, Godzilla,[4] *Takeshi's Castle*,[5] cosplay,[6] or Japan's office workers. Regardless of their consistent appearance, the images that are supposedly Japanese in origin are very often just based on Western mainstream stereotypes about Japan and rarely deeply relate to accurate knowledge about the Far Eastern country's culture. What is displayed, and what the present volume intends to discuss in more detail, is a kind of Western Japaneseness. That means Western imaginations about Japan are displayed, especially in popular media, which address the preassumptions of the consumers rather than the cultural realities as they exist in Japan. What is consequently achieved is a construction of Japaneseness that is solely based on stereotypes and prejudices. It has to be highlighted here as well that being Japanese, like being Italian, German, etc., is imagined because many elements of Japanese culture have been imported from other Asian regions, especially from China. Nevertheless, there is a "cultural conglomerate," based on a set of values, traditions, self-perceptions, as well as identifications of Japaneseness by foreigners that creates the identity that is usually brought in connection with Japan. In a foreign and often Western context, what is supposed to be Japanese is similarly imagined, yet is considered, to refer to the present topic once more, by those who consume things, e.g., popular media, as something particularly Japanese.

The famous French semiotician Roland Barthes (1915-1980) visited Japan in the 1960s, and he would later describe his experiences in his *Empire of Signs*[7] in which the bodies of the Japanese create a larger union, a community that is very much defined by the signs that surround individuals.[8] The semiotics of Japan seemed to be quite different from those in the Western world, with other

---

[4] On Godzilla as a global icon of Japanese descent, see Frank Jacob, "From Tokyo's Destroyer to International Icon: Godzilla and Japanese Monstrosity in the Postwar Age," in All Around Monstrous: Monster Media in Their Historical Contexts, ed. Verena Bernardi and Frank Jacob (Wilmington, DE: Vernon Press, 2019), 211-244.

[5] Fūun! Takeshi-jō (Takeshi's Castle) was a popular game show broadcast in Japan between 1986 and 1989, hosted by Takeshi Kitano.

[6] A Japanese fan practice in which people dress up as characters from famous anime or manga. This cultural practice has also gained popularity in Europe and North America in the last two decades. Theresa Winge, "Costuming the Imagination: Origins of Anime and Manga Cosplay," Mechademia 1 (2006): 65-76.

[7] Roland Barthes, *L'Empire des signes* (Paris: Flammarion, 1966). For a discussion of Barthes' intercultural experiences in Japan, Antje Landmann, *Zeichenleere: Roland Barthes' interkultureller Dialog in Japan* (Munich: Iudicium, 2003) is recommended. On Barthes' theoretical concepts, see also Gianfranco Marrone, *Roland Barthes: Parole Chiave* (Rome: Carocci, 2016).

[8] Barthes, *L'Empire*, 133.

forms of traditional symbolism at work. An image of Mt. Fuji[9] evokes quite different feelings than it would for a Western spectator, appearing similar to a wave (Fig. X.1), as do other famous images like the "Dream of the Fisherman's Wife" (ca. 1814, Fig. X.2), depicted in an *ukiyo-e*[10] by Katsushika Hokusai (1760-1849).[11] The latter image reminds people of the famous Edo-period story about Princess Tamatori, a semiotic message or encoding that could only work in a Japanese context. In the West, an octopus raping a woman was and probably still would be considered some kind of perversion that originated in an artist's mind.

Fig. X.1: Hokusai: The Great Wave off Kanagawa

---

[9] Jocelyn Bouquillard, ed., *Hokusai: 36 Ansichten des Berges Fuji*, trans. Matthias Wolf (Munich: Schirmer Mosel, 2007).

[10] On Japanese woodblock prints (*ukiyo-e*) see, among others, Renée Violet, *Japanische Farbholzschnitte*, 2nd ed. (Leipzig: Insel Verlag, 1984); Museen der Stadt Regensburg, eds. *Ukiyo-E: Bilder der vergänglichen Welt* (Regensburg: Museen der Stadt Regensburg, 1990); Hans-Günther Schwarz, Geraldine Gutiérrez de Wienken, and Frieder Hepp, eds. *Schiffbrüche und Idyllen: Mensch, Natur und die vergängliche, fließende Welt (ukiyo-e) in Ost und West* (Munich: Iudicium, 2014).

[11] On Hokusai's life and work, see Nagata Seiji, *Hokusai* (Tokyo: Heibonsha, 1984); Edmond De Goncourt, *Hokusai* (New York: Parkstone International, 2014).

Fig. X.2: Hokusai: The Dream of the Fisherman's Wife.

Of course, the import of Japanese artworks, like the famous woodblock prints displayed during the first World Exhibition in Paris in 1855,[12] created a wave of influence from abroad, and a so-called "Japonisme" was reflected in Western and especially French art in the second half of the 19th century as well.[13] This was not the first time that images and stories were told about Japan, as they became more well-known due to the opening of the Asian country in 1853 by an American expedition, and the first diplomatic missions' reports provided many stories and determined stereotypes about the nation in the decades to come.[14] Already in the medieval age, stories about the island were spread in the

---

[12] Charles Robin, Histoire illustrée de l'Exposition universelle (Paris: Furne, 1855).

[13] Gabriel P. Weisberg et al., eds. *Japonisme: Japanese Influence on French Art, 1854-1910* (Cleveland, OH: Cleveland Museum of Art, 1975); Siegfried Wichmann, *Japonisme: The Japanese Influence on Western Art since 1858* (London: Thames and Hudson, 2007). On the influence of erotic woodblock prints (*shunga*) on Western art, see Ricard Bru, *Erotic Japonisme: The Influence of Japanese Sexual Imagery on Western Art* (Leiden: Hotei Publishing, 2014).

[14] On the Prussian expedition and the stereotypes it would later report with regard to Japan, Frank Jacob, "Die Eulenburg-Expedition — Preußische Direktheit trifft Japanische Zurückhaltung," in *Fremdbilder — Selbstbilder: Paradigmen japanisch-deutscher Wahrnehmung (1861-2011)*, ed. Stephan Köhn (Wiesbaden: Harrassowitz, 2013), 25-40 is

report given by Marco Polo (1254-1324), who had supposedly been in China where he had heard a lot about Japan.[15] Another wave of knowledge was provided by Portuguese traders and Jesuit missionaries[16] who had visited the East Asian region before Japan was eventually almost totally secluded from Western influence by Tokugawa Ieyasu in the early 1600s.[17]

When Japanese art and, later, popular media reached the West, it usually had some impact, similar to that which Western art or literature would have in the years following the opening of Japan as well.[18] Like the imports from abroad, Japanese exports also needed to be adjusted to the semiotic context and environment of Europe and North America. Famous films by Kurosawa Akira (1910-1998) would therefore be reproduced in a more suitable, i.e., sellable, fashion. *Seven Samurai* (1954) turned into the *Magnificent Seven* (1960), and Mifune Toshirō (1920-1997) in *Yojimbo* (1961)[19] turned into Clint Eastwood in *A Fistful of Dollars* (1964).[20]

When Japanese figures actually appeared in Western popular media throughout the 20th century, they often served to deliver a specific stereotype

---

recommended. Many early Western visitors would later publish their impressions of the Asian country as well. See, for example, Gustav Spiess, *Die preussische Expedition nach Ostasien während der Jahre 1860-1862. Reise-Skizzen aus Japan, China, Siam und der indischen Inselwelt* (Berlin: Otto Spamer, 1864).

[15] John Larner, *Marco Polo and the Discovery of the World* (New Haven, CT: Yale University Press, 1999).

[16] St. Francis Xavier, "Letter from Japan, to the Society of Jesus in Europe, 1552." Accessed March 22, 2020. https://my.tlu.edu/ICS/icsfs/EurosinAsiaSources9pg.pdf?target=f95413e2-209d-4e7f-a324-456e70da7a3d.

[17] Trade control and the prevention of an influx of Christian ideas were measures Tokugawa Ieyasu took to protect and strengthen his familiy's rule over Japan. For a more detailed discussion of these measures, see Frank Jacob, "Tokugawa Ieyasu, Reichseiniger, Shōgun oder Japans Diktator?" in *Diktaturen ohne Gewalt? Wie Diktatoren ihre Macht behaupten*, ed. Frank Jacob (Würzburg: Königshausen & Neumann, 2013), 79-102.

[18] For a detailed discussion of modern Japanese literature and the impact of Western knowledge and literature see the chapters in Frank Jacob, ed., *Critical Insights: Modern Japanese Literature* (Ipswich, MA: Salem Press, 2017).

[19] Charles Silver, "Akira Kurosawa's *Yojimbo*," *Inside/Out, a MOMA Blog*, September 10, 2013,
https://www.moma.org/explore/inside_out/2013/09/10/akira-kurosawas-yojimbo/

[20] For a detailed analysis of the adaptions from Japanese cinema within the American Western genre, see Kyle Keough, "Cowboys and Shoguns: The American Western, Japanese Jidaigeki, and Cross-Cultural Exchange," accessed March 20, 2020, https://digitalcommons.uri.edu/cgi/viewcontent.cgi?article=1109&context=srhonorsprog

related to Japan. What was thereby collectively created was what we refer to in the present volume as "Western Japaneseness." The chapters in this volume will highlight how images of Japan were constructed and used in modern Western popular media and give an insight into how far the entertainment industry is still using such artificial images when talking about presenting a foreign otherness.

The Contributions

Bruno Surace's chapter opens the volume by investigating the myth of Japan – a country visited every year by several million tourists, a number that is also constantly growing – as it is conveyed by the Western media, and then exploring the points of contact between an aesthetic of Japaneseness and various types of Western media products: cartoons, cinema forms, digital content, etc. The chapter highlights the mutual influences between the two contexts, often such as to generate real interpolations, which are heightened in the globalized world and its imaginaries.

Giacomo Calorio's chapter proceeds with an in-depth analysis dedicated to Japanese cinema. Nevertheless, the goal is not to present another history of Japanese cinema, but to develop a study on how Japanese cinema is received in the West in a cultural key. In this way, the processes of the dislocation and relocation of a distant cinema are explored in terms of their aesthetic mutations and shifts from one receptive context to another. These pages also take into account how the "J-pop" imaginary and the halo of *otherness* that is associated with it not only reverberate in contexts of close textual production, but also in a whole universe of urban life practices, treating the exchange of aesthetics from Japan to the West not only as being pertinent to films, books, and comics, but also as being capable of reconfiguring some ways of reading reality.

The reflection on cinema continues in the chapter by Remo Gramigna, which centers on Jim Jarmusch's film *Ghost Dog* (1999). Gramigna studies Jarmusch's film from a semiotic perspective as the fruit of a multifaceted syncretism: of inspiration, of genre, of form. The film thus becomes a laboratory for the author to verify a particular postmodern and transnational declination of the ancient code of the Samurai. The textual analysis provides meaningful data not only about the film, but also about a more general transcoding system from Japan to the West and back.

The chapter by Mattia Thibault is also configured in this direction, again starting from cinematographic cases, namely the animated film *Big Hero 6* (Don Hall and Chris Williams, 2014) and the television series *The Man in the*

High Castle (Frank Spotnitz, 2015-2019). The author specifically focuses on the representation in both these cases of a San Francisco imbued with Japaneseness, to the point of it being renamed San Fransokyo. The author's analysis extrapolates from the useful indicator texts in terms of real urban semiotics and culture, capable of accounting for the meaning of increasingly multicultural cities, where the dominant isotope is that of a fusion, a hybridization made of constant references to a Japanese aesthetic. The city therefore stands as a place for writing and reading relationships between distant cultures.

Frank Jacob's chapter continues the discourse on audiovisual media, focusing specifically on the 1980s television series *The Master* (Michael Sloan, 1984). This series is in fact the result of the era of the massive advent of Japanese characters in Western television and cinema, and the chapter detects stereotyping processes that the author identifies by focusing on the figure of the ninja as the result of a radical resemanticization in the transition from the Japanese context to the Western one.

Gianmarco Thierry Giuliana shifts the perspective further by focusing on *anime* and *manga*. For several decades, Japanese cartoons and comics have been, in an increasingly pervasive way, objects of Western fetishism, around which vast markets and imaginaries revolve. Giuliana thus proposes a rich exploration of the processes of contamination that underlie the production of *anime*, often already originally characterized by more or less immediately identifiable Western elements. The chapter is therefore configured as a complex work on the dynamics of intercultural translations from Japan to the West and vice versa, starting from the increasingly popular texts shared by both contexts.

Finally, the chapter by Juan Manuel Montoro extends the media overview by investigating the video game sphere using the case study of *Super Mario*, one of the most famous video game series in history. Montoro begins by providing a detailed definition of Japaneseness, which he then uses to study a relevant case of a product of Japanese origins with strong Western connotations (Mario is in fact an Italian plumber), and continues by studying the worldbuilding processes that have contributed to making it so iconic. The series and the brands that derive from it are analyzed in detail, with attention being paid at the same time to the internal mechanisms of the construction of the character and the world it inhabits and its forms of transmedia outsourcing.

A journey through various forms of media – cinema, TV, comics, video games, and digital media – and texts is thus proposed in this volume through a plurality of voices and approaches that share a vocation for the analysis of specific texts and, at the same time, a willingness to make these texts speak as bearers of values, imaginaries, and ideologies, deriving from their primary structure of intercultural translations what we have called "Western Japaneseness."

Works Cited

Barthes, Roland. _L'Empire des signes_. Paris: Flammarion, 1966.

Bouquillard, Jocelyn, ed. _Hokusai: 36 Ansichten des Berges Fuji_. Translated by Matthias Wolf. Munich: Schirmer Mosel, 2007.

Bru, Ricard. _Erotic Japonisme: The Influence of Japanese Sexual Imagery on Western Art_. Leiden: Hotei Publishing, 2014.

Condry, Ian. _The Soul of Anime: Collaborative Creativity and Japan's Media Success Story_. Durham, NC: Duke University Press, 2013.

De Goncourt, Edmond. _Hokusai_. New York: Parkstone International, 2014.

Dobson, Hugo. "Mister Sparkle Meets the Yakuza: Depictions of Japan in The Simpsons." _The Journal of Popular Culture_ 39, no. 1 (2006): 44-68.

Jacob, Frank, ed. _Critical Insights: Modern Japanese Literature_. Ipswich, MA: Salem Press, 2017.

———. "From Tokyo's Destroyer to International Icon: Godzilla and Japanese Monstrosity in the Postwar Age." In _All Around Monstrous: Monster Media in Their Historical Contexts_, edited by Verena Bernardi and Frank Jacob, 211-244. Wilmington, DE: Vernon Press, 2019.

———. "Die Eulenburg-Expedition — Preußische Direktheit trifft Japanische Zurückhaltung." In _Fremdbilder — Selbstbilder: Paradigmen japanisch-deutscher Wahrnehmung (1861-2011)_, edited by Stephan Köhn, 25-40. Wiesbaden: Harrassowitz, 2013.

———. "Tokugawa Ieyasu, Reichseiniger, Shōgun oder Japans Diktator?" In _Diktaturen ohne Gewalt? Wie Diktatoren ihre Macht behaupten_, edited by Frank Jacob, 79-102. Würzburg: Königshausen & Neumann, 2013.

Keough, Kyle. "Cowboys and Shoguns: The American Western, Japanese Jidaigeki, and Cross-Cultural Exchange." Accessed March 20, 2020. https://digitalcommons.uri.edu/cgi/viewcontent.cgi?article=1109&context=srhonorsprog.

Köhn, Stephan. _Traditionen visuellen Erzählens in Japan: Eine paradigmatische Untersuchung der Entwicklungslinien vom Faltschirmbild zum narrativen Manga_. Wiesbaden: Harrassowitz, 2005.

Landmann, Antje. _Zeichenleere: Roland Barthes' interkultureller Dialog in Japan_. Munich: Iudicium, 2003.

Larner, John. _Marco Polo and the Discovery of the World_. New Haven, CT: Yale University Press, 1999.

Marrone, Gianfranco. _Roland Barthes: Parole Chiave_. Rome: Carocci, 2016.

Museen der Stadt Regensburg, eds. _Ukiyo-E: Bilder der vergänglichen Welt_. Regensburg: Museen der Stadt Regensburg, 1990.

Robin, Charles. _Histoire illustrée de l'Exposition universelle_. Paris: Furne, 1855.

Schwarz, Hans-Günther, Geraldine Gutiérrez de Wienken, and Frieder Hepp, eds. *Schiffbrüche und Idyllen: Mensch, Natur und die vergängliche, fließende Welt (ukiyo-e) in Ost und West*. Munich: Iudicium, 2014.

Seiji, Nagata. *Hokusai*. Tokyo: Heibonsha, 1984.

Silver, Charles. "Akira Kurosawa's *Yojimbo*." *Inside/Out, a MOMA Blog*, September 10, 2013. https://www.moma.org/explore/inside_out/2013/09/10/akira-kurosawas-yojimbo/.

Spiess, Gustav. *Die preussische Expedition nach Ostasien während der Jahre 1860-1862. Reise-Skizzen aus Japan, China, Siam und der indischen Inselwelt.* Berlin: Otto Spamer, 1864.

St. Francis Xavier, "Letter from Japan, to the Society of Jesus in Europe, 1552." Accessed March 22, 2020. https://my.tlu.edu/ICS/icsfs/EurosinAsiaSources9pg.pdf?target=f95413e2-209d-4e7f-a324-456e70da7a3d.

Violet, Renée. *Japanische Farbholzschnitte*. 2nd ed. Leipzig: Insel Verlag, 1984.

Weisberg, Gabriel P. et al., eds. *Japonisme: Japanese Influence on French Art, 1854-1910*. Cleveland, OH: Cleveland Museum of Art, 1975.

Wichmann, Siegfried. *Japonisme: The Japanese Influence on Western Art since 1858*. London: Thames and Hudson, 2007.

Winge, Theresa. "Costuming the Imagination: Origins of Anime and Manga Cosplay." *Mechademia* 1 (2006): 65-76.

Films and TV Series

Kitano, Takeshi, dir. *Fūun! Takeshi-jō* (Takeshi's Castle). 1986-1989.

Miyazaki, Hayao, dir. *Kaze no Tani no Naushika* (Nausicaä of the Valley of the Wind). 1984.

———. *Sen to Chihiro no kamikakushi* (Spirited Away). 2001.

Sheetz, Chuck, dir. *The Simpsons*. Season 8, episode 11, "The Twisted World of Marge Simpson." Aired January 19, 1997.

Chapter 1

Big in Japan:
The Myth of Japan in
Western Audiovisual Media

Bruno Surace

University of Turin, Italy

Abstract

This chapter will take a closer look at the global spread of "Japaneseness" through anime and manga, but also leading to the global phenomenon of Pokémon, which has been on the crest of a wave for over twenty years, able to span various generations, pervasive, and crossmedial. The example of Pokémon will be useful for understanding a mixed imaginary, totally hybridized, in which components specifically drawn from the aesthetics of Japanese manga are fused with elements coming from other semiospheres. The chapter will then also take a look at the growing value of Japanese cinema in the West, concentrating initially on the direct relationship between the works of Yasujiro Ozu (1903-1963) and classic American cinema, and then on the importance of the "J-horror" genre in the definition of a globalized aesthetics of terror, and on the growing appreciation of the Japanese cinematographic context in the rest of the world.

Keywords: Pokémon, Japanese horror film, Yasujiro Ozu.

* * *

The Birth of a Myth

In 2017, as recorded by the UNWTO (United Nations World Tourism Organization), almost 30 million tourists visited Japan. This is an amazing amount of people, considering that Japan has approximately 127 million inhabitants and, above all, that only five years before there were around 20 million fewer tourists. Japan has become a mythical country, a land whose mixture of exoticism and familiarity induces an increasing number of people to visit it.[1] The forthcoming Tokyo 2021 Summer Olympics, projected as an event where Japanese imaginary – especially manga – and reality – the barnstormer athletes of the games – are completely fused, will presumably further increase these statistics.[2]

In the eyes of Westerners, for a series of reasons which will be investigated in this chapter and which are intimately interrelated with the global media system, today's Japan is not only a country in Eastern Asia like China, Malaysia, the Philippines, Laos, Cambodia, and many others.[3] It is also a symbolic place, deeply connected with an ensemble of beliefs and, often, stereotypes, conveyed by many texts which have been grafted onto Western media for decades. This diversified set of texts has created what Walter Lippman (1889-1974) called a pseudo-environment,[4] a widespread idea of Japan as a sort of fancy utopia, an island full of polite people, with a very fascinating traditional apparatus, reverberated in the iconic temples and beautiful landscapes of the rural part of the country, and most of all a place where magical creatures, like those from manga, dainty and whimsical food, and other wonders live in their authentic condition. It is not by chance that lots of people go to Japan in order to taste "original sushi," or to visit "real Buddhist temples," or to see the place where "authentic manga art" originated. These are all things, it must be said, which, however, were imported to Japan centuries ago, especially from China, but today are fully associated with Japan.[5]

---

[1] For a critical approach to the possible origins of this phenomenon, see Edward Said, *Orientalism* (New York: Vintage Books, 1979).

[2] The official website of the Olympic Games presents several images with the most iconic characters from *manga* and *anime*, utilized to sponsor the event, and the official mascots Miratowa and Someity are designed with the specific traits of Japanese cartoons.

[3] On the relationship between Western imaginaries and Japanese culture, see William M. Tsuitsui, "Soft Power and the Globalization of Japanese Popular Culture," in *Japan in the Age of Globalization*, ed. Carin Holroyd and Ken Coates (London: Routledge, 2011), 136-147.

[4] See Walter Lippman, *Public Opinion* (London: G. Allen & Unwin, 1929).

[5] On the deepening historical relationship between China and Japan, see Christopher Howe and Brian Hook, *China and Japan: History, Trends, and Prospects* (Oxford/New York: Oxford University Press, 1996); Michael Heazle and Nick Knight, eds., *China-Japan Relations in the Twenty-first Century* (Cheltenham/Northampton: Edward Elgar, 2007); Ryōsei Kokubun et al., *Japan-China Relations in the Modern Era* (London/New York: Routledge, 2017).

The influential tourist guide *Lonely Planet* describes Japan in the following way: "Japan is a world apart – a cultural Galápagos where a unique civilization blossomed, and thrives today in delicious contrasts of traditional and modern. The Japanese spirit is strong, warm and incredibly welcoming."[6] As Italian Japanese Studies researcher Paolo Barbaro sustains, these few words contain three "mythological tales at the foundation of Japanese identity …: the clear proposition of the very fortunate but totally groundless ideology which postulates the existence of an ethnic-national spirit; the modern/ancient dichotomy; the myth – historically baseless – of the seclusion that is supposed to have generated … a race distinct from all others."[7]

What is extremely important in Japanese tourism is therefore the phase of *Imaginary Japan*, as Arthur Asa Berger calls it in his ethno-semiotic analysis of tourism in the country, "the imagined or pre-visualized trip,"[8] which will be juxtaposed with the third phase, the post-trip memories referred to as *Remembered Japan*, "the recollected trip, via journals, postcards, photographs, videos and souvenirs."[9] *Imaginary Japan* is, by definition, an idea of Japan as a collection of stereotypes, neither necessarily positive nor negative, but based on the meta-myth of *alterity*,[10] taken from several texts, which configurate the country as a land of myth.

Our purpose in this introductory text is, therefore, to explore how this meta-myth is constructed, by means of certain media products which are in some way seminal on account of their diffusion in the West. Our interest is not so much the presence of Japan in Western media as, rather, the spread of a certain "Japaneseness," that is, a series of features which contribute to defining those specific atmospheres which underlie the great success of the imaginary of Japan. For this reason, we will initially concentrate on manga and anime, which do not simply constitute fads but extremely varied and complex semiotic

---

[6] Chris Rowthorn and Ray Bartlett, eds., *Lonely Planet Japan* (Melbourne: Lonely Planet Publications, 2015), 17.

[7] Paola Barbaro, "Dicotomie identitarie: l'immaginario del Giappone nelle rappresentazioni turistiche occidentali," *Lingue Culture Mediazioni – Languages Cultures Mediation* 380 (2013): 46. My translation.

[8] Arthur Asa Berger, *Tourism in Japan: An Ethnosemiotic Analysis* (Bristol / Buffalo / Toronto: Channel View Publications, 2010), 10.

[9] Ibid.

[10] Marco Pellitteri, *Il drago e la saetta: Modelli, strategie e identità dell'immaginario giapponese* (Latina: Tunué, 2008), 527.

phenomena, and on their reciprocal hybridization with the tradition of the Western comic.

> At first sight it seems like just another *made in Japan* fad... In reality we believe that familiarity with this particular type of comic condenses numerous qualifying characteristics of the *cult:* the peripheral origins in relation to the big mass trends, the product as a solidifier or catalyst of behaviors of attachment, the circuit of meaning which presents itself as a system of heterogeneity around the central body represented by the product itself, the arcane nature, mysterious and not very transparent, of the characters, customs, languages and artifacts represented and of the graphic cut of the images, and finally the presence of "tribes" of enthusiasts who turn the object into an opportunity for forms of ritual collective behavior.[11]

The exploration of the universe of manga and anime will lead us to launch the hypothesis of a branch of studies entirely devoted to the global phenomenon of Pokémon, which has been on the crest of a wave for over twenty years, able to span various generations, pervasive and crossmedial. For our purposes, the example of Pokémon will be useful for understanding a mixed imaginary, totally hybridized, in which components specifically drawn from the aesthetics of Japanese manga are fused with elements coming from other semiospheres, generating a real "epidemic of the imaginary."[12]

Thereafter we will address the growing value of Japanese cinema in the West, concentrating initially on the direct relationship between the works of Yasujiro Ozu (1903-1963) and classic American cinema, and then on the importance of the "J-horror" genre in the definition of a globalized aesthetics of terror, and on the growing appreciation of the Japanese cinematographic context in the rest of the world, such that it gave rise from the Eighties on to the massive production of films with more or less explicit references to a Japan that was more imagined than real.

Finally, we will devote a section to the transliteration of the protocols of Japan-West hybridization from traditional media to new media, with a glance at the activities of certain Italian YouTubers and vloggers who, in the wake of a

---

[11] Fulvio Carmagnola and Mauro Ferraresi, *Merci di culto: Ipermerce e società mediale* (Rome: Castelvecchi, 1999), 189. My translation.
[12] The reference is to the particularly effective Italian translation of the title of Slavoj Žižek's book *The Plague of Fantasies* (London: Verso, 1999).

trend which continues to be all the rage, exploit the appeal of Japaneseness to produce *ad hoc* content based on the Japanese imaginary in the West.

Comics Meet Manga

The universe of manga, and consequently that of anime, constitute an expansive and extraordinarily rich pool of texts, both from an artistic and a narrative perspective. Dozens of genres and subgenres (starting from the macro-categories of *kodomo*, *shōjo-josei*, *shōnen-seinen*, and *seinen-josei*) articulate a complex semiosphere where values and meaning circulate from the drawings of graphic artists to the minds of millions of readers and spectators. Not only Japanese readers, but people from all over the world. Manga is able to create a deep culture, which continues to expand.[13]

Although the origin of Western comics is of course situated in a pre-modern era, officially around 1895 with the *Yellow Kid* character by Richard Felton Outcault (1863-1928) but traceable in a history of illustrations – characterized by a sort of pre-cinematographic ideal editing – from Egyptian papyrus to medieval miniatures, from monastic illustrations to the *Histoire de M. Vieux Bois* by Swiss author Rodolphe Töpffer (1799-1846),[14] the age of the canonization of comics as an autonomous form of expression is certainly the 20th century.[15] This was the period when the market in comics boomed, starting in the US and defining one of the most persistent post-modern myths: that of the superhero.[16] Superheroes are the highest common denominator in the history of classic comics, together with another current which is related to the Disney comics style. Today, Spiderman and his colleagues, gathered in the so-called Marvel Cinematic Universe, and Batman and his associates, in the similar ensemble called the DC Universe, are able to create strong fandoms and an immense circulation of money. But who are the superheroes? They are men or women who defeat despicable villains, helped by some kinds of superpowers, from the most codified (flying, hyper-strength, invisibility) to the most peculiar (shooting deadly rays from their eyes, pausing time, and so on). Superman is, in this multi-colored panorama, the first archetype, who defines

---

[13] See, for example, Jacqueline Berndt and Bettina Kümmerling-Meibauer, eds., *Manga's Cultural Crossroads* (New York/London: Routledge, 2013).

[14] Rodolphe Töpffer, *Histoire de Mr. Vieux Bois* (Geneva: Cherbuliez, 1833).

[15] See, for example, Susan Doyle, Jaleen Grove, and Whitney Sherman, *History of Illustration* (New York: Fairchild Books, 2018).

[16] On the post-modern myths, see Peppino Ortoleva, *Miti a bassa intensità: Racconti, media, vita quotidiana* (Turin: Einaudi, 2019).

the *tòpoi* related to the superhero: a man, with human sentiments, but also something more than a man (he comes from another planet), who is able to fly, incredibly strong, and summoned to fight against terrible threats that could destroy the whole of mankind, and perhaps the entire universe.

This portrait is incredibly analogous to that of Son Goku, the hero of *Dragon Ball*,[17] one of the most famous manga and anime characters of all time: a human but a non-human, coming from another planet, who flies, has immense power, and fights in order to save the Earth and the universe from dangerous, evil creatures. Like Superman, he was rescued by kind people after being left on the Earth by his family. Son Goku, born from the pen of Toriyama Akira, and Superman, created by Jerry Siegel (1914-1996) and Joe Shuster (1914-1992), are the ideal brothers who represent a   cultural intersection in the era of the internet, manifested by the thousands of fanworks that see them together. Moreover, the two superheroes, whose individual traits reflect their countries of origin, on the one side tights and a red mantle, on the other an orange karate suit, reflect the crosscultural fascination with figures who represent Good and who are gifted with magnificent skills. The roots of *Dragon Ball* stories are in fact both *Journey to the West*, an ancient Chinese tale about the "Monkey King," and *Superman*.[18] These dual and geographically antipodal references convey the idea of how the exoticism usually associated with Japan is not a uni-directional process, but is organized in a mutual exchange of seminal figures, values, aesthetics. What Mark I. West calls the "Japanification of ... popular culture"[19] in the West is also the "Westernization of popular culture" in the East.

Westerners' fascination with Japan is, in other words, a sort of mirror-like operation, which serves also to confirm their identity, by looking at myths that are already the result of a hybridization. In the case of *Dragon Ball* this is glaring, but it is also found in other forms of expression, such as the cinema of one of the most famous Japanese directors of all time: Ozu Yasujirō. We will come back to this pre-eminent figure later, but now we will continue our brief exploration of the mutual contamination between Western and Japanese culture through manga and comics by moving our gaze to other emblematic

---

[17] For a semiotic approach to *Dragon Ball*, see Vincenzo Idone Cassone, "'It's Over 9000!!!' Apeiron Narrative Configurations in Contemporary Mediascape," *Digital Age in Semiotics and Communication* 1, no. 1 (2018): 79-94.

[18] Brian Camp and Julie Davis, *Anime Classics Zettai! 100 Must-See Japanese Animation Masterpieces* (Berkeley, CA: Stone Bridge Press, 2007).

[19] Mark I. West, *The Japanification of Children's Popular Culture. From Godzilla to Miyazaki* (Lanham, MD/Toronto/Plymouth: The Scarecrow Press, 2009).

examples. *Detective Conan*, a very well known manga and anime by Aoyama Gōshō, is clearly inspired by Arthur Conan Doyle's (1859-1930) Sherlock Holmes, with the addition of some engaging features from *shōjo* manga, for instance, the emphasized teenage dimension and the troubled love story between the protagonist and his female counterpart Ran, and from *shōnen manga*, like the insertion of highly technological instruments. These narrative components occupy a prominent position in the diegetic architecture of the text, together with the detective stories, while in Sherlock Holmes' adventures, although present (think of the character of Irene Adler or the ability of the detective to utilize tools in a futuristic way), they are somehow subservient to the investigations. So, semiotically, *Detective Conan* is an operation of intersemiotic translation,[20] which triggers – technically, *pertinentizes* – some of the traits partially dormant in the original text, and in the meanwhile narcotizes certain others. This is an operation that shares some instances with *Dragon Ball* as a cultural redefinition and a kind of adjusted translation of *Superman*, although in the latter case, the translation appears situated on a different level. Basically the axiologies remain the same (while in *Detective Conan* it is possible to perceive a light *décalage* due to its emphasis on the dimension of youth); the most significative shift is in the more superficial, in Greimasian terms, level of spatialization: whereas Superman lives in Metropolis, a typical US-like megalopolis, and experiences the problems of sophisticated life, Son Goku inhabits a strange world where very pre-historical elements – such as the presence of dinosaur-like monsters – live in an ultra-technological society, far from the protagonist's personality, which remains pure and genuine from childhood to adulthood like a sort of *noble savage*. Substantially what changes most between the two interrelated texts are the semantic components which enrich the settings and contribute, together with the axiological level, to defining two different aesthetics, equally exotic and specular. Analogous considerations could be made about the relationship between *Slam Dunk* by Inoue Takehiko and the NBA mythology in the US, or about *One Piece* by Oda Eiichirō and the tales of Caribbean pirates, or about the anime *Heidi* by Takahata Isao (1935-2018), which is the translation of the novel by the Swiss author Johanna Spyri (1827-1901), or *Lady Oscar* by Ikeda Riyoko, the epic and tough life story of Oscar François de Jarjayes at the Versailles court during the Ancien Régime.

These last two cases are truly symbolic of an interest in Western culture on the part of Japanese people. *Heidi* is, to all effects, an animated series totally

---

[20] See Roman Jakobson, *Essais de linguistique Générale* (Paris: Editions de Minuit, 1963).

free from Japanese influences on the diegetic level. The story is set in the Swiss Alps and is configurated as a sort of *Bildungsroman*, full of atmospheres which are somehow reminiscent of Edmondo De Amicis' (1846-1908) *Cuore* (1886) ideology,[21] mixed with rural adventures. What is Japanese in *Heidi* is the visual style, which corresponds to the Japanese animation of the second part of the 20th century. In *Lady Oscar*, similarly, there are no explicit references to Japan, but some thematic roles are more easily amenable to the manga semiosphere, for example, certain emotional affectations, and the clearly Japanese "big-eye style," once again, in its turn, already the fruit of a cultural exchange of the West-East kind, starting from Western models like Betty Boop (1930) and Felix the Cat (1919).[22] The intimate connection between these texts, as well as others like *Anne of Green Gables* (Takahata Isao, based on the homonymous novel by Lucy Maud Montgomery, 1874-1942), *Belle and Sebastian* (inspired by Cécile Aubry, 1928-2010) or *Remi* (by Hector Malot, 1830-1907), and a certain US-European culture is such that several Western viewers in the past testified to having felt a strong sensation of familiarity when watching them,[23] as if they had actually been realized in their country of origin: "the most interesting aspect of anime and manga is the extent to which they are able to blur cultural origin and loosen the requirements of cultural representation."[24]

In this dappled scenario of hybridizations and contaminations, a peculiar case of global phenomenon stands out, which properly manifests the post-modern nature of the reciprocal grafting between Japan and the West. The Pokémon brand, initially born as a video game by Tajiri Satoshi in 1996, is the perfect realization of the "Americanization of Japanization,"[25] or, similarly, of

---

[21] See Pino Boero and Giovanni Veronesi, *Cuore: De Amicis tra critica e utopia* (Milan: Franco Angeli, 2009).

[22] Anne Cooper-Chen, *Cartoon Cultures: The Globalization of Japanese Popular Media* (New York: Peter Lang, 2010), 26. See also Pellitteri, *Il drago e la saetta*, 417.

[23] We are dealing with an era without internet connections and at the beginning of globalization, when people usually acquired knowledge through traditional mass media.

[24] Fabienne Darling-Wolf, *Imagining the Global: Transnational Media and Popular Culture Beyond East and West* (Ann Arbor, MI: University of Michigan Press, 2015), 121. In the chapter "What West Is It? Anime and Manga according to Candy and Goldorak," Darling-Wolf collects some interviews from viewers of *Heidi*: "*Heidi*, it was – quote unquote – 'our mountains'" (42-year-old woman) or "*Heidi* it was for me, so faithful to our own lives, I mean for me, I lived in the Alps, in the mountains, it was so faithful to the Alps, the Alpine pasture" (32-year-old woman)."

[25] Kōichi Iwabuchi, *Recentering Globalization: Popular Culture and Japanese Transnationalism* (Durham, NC/London: Duke University Press, 2002), 38.

the "Orientalized West."[26] Although the origin of this brand was formulated on very codified Japanese values and style, i.e., a certain interest in monstrous creatures and the emphasis on child-teenager characters who live incredible adventures in a context where nature and hyper-technology are fully harmonized (which were, however, already the result of a millenary history of mercantile and, above all, cultural exchanges), the success of the "pocket monsters" immediately boomed around the world through a complex and stratified apparatus of video games, action figures, animated series, collectible cards, up to the recent success of the augmented reality game for smartphones *Pokémon Go* and the pairs of games (in order to re-evoke the tradition of the first video games, which were usually released in pairs) for the Nintendo Switch console, *Pokémon Let's go Pikachu* and *Pokémon Let's go Eevee*, and *Pokémon Sword* and *Pokémon Shield*. As I have already outlined elsewhere, the global success of this brand, which in a certain way betrays the idea of Japanese people as intrinsic nationalists,[27] can be explained with the help of some semiotic concepts:

> Pokémons, even if they were born in a specific historic-cultural Japanese context, are built starting from a series of narrative patterns which are typical of the culture of the so-called "global village." These patterns are easy to export because of their permeability to almost every culture, and it is Anne Allison who identifies the two principal ones: firstly, "cuteness as a national export and cultural capital," which takes advantage of a "universal appeal" and, secondly, the narrative structure whereby the exportation of a single Pokémon involves a trail of constructions that gravitate around it, configuring the exportation of the world itself, which can be actorialized and spatialized with the values of the receiving culture. … Indeed the Pokémon world, be it placed in Japan or exported to Italy, Canada or Nigeria, is dynamized through the implementation of a society where some fundamental rules are applied, whose principal commandment, which also topicalizes the title of the series and which

---

[26] Toshio Miyake, *Occidentalismi: la narrativa storica giapponese* (Venice: Cafoscarina, 2010).

[27] "As 'Japanese' *Transformers* was a regional success story in opposition to the media barrage of American and Western cultural imperialism." Derek Johnson, *Media Franchising: Creative License and Collaboration in the Culture Industries* (New York/London: New York University Press, 2013), 187.

is the primary objective of all Pokémon videogames, is: "Gotta catch 'em all!"[28]

These are the reasons why Pokémon are often utilized out of their "natural" environment, as for example happens with the minigame *Pokémon Black and Blue*, developed for proselytistic reasons by PETA (People for the Ethical Treatment of Animals), which capsizes the axiology contained in the slogan "Gotta catch 'em all!" into the reverse formula "Gotta free 'em all," while maintaining very firmly the main values related to the intrinsic cuteness of the little "animaloids": "It must be pointed out that *Pokémon Black and Blue* is not the only example of exploitation of fiction on the part of PETA in order to convey the 'animal rights message.' Reality and fiction, joined by the thread of extremeness, frequently share the same ideal of battle against the injustices perpetrated by those who ill-treat animals or animaloids."[29]

The pervasiveness of the Pokémon brand and its permeability and adaptivity to every context, as well as the nostalgia effect it produces in the older generations while inculcating an unprecedented fascination in the younger ones, makes Pokémon a strong cultural ecosystem, which deserves to be systematized by proper studies, both cultural and semiotic: "Though Pokémon was originally designed to target young Japanese boys, its double nature of intimacies and cooperation along with its goal of continual accumulation and acquisition (which somewhat parallel the Western capitalistic ethos) has allowed it to dominate both Asian and Western global culture."[30]

Cinematic Japaneseness

Cinema deserves a special mention in this brief reconnaissance of the textualities that trace some of the symbolic features of Japanese-Western "brotherhood." Nowadays, Asian cinema, especially from Japan, is well known in Western countries and generates niches of enthusiasts. These admirers can

---

[28] Bruno Surace, "Zoosemiotica dei Pokémon," in *Zoosemiotica 2.0. Forme e politiche dell'animalità*, ed. Gianfranco Marrone (Palermo: Edizioni Museo Pasqualino, 2017), 609-610. My translation.

[29] Bruno Surace, "Pokémon and the PETA: Viral Extremeness as a Semiotic Strategy," in *Virality and Morphogenesis of Right-Wing Internet Populism*, ed. Eva Kimminich, Julius Erdmann, and Amir Dizdarević (Berlin: Peter Lang, 2018), 158.

[30] Anthony Y. H. Fung, *Asian Popular Culture: The Global (Dis)continuity* (London/New York: Routledge, 2013), 13. See also Martin Lister et al., *New Media: A Critical Introduction* (London/New York: Routledge, 2003), 293.

gather, for example, at important film festivals such as the Far East Film Festival (FEFF), which is held every year in Udine, Italy, and together watch the latest films by Kore'eda Hirokazu, Sono Sion, Tsukamoto Shin'ya, Nakata Hideo, Miike Takashi, Kitano Takeshi, and many others, all names that are highly appreciated in the West: Hayao Miyazaki and Studio Ghibli's products, memorable directors like Kurosawa Akira (1910-1998), Mizoguchi Kenji (1898-1956), Fukasaku Kinji (1930-2003),[31] and so on up to Ozu Yasujirō (1903-1963), rightly considered not only probably the most important director in the history of Japanese cinema, but also one of the most important in the *entire* history of cinema.[32]

Founder of a poetic of the filmic image where stylistic components are fused with a wide-ranging artistic vision of the relation between nature and culture, in Ozu's cinema, lots of autochthonous codified genres are interpolated, as happens with *gakusei mono* (student life-based movies), *ero guro nansensu* (grotesque films with erotic background gags), and primarily *shomin-geki* (realist movies about common people) and *sararimen eiga* (movies about the life of office workers). Nevertheless, in this very Japanese context, the Western presence manifests itself prominently.

Ozu, who crossed all the principal stages of the twentieth-century history of cinema, from silent to sound, from black-and-white to color, was a true cinephile, captivated by Hollywood movies and directors, especially the genres and topics developed in or related to the West, such as comedy and the comic, melodrama deriving from the European *melò*, the gangster movie and the movie based on social issues. This is of course related also to the historical phase in which Ozu lived, made up of a juxtaposition between an authoritarian regime and strong Westernalization processes in Japan. So in Ozu's movies, it is common to see, more or less disguised and more or less parodic, references to the Western cinema or to specific Hollywood movies, more manifestly in some pseudo-remakes: *Tōkyō no onna* (1933) contains an explicit revisiting of *If I Had a Million*, a movie by Ernst Lubitsch (1892-1947) in 1932, and sometimes it is

---

[31] An excellent introduction to Japanese cinema, both from a historical and from a stylistic point of view, is provided in Joseph L. Anderson and Donald Richie, *The Japanese Film: Art and Industry* (Princeton, NJ: Princeton University Press, 1982). For a more recent overview, see Yomota Inuhiko, *What is Japanese Cinema? A History* (New York: Columbia University Press, 2019).

[32] For further information about this director, see Dario Tomasi, *Ozu Yasujiro* (Turin: Lindau, 1996), the volume from which the material concerning him supplied in the text has been drawn.

possible to identify in the comic movies an out-and-out parallelism with Charlie Chaplin (1889-1977) or Buster Keaton's (1895-1966) slapstick comicality.

At the same time, Western cinema manifests several contributions from Japanese movies, both in terms of themes and narrative archetypes and of formal components. These relations, previously usually hidden under the filmic image (except for rare cases of explicit reference), are proudly displayed in the phase of post-modern cinema in the awareness that contemporary audiences are thrilled by the exotic that becomes familiar and by their manifest quotation. This is one of the reasons for the global success of *Kill Bill*, the pair of movies shot by Quentin Tarantino in 2003 and based on a story of revenge where the US and Japan clash in a new aesthetics, where Western archetypes and kung fu, but also live-action sequences and anime, live together.[33]

Similarly, in the same years, "J-horror" – the way in which non-Japanese people refer to Japanese horror movies – arrived in the West in the form of remakes. The most iconic cases are certainly *The Ring* (Gore Verbinski, 2002),[34] an adaptation of *Ringu* (1998) by Hideo Nakata which was itself the intersemiotic translation of a 1991 novel by Suzuki Kōji, and *The Grudge*, which is an interesting case of an overseas remake realized by the same director who made the original. Shimizu Takashi, in fact, who had already directed *Juon* in 2000 (as well as another movie with the same title in 2002, because the first one circulated only on the home video market), decided in 2004 to direct the American remake, working with the famous actress Sarah Michelle Gellar, well-known because of her lead role in the TV series *Buffy the Vampire Slayer* and so already sutured to an exoteric imaginary. This operation of a remake by the same director is unique in the case of J-horror and very rare in connection with Japanese directors; other examples are *The Burmese Harp*, made in 1956 and subsequently remade in 1985 as *Biruma no tategoto* by Ichikawa Kon (1915-2008), Inagaki Hiroshi's (1905-1980) *Muhomatsu no issho* (1943), remade by him in color in 1958, and Ozu's pair of films *A Story of Floating Weeds* (1934 and 1959). Of these, only *Biruma no tategoto*, presented in Venice in 1984, was probably made with the partial intention of translating it for a Western audience. *The Grudge* thus represents today a *unicum*, because of the clear will of its director to export it to the West.

---

[33] See for example Leon Hunt and Leung Wing-Fai, *East Asian Cinemas: Exploring Transnational Connections on Film* (New York: I.B. Tauris, 2011).

[34] Colette Balmain, *Introduction to Japanese Horror Film* (Edinburgh: Edinburgh University Press, 2008), 2.

J-horror became a golden seam in the years after 2000, mined by lots of Western directors and scriptwriters. The theme of demonic or cursed children with all the restlessness they convey started to appear on the cinematic agenda.[35] Nevertheless, it must be said, once again, that this horror trend, although springing from Japan, was in its turn more ancient, and already the result of contamination which can be traced, for example, in the very Western *The Exorcist* (William Friedkin, 1973), where a child is the incubator of evil, or similarly in *Rosemary's Baby* (Roman Polański, 1968). Japanese audiences, in fact, after the Second World War "showed an increasing interest in Western (horror) movies," and turned the classic Japanese ghost story, called *kaidan*, mixed with urban legends which sounded like "true ghost stories" (*shinrei jitsuwa*), into movies based on "horrific creatures of Western origin, such as monsters, vampires and serial killers."[36] This mutual relationship, whose origin is difficult to trace through philology because of the sort of universality of the underlying issues of fear and horror, shows us once again how Japanese and Western stylemes and themes are intertwined, and how J-horror is not a manifestation of a pure part of Japanese culture, nor something *authentic* (a notion which is truly problematic), but rather a manifestation of a codified but mercurial Japaneseness, as the scriptwriter of *Ringu* affirmed in an interview about the genealogy of J-horror: "In my movies ... this [taste for true ghost stories] was well received in America and Europe. ... That kind of expression became popular overseas. I think it was interpreted as the 'Japanese taste' and spread as 'J-horror,' but we don't think of it as 'Japanese' by any means. On the contrary, this type of 'true ghost story' was first done in British ghost movies and American ghost movies...."[37]

---

[35] On the cinematic relationship between children and evil, see Bruno Surace, "Baby Simulacra: Semiotica dei cuccioli al cinema come incubatori di assiologie," in "Cuccioli, pets e altre carinerie," ed. Francesco Mangiapane, special issue, *E|C – Rivista online dell'AISS. Associazione italiana di studi semiotici* 22 (2018), http://www.ec-aiss.it/monografici/22_cuccioli.php.

[36] Elisabeth Scherer, "Well-Traveled Female Avengers: The Transcultural Potential of Japenese Ghosts," in *Ghost Movies in Southeast Asia and Beyond: Narrative, Cultural Contexts, Audiences*, ed. Peter J. Bräunlein and Andrea Lauser (Leiden: Brill, 2016), 69. See also Kitajima Akihiro, "Nihon kaidan eiga no shuyaku wa yūrei, yōkaitachi" [The Protagonists of kaidan Films are yūrei and yōkai], in *Nihon kyōfu (horā) eiga e no shōtai* [Invitation to Japanese Horror Films], ed. Haraguchi Tomo'o and Murata Hideki (Tokyo: Heibonsha, 2000), 25.

[37] Takahashi Hiroshi, "Interview with Producer Hiroshi Takahashi," *Marebito*, directed by Shimizu Takashi (2004), subtitled DVD (Los Angeles, CA: Tartan Video, 2006), translation

Thus the result of this continuous cultural exchange, which is somehow the genetic functioning of culture made clear in the era of globalization, is a juxtaposition between an idea of authenticity, which is a concept that displays its strength on an ideological level while being very difficult to place on an ontological one (in simple terms: it is not possible to establish what is authentic and what is not), and a series of stereotypes and other cultural deposits. Sushi, for example, a dish which is traditionally thought of as Japanese, is nowadays eaten by people all over the world and has become the *escamotage* for making movies such as *Sushi Girl* (Kern Saxton, 2012), an American thriller film based on "body sushi" (*nyotaimori*), the practice of eating sushi on the naked body of a beautiful woman, mentioned in the movie principally for its exotic extravagance.[38] The brand *Teenage Mutant Ninja Turtles*, very famous from the mid-1980s, transliterates an alleged ninja and zen culture into a trash story of giant warrior turtles who love eating pizza and are trained by a huge sewer rat. *The Karate Kid* cinematographic series, starting in 1984 with the movie directed by John G. Avildsen (1935-2017), rode on the increasing success of martial arts movies. *Transformers*, an American animated series of the 1980s and then a toy brand and a successful cinematographic series of blockbusters by Michael Bay, is certainly indebted to the Japanese robotic aesthetics of *Great Mazinger* (Go Nagai, 1974) and similar works. And analogous considerations could be made in regard to Steven Spielberg's *Jurassic Park* (1993), based on a diffuse dinosaur craze, and the infinite series of *Godzilla*-based texts.[39]

If in the years preceding the turn of this century, when post-modernism was certainly already *in auge* but without that widespread sense of irony which is typical of contemporaneity, the exchange of values, form, and diegetic patterns

---

taken from Steven T. Brown, *Japanese Horror and the Transnational Cinema of Sensations* (Cham: Palgrave Macmillan, 2018), 3-4.

[38] Elisa Gasti and Bruno Surace, "Immaginari del cibo, cibi dell'immaginario: Riflessioni semiotiche attorno alla rappresentazione cinematografica del sushi," in "Cibo e identità culturale," ed. Simona Stano, special issue, *Lexia* 19-20 (2016): 299-310. For a semiotic overview of the relationship between Japanese food and alterity, see also Simona Stano, *Eating the Other: Translations of the Culinary Code* (Newcastle upon Tyne: Cambridge Scholars Publishing, 2015).

[39] The relationship between the two texts is moreover proven by the fact that these stories are connected to several other films or TV shows, such as *The Return of Ultraman* (1971), whose storyline was written by Shinichiro Kobayachi, related to the *Godzilla* series. Justin Mullis, "Notes from the Land of Light: Observations on Religious Elements in *Ultraman*," in *Essays on Kaiju and American Popular Culture*, ed. Camille D. G. Mustachio and Jason Barr (Jefferson: McFarland & Company, 2017), 42.

between Japan and the US was maintained at a serious level, today the sclerotization of the media system through new media (just think of phenomena like internet memes, true ferrymen of instantaneous contents around the world)[40] and the rise of a new aesthetics based on the absurd for its own sake, generate interesting new products. *Thermae Romae* is absolutely one of them. Born in 2008 as a manga by Yamazaki Mari and then becoming a pair of films by Takeuchi Hideki in 2012 and 2014, it tells the story of Lucius Modestus, an architect living in 135 CE in ancient Rome, who, due to a space-time warp, ends up in contemporary Japan, where he learns the art of modern thermal baths. As Luciana Cardi writes:

> rather than the love story between Lucius and a Japanese woman, the principal element which is the basis of the success of the manga [and of the film] is the modality through which Japan and ancient Rome are represented and relate to each other. In fact, going through a series of filters, Japanese contemporaneity and Roman antiquity are specularly opposed, until one becomes the reflection of the other.[41]

Vlogging in Japan

Favij, St3pNy, Anima, Surry, LaSabri, Matt & Bise, Jack Nobile … These are the names of some of the most followed YouTubers in Italy, with channels that record millions of views and have vast communities of fans. They certainly have something in common because they are young and specialized in creating entertaining content, usually targeted at very young users (mostly children), they create and follow the most significant trends of the moment in the web sphere, and sometimes they collaborate in order to help one another grow in terms of notoriety. Nonetheless, each of them has created a strong personal identity, not so easy to mistake. What is interesting to notice is that despite their differences, all these personages have created vlogs (a crasis of video and blog) in Japan, as has PewDiePie (1989), the most popular YouTuber in the world with over 100 million subscribers, contributing to the increase in interest in this land. And, of course, on the other side, these names, like many others,

---

[40] Gabriele Marino, "Semiotics of Spreadability: A Systematic Approach to Internet Memes and Virality," *Punctum* 1, no. 1 (2015): 43-66.

[41] Luciana Cardi, "Riconfigurazioni dell'antica Roma nel manga *Thermae Romae* e nei suoi adattamenti cinematografici," in *Riflessioni sul Giappone antico e moderno*, vol. II, ed. Maria Chiara Migliore, Antonio Manieri, and Stefano Romagnoli (Rome: Aracne, 2016), 278-279. My translation.

sometimes propose a format based on the consumption of stereotyped products and food from Japan exported to Italy. In all their videos, both the ones shot in Japan and those shot in Italy where Japanese snacks or objects are consumed and reviewed, Japan is presented as a strange place, full of things very far from Western culture. Most of all, Japan is presented as a mythical land that cannot be seen without fulfilling certain symbolic assignments.

In the culinary semiosphere, for example, Japan is presented as a place where you can find authentic sashimi and sushi and eat them (after having taken a picture and posted it on Instagram), but of course, it is also the place where you can easily taste exotic fruits, bizarre snacks, and the *truly* mythical Kobe beef. This is a fine and very expensive cut of meat, with a characteristic marbling, derived from a bovine named *Wagyū*, whose "pedigree" has to be rigidly certified, as do the breeding procedures. If, not so many years ago, only specialists in the gastronomic sector were aware of the existence of this food, which was destined for only very special occasions or high-quality consumption, nowadays it is definitely part of the ideal list of experiences for every Western tourist in Japan, including because of the rise of YouTubers as opinion leaders or, to use a more recent appellation, influencers. Almost all the vlogs shot in Japan contain at least one episode fully dedicated to Kobe beef, which is usually topicalized with enthusiastic titles and constructed with a standard diegetic architecture: the arrival at the typical little eatery where the YouTuber is going to eat this dainty food, the chef's exotic cooking operations executed on a peculiar hot-plate – the *teppanyaki* – in front of the clients, a series of close-ups on the cooked beef, in order to increase the viewer's expectations, a close-up of the first bite of the dish as well as the rotating eyes of the YouTuber, who – unless there is a desire to dismantle the myth – publicly externalizes how impossible it is to describe with words the unbelievable pleasure the beef is giving him or her. This pattern, reiterated by many Western Youtubers, with some small variants, contributes not only to suggesting Japan as a possible tourist destination, but also to inducing viewers to go there and replicate what they have seen in the vlogs which become, in some way, pedagogues of *aesthesia*, inasmuch as not only do they offer young viewers advice, but they also provide implicit instructions on how to feel.[42] The consequences of this "moral suasion" are of course an increment in tourism in Japan, but also a modification of the market, as today it is not so difficult to find

[42] For an extensive approach to the online creation of lifestyles and identities, see Mattia Thibault, "Untag Yourself: Opacità e trasparenze negli stili di vita online," *Carte semiotiche* 4 (2016): 103-118.

Kobe beef in Western shops: "the influencer phenomenon is an intermediate step between brands and consumers that is attracting interest from marketers."[43]

To this mapping must be added travel vloggers, who specialize in making videos about tourist experiences, as in the case of HumanSafari, alias Nicolò Balini, the best-known Italian travel vlogger, and also the channels opened by Westerners now living in Japan, who tell their personal stories of living in the country while being non-autochtonous, like Marco Togni, or *Tommaso in Giappone*, who has a channel with his Japanese wife Juri.

It is not only food that is subject to processes of hypermediation and stereotypization. For the younger targets YouTube has replaced tourist guides, so places to see and activities to do are also vigorously promoted by the vloggers. This means that there has been a sort of re-translation of priorities, and a consequent re-building of the imaginary of Japan and of the pseudo-environments related to it. Of course there are points of contact between the two forms of tourist guidance, but there are also very important differences. Unless you are watching a very sectorial video, images of Japan made by the most followed YouTubers often focus on pop activities, on the reiteration of the clichés already established by precedent videos, and on what a Westerner could consider eccentric. So, of course, there will be an emphasis on Tokyo, with the classic time-lapse on Shibuya Crossing, "the busiest crossing in the world," the trip to the Tsukiji Market, the curious images of ladies with kimonos, the visit to Akihabara where you can find all kinds of *otaku* stuff,[44] Mount Fuji, Tokyo Disneyland, cherry trees in bloom, the free deer in the parks, the temples, and the *Burusera* shops (for fetishists who like used panties). Visiting these places, living these experiences, completes the ideal postcard carefully projected by an imaginary colonized by YouTubers and new media. This does not mean that

---

[43] Angeriñe Elorriaga Illera and Sergio Monge Benito, "La profesionalización de los YouTubers: el caso de Verdeliss y las marcas," *Revista Latina de la Comunicación Social* 73 (2018): 37-54.

[44] "An otaku is a culturally-specific instance of the fan phenomenon, something more specific than just 'geek' but (very) roughly translatable into English as 'fanboy.' The word itself refers to the home, so may suggest someone who stays inside, and it connotes overly obsessive fandom, especially of manga (comics) and anime (animated films), as well as of games and game-related merchandise." Steven E. Jones, *The Meaning of Video Games. Gaming and Textual Strategies* (New York/London: Routledge 2008), 60. For further insights see Patrick W. Galbraith, Thiam Huat Kam, and Björn-Ole Kamm, eds., *Debating Otaku in Contemporary Japan: Historical Perspectives and New Horizons* (London/New York: Bloomsbury 2015).

these experiences are wrong, but rather that they are not really representative of what Japanese culture is because of their clear Tokyo-centrism (it would be like saying that you know America because you have been to New York) and their strong relationship with a very narrow slice of Japanese culture, based on previous stereotypes and on a constant adhesion to the post-modern text culture of sensation. It is a culture interested above all in the colorful, the gaudy, the strong,[45] which physiologically and ideologically expunges other significant domains of Japanese identity.

Big in Japan

The "Japaneseness" conveyed by the media thus engenders a pseudo-representation of Japan which is necessarily semantically impoverished and often distorted or lacking in any of the characteristics that contribute to defining the identity of this country: its history, both ancient and recent, its languages – which so captivated Roland Barthes (1915-1980), as *L'Empire des signes* (1970)[46] testifies – and all the related fascinating art of calligraphy, the theatrical traditions of *kabuki* and *nō*, the cinema, the ceramics, the tea ritual, the literature, which is of course made up of manga but also of such works as *The Pillow Book* by Sei Shōnagon (c.966-c.1025), the culture of whiskey, the social practices which are to be understood as surpassing every schematization like that, nowadays pretty well-known in West, of *hikimori* (people who deliberately isolate themselves from everyone), the poetry, and so on. Japanese poetry can help us understand how the system of homologated differences hinted at by YouTube aesthetics could be refined through an ideal journey based on less mainstream objectives, no longer plotting the exploration on our commonplaces related to Japan, but directing our gaze on its inner *loci communes*, which are strong cultural markers:[47]

> The favourite subjects of the Japanese muse are the flowers, the birds, the snow, the moon, the falling leaves in autumn, the mist on the mountains …, love of course, and the shortness of human life. Many of our Western commonplaces are conspicuously absent: no Japanese

---

[45] See Cristoph Türcke, *Erregte Gesellschaft. Philosohie der Sensation* (Munich: C. H. Beck, 2002).
[46] Roland Barthes, *L'Empire des signes* (Geneve: A. Skira, 1970).
[47] This idea is related to concepts like "rumor" and gossip, which can reveal the inner beliefs of a certain culture. See Marino Livolsi and Ugo Volli, eds., *Rumor e pettegolezzi: L'importanza della comunicazione informale* (Milan: Franco Angeli, 2005).

poet has expatiated on the beauties of sunset or starlight, or has penned sonnets to his mistress's eyebrows, or even so much alluded to her eyes; much less would he be so improper as to hint at kissing her. Japanese poetry has commonplaces of its own.[48]

These commonplaces account for why the lever of the imaginary of Japan nowadays does not reflect the dense network of cultural veins that are rooted in this country. On the other hand, it must be said that "authenticity," too, is a post-modern myth. Authenticity is epistemically unattainable, and its rhetoric is often misleading. And yet the total distortion and radical commercialization of a place or a culture risks sterilizing all its values and charms, flattening aesthetic experience to the level of mere performance of consumer models. In this light the case of global "Japaneseness" becomes an archetype, both of an approach to knowledge that is increasingly linked to forms of show business and of a sort of widespread need for alterity, as a response to social instances of the most different kinds, perhaps first of all of contemporary boredom in the face of a world which now appears to us to be completely accessible. This is not, however, exclusive to today's world, as we can see from the song with which we will conclude our exploration.

"You're big in Japan." This iconic verse derives from a 1984 disco song by the German group Alphaville, but was made famous by the rock cover by Guano Apes in 2000, and then re-covered various other times. The meaning of the idiomatic expression is a sort of veiled insult directed at someone who is considered famous in another country than his or her native land, like a singer who was born in the US and reached success in Japan.[49] It is interesting to ascertain that this slang expression uses Japan as a symbolic place, an *elsewhere* – and at the same time a *nowhere* – distinct from here. The reputation of Japan, as we have seen, is related to the *otherness* the West has sewn onto it. It is this otherness that is represented in *Lost in Translation* (Sofia Coppola, 2003), *The Last Samurai* (Edward Zick, 2003), or *Black Rain* (Ridley Scott, 1989), "films that

---

[48] Basil Hall Chamberlain, *Things Japanese: Being Notes on Various Subjects Connected with Japan* (Berkeley, CA: Stone Bridge Press, 2007), 401.
[49] The expression is utilized as an example under the entry "big in *sth*" in the *Cambridge Dictionary of American Idioms*: "The band is still unknown in the US but they're very big in Japan." Paul Heacock, ed., *Cambridge Dictionary of American Idioms* (Cambridge: Cambridge University Press, 2003), 30.

depict Japan as a site of inscrutable mystery."[50] It is an otherness which is domesticated by the dynamic connection of previously treated cultural exchanges, which must be understood by a comparative approach, identifying their functioning from a structuralist perspective as the basis of a form of self-aware cultural study.

Japan could nowadays be thought of as a "low intensity myth,"[51] as Peppino Ortoleva says in the wake of thinkers like Claude Lévi-Strauss (1908-2009) and Roland Barthes,[52] a system of narrations "not generally sustained by apparatuses and ceremonials, but spread in all the areas of our culture. They are omnipresent, their consumption can also unite people and communities that are otherwise separate, even opposite, in national or ethnic identity, religious beliefs, political ideologies."[53] Some of the strengths and mechanisms of this myth have been analyzed in this paper, which has mostly aimed to show how the media system and the contemporary proliferation of textualities through new media not only help in the circulation of the values necessary for the sedimentation of the myth itself, but also validate its perpetuation and change its facets.

Works Cited

Akihiro, Kitajima. "Nihon kaidan eiga no shuyaku wa yūrei, yōkaitachi" [The Protagonists of Kaidan Films are Yurei and Yokai]. *Nihon kyōfu (horā) eiga e no shōtai* [Invitation to Japanese Horror Films], edited by Haraguchi Tomoo and Murata Hideki. Tokyo: Heibonsha, 2000.

Anderson, Joseph L., and Donald Richie. *The Japanese Film: Art and Industry.* Princeton, NJ: Princeton University Press, 1982.

Balmain, Colette. *Introduction to Japanese Horror Film.* Edinburgh: Edinburgh University Press, 2008.

Barbaro, Paola. "Dicotomie identitarie: l'immaginario del Giappone nelle rappresentazioni turistiche occidentali." *Lingue Culture Mediazioni – Languages Cultures Mediation* 380 (2013): 35-54.

Barthes, Roland. *L'Empire des signes.* Geneve: A. Skira, 1970.

———. *Mythologies.* Paris: Editions du Seuil, 1957.

---

[50] Todd McGowan, "Psychoanalytic Criticism," in *The Craft of Criticism. Critical Media Studies in Practice,* ed. Michael Kackman and Mary Celeste Kearney (New York/London: Routledge, 2018), 152.

[51] Ortoleva, *Miti a bassa intensità.*

[52] Claude Lévi-Strauss, *Mythologiques* (Paris: Plon, 1964); Roland Barthes, *Mythologies* (Paris: Editions du Seuil, 1957).

[53] Ortoleva, *Miti a bassa intensità,* viii-ix. My translation.

Berger, Arthur Asa. *Tourism in Japan: An Ethno-Semiotic Analysis*. Bristol et al.: Channel View Publications, 2010.

Berndt, Jacqueline, and Bettina Kümmerling-Meibauer, eds. *Manga's Cultural Crossroads*. New York/London: Routledge, 2013.

Boero, Pino, and Giovanni Veronesi. *Cuore: De Amicis tra critica e utopia*. Milan: Franco Angeli, 2009.

Brown, Steven T. *Japanese Horror and the Transnational Cinema of Sensations*. Cham: Palgrave Macmillan, 2018.

Camp, Brian, and Julie Davis. *Anime Classics Zettai! 100 Must-See Japanese Animation Masterpieces*. Berkeley, CA: Stone Bridge Press, 2007.

Cardi, Luciana. "Riconfigurazioni dell'antica Roma nel manga *Thermae Romae* e nei suoi adattamenti cinematografici." In *Riflessioni sul Giappone antico e moderno*, vol. II, edited by Maria Chiara Migliore, Antonio Manieri, and Stefano Romagnoli, 275-297. Rome: Aracne, 2016.

Carmagnola, Fulvio, and Mauro Ferraresi. *Merci di culto: Ipermerce e società mediale*. Rome: Castelvecchi, 1999.

Chamberlain, Basil Hall. *Things Japanese. Being Notes on Various Subjects Connected with Japan. For the Use of Travellers and Others*. Berkeley: Stone Bridge Press, 2007.

Cooper-Chen, Anne. *Cartoon Cultures: The Globalization of Japanese Popular Media*. New York: Peter Lang, 2010.

Darling-Wolf, Fabienne. *Imagining the Global: Transnational Media and Popular Culture Beyond East and West*. Ann Arbor, MI: University of Michigan Press, 2015.

Doyle, Susan, Jaleen Grove, and Whitney Sherman. *History of Illustration*. New York: Fairchild Books, 2018.

Elorriaga Illera, Angeriñe, and Sergio Monge Benito. "La profesionalización de los YouTubers: El caso de Verdeliss y las marcas." *Revista Latina de la Comunicación Social* 73 (2018): 37-54.

Fung, Anthony Y. H. *Asian Popular Culture: The Global (Dis)continuity*. London/New York: Routledge, 2013.

Galbraith, Patrick W., Thiam Huat Kam, and Kamm Björn-Ole, eds. *Debating Otaku in Contemporary Japan: Historical Perspectives and New Horizons*. London/New York: Bloomsbury, 2015.

Gasti, Elisa, and Bruno Surace. "Immaginari del cibo, cibi dell'immaginario: Riflessioni semiotiche attorno alla rappresentazione cinematografica del sushi." In "Cibo e identità culturale," edited by Simona Stano. Special issue, *Lexia* 19-20 (2016): 299-310.

Heacock, Paul, ed. *Cambridge Dictionary of American Idioms*. Cambridge: Cambridge University Press, 2003.

Heazle, Michael, and Nick Knight, eds. *China-Japan Relations in the Twenty-first Century*. Chelenham-Northampton: Edward Elgar, 2007.

Howe, Christopher, and Brian Hook. *China and Japan: History, Trends, and Prospects*. Oxford/New York: Oxford University Press, 1996.

Hunt, Leon, and Leung Wing-Fai. *East Asian Cinemas: Exploring Transnational Connections on Film.* New York: I.B. Tauris, 2011.

Idone Cassone, Vincenzo. "'It's over 9000!!!' Apeiron Narrative Configurations in Contemporary Mediascape." *Digital Age in Semiotics and Communication* 1, no. 1 (2018): 79-94.

Inuhiko, Yomota. *What is Japanese Cinema? A History.* New York: Columbia University Press, 2019.

Iwabuchi, Kōichi. *Recentering Globalization: Popular Culture and Japanese Transnationalism.* Durham, NC/London: Duke University Press, 2002.

Jakobson, Roman. *Essais de linguistique générale.* Paris: Editions de Minuit, 1963.

Johnson, Derek. *Media Franchising: Creative License and Collaboration in the Culture Industries.* New York/London: New York University Press, 2013.

Jones, Steven E. *The Meaning of Video Games: Gaming and Textual Strategies.* New York/London: Routledge, 2008.

Kokubun, Ryōsei et al. *Japan-China Relations in the Modern Era.* London/New York: Routledge, 2017.

Lévi-Strauss, Claude. *Mythologiques.* Paris: Plon, 1964.

Lippman, Walter. *Public Opinion.* London: G. Allen & Unwin, 1929.

Lister, Martin et al. *New Media: A Critical Introduction.* London/New York: Routledge, 2003.

Livolsi, Marino, and Ugo Volli, eds. *Rumor e pettegolezzi: L'importanza della comunicazione informale.* Milan: Franco Angeli, 2005.

Marino, Gabriele. "Semiotics of Spreadability: A Systematic Approach to Internet Memes and Virality." *Punctum* 1, no. 1 (2015): 43-66.

McGowan, Todd. "Psychoanalytic Criticism." In *The Craft of Criticism: Critical Media Studies in Practice,* edited by Michael Kackman and Mary Celeste Kearney, 146-156. New York/London: Routledge, 2018.

Miyake, Toshio. *Occidentalismi: La narrativa storica giapponese.* Venice: Cafoscarina, 2010.

Mullis, Justin. "Notes from the Land of Light: Observations on Religious Elements in *Ultraman.*" In *Essays on Kaiju and American Popular Culture,* edited by Camille D. G. Mustachio and Jason Barr, 35-58. Jefferson: McFarland & Company, 2017.

Ortoleva, Peppino. *Miti a bassa intensità.* Turin: Einaudi, 2019.

Pellitteri, Marco. *Il drago e la saetta: Modelli, strategie e identità dell'immaginario giapponese.* Latina: Tunué, 2008.

Rowthorn, Chris, and Ray Bartlett, eds. *Lonely Planet Japan.* Melbourne: Lonely Planet Publications, 2015.

Said, Edward. *Orientalism.* New York: Vintage Books, 1979.

Scherer, Elisabeth. "Well-Traveled Female Avengers: The Transcultural Potential of Japanese Ghosts." In *Ghost Movies in Southeast Asia and Beyond: Narrative, Cultural Contexts, Audiences,* edited by Peter J. Bräunlein and Andrea Lauser, 61-82. Leiden: Brill, 2016.

Stano, Simona. *Eating the Other: Translations of the Culinary Code.* Newcastle upon Tyne: Cambridge Scholars Publishing, 2015.

Surace, Bruno. "Baby Simulacra: Semiotica dei cuccioli al cinema come incubatori di assiologie." In "Cuccioli, pets e altre carinerie," edited by Francesco Mangiapane. Special issue, *E|C – Rivista online dell'AISS. Associazione italiana di studi semiotici* 22 (2018). http://www.ec-aiss.it/monografici/22_cuccioli.php).

———. "Pokémon and the PETA: Viral Extremeness as a Semiotic Strategy." In *Virality and Morphogenesis of Right-Wing Internet Populism*, edited by Eva Kimminich, Julius Erdmann, and Amir Dizdarević, 151-162. Berlin: Peter Lang, 2018.

———. "Zoosemiotica dei Pokémon." In *Zoosemiotica 2.0. Forme e politiche dell'animalità*, edited by Gianfranco Marrone, 609-619. Palermo: Edizioni Museo Pasqualino, 2017.

Thibault, Mattia. "Untag Yourself. Opacità e trasparenze negli stili di vita online." *Carte semiotiche* 4 (2016): 103-118.

Tomasi, Dario. *Ozu Yasujiro.* Turin: Lindau, 1996.

Töpffer, Rodolphe. *Histoire de Mr. Vieux Bois.* Geneva: Cherbuliez, 1833.

Tsuitsui, William M. "Soft Power and the Globalization of Japanese Popular Culture." In *Japan in the Age of Globalization*, edited by Carin Holroyd and Ken Coates, 136-147. London: Routledge, 2011.

Türcke, Cristoph. *Erregte Gesellschaft: Philosohie der Sensation.* Munich: C. H. Beck, 2002.

West, Mark I. *The Japanification of Children's Popular Culture: From Godzilla to Miyazaki.* Lanham, MD et al.: The Scarecrow Press, 2009.

Žižek, Slavoj. *The Plague of Fantasies.* London: Verso, 1999.

Chapter 2

Digital Japaneseness for Distant Observers: Contemporary Japanese Cinema Through the Lens of Our Screens

Giacomo Calorio

University of Turin and University of Bergamo, Italy

Abstract

Rethinking at Noël Burch's *To the Distant Observer*, one thing that is worth underlining is that, following the spread of the latest technology aimed at media consumption and telecommunications, today the distance evoked by the American scholar has grown thinner. Undoubtedly, the digital revolution has had a considerable impact on Japanese cinema at the level of production and distribution processes, but new technologies played an even more crucial part in redefining the image of Japanese cinema abroad. This new image is very bright, colorful and striking, consistent with a Japan that is no longer seen as only a tradition-keeper, but also a pioneer and exacerbator of pop trends. Yet, all things considered, it is equally partial and not necessarily in contradiction with deeply-rooted images of Japan and Japanese cinema. Moreover, it would appear that following this new condition of global proximity, Japanese cinema itself is changing. For instance, the new "pictorial" approach in manga adaptations is erasing part of the cultural odor closely connected to cinema's photographic nature, but it shows traces of a new odor as well. This belongs to the two-dimensional "anime fantasy-scape" which we may consider as equally Japanese. Nevertheless, as manga aesthetics is becoming a shared heritage, things are also evolving in the global cinema context.

Keywords: Japanese cinema, manga adaptations, manga aesthetics, anime.

* * *

To the Digital Observer

In line with global trends but in very specific ways, the digital revolution has had a considerable impact on Japanese cinema at the level of production and distribution processes[1] contributing, together with other factors, to redrawing the contours of a national cinema that during the two previous decades had gone through a phase of an apparently relentless decline.[2] However, new technologies played an even more crucial part in redefining the image of Japanese cinema abroad. On the one hand, by drawing the cinephiles' attention again to a national cinema that once had enjoyed high prestige and then was eclipsed in the eyes of the rest of the world; on the other, by revealing to the new audiences of the small screens (always in advance of the initiatives taken by the industry and the institutions in order to promote Japanese cinema abroad),[3] unexplored areas, strictly local phenomena and aesthetic peculiarities different from the ones that had emerged in previous periods and sedimented over the decades. The relocation[4] of Japanese cinema on our screens has allowed it to reach viewers all over the world through ways other than the official consolidated channels, and in doing so has brought to light something different from the outburst of interest in samurai films in the 1950s and 1960s (which returned an archaic image of Japan),[5] from the subsequent discovery of Ozu Yasujirō's cinema (which, even though it made adjustments toward a more realistic, contemporary and everyday image of Japan through cinema, was well suited to be read in terms of an equally exotic Japaneseness based on transcendence, simplicity, the small things in life, and the relation to nature and its cycles), and from the art cinema that sporadically appeared in

---

[1] Mitsuyo Wada-Marciano, *Japanese Cinema in the Digital Age* (Honolulu, HI: University of Hawai'i Press, 2012).

[2] What Alexander Zahlten refers to as "the end of Japanese cinema." Alexander Zahlten, *The End of Japanese Cinema: Industrial Genres, National Times, and Media Ecologies* (Durham, NC: Duke University Press, 2017).

[3] Yoshiharu Tezuka, *Japanese Cinema Goes Global* (Hong Kong: Hong Kong University Press, 2008). Also see Andrew Dorman, *Paradoxical Japaneseness: Cultural Representation in 21st Century Japanese Cinema* (London: Palgrave Macmillan, 2016).

[4] "The process by which the experience of a medium is reactivated and reproposed elsewhere than the place in which it was formed, with alternate devices and in new environments." Francesco Casetti, *The Lumière Galaxy: Seven Key Words for the Cinema to Come* (New York: Columbia University Press, 2015), 28.

[5] Nolwenn Le Minez, "Histoire du cinéma asiatique en France (1950-1980): Etude d'une réception interculturelle et réflexion sur l'exotisme cinématographique" (PhD diss., Université Paul Verlaine, 2009).

the film festivals' selections. Even though something of those images survives to this day, the real precursor of the new image of Japanese cinema that now and here strongly emerges from our distant screens, obscuring the complexity of the landscape which extends beyond them, can perhaps be found in the camp taste for the monstrous, cute, weird, and bindings to the present products of what William M. Tsutsui calls "prehistory of soft-power":[6] *tokusatsu*[7] movies. The new image is very bright, colorful, and striking, consistent with a Japan that is no longer seen as *only* a tradition-keeper, but *also* a pioneer and exacerbator of pop trends. In this chapter, I would like to explore the origin of this image, its nature, its composition, its connection with reality and its impact on it, and finally, its reception and effects abroad.

Rethinking Noël Burch's well known and discussed book about Japanese cinema, *To the Distant Observer – Form and Meaning in the Japanese Cinema*,[8] one thing that is worthwhile underlining is that, following the spread of the latest technology aimed at media consumption and telecommunications, today the *distance* evoked by the American scholar has grown thinner. What has been almost erased in the digital age is, of course, *geographical distance*, as today, unlike Burch, one can see, without leaving one's home, a number of Japanese films far superior to those examined by the American scholar in Japan. However, it includes also a *chronological distance* since, unlike Burch, who "discovered" an entire golden age of this national cinema decades after it actually took place, one can see those movies almost immediately, for instance, if they are directly streamed online, or if one buys them on DVD through Amazon or downloads them from the Web before someone resolves to export or import them. Then there is the erasure of a certain *linguistic distance*, because, in the absence of local distribution, to enjoy those movies it is no longer necessary to know the Japanese language or to have a pool of interpreters on the spot. Indeed, we can now rely on the generosity of some

---

[6] William M. Tsutsui, "The Prehistory of Soft Power: Godzillla, Cheese, and the American Consumption of Japan," in *Introducing Japanese Popular Culture*, ed. Alisa Freedman and Toby Slade (London/New York: Routledge, 2018), 193-203.

[7] The term refers to those sci-fi movies and TV dramas dealing with *kaijū* monsters and superheroes, characterized by rudimentary special effects.

[8] Noël Burch, *To the Distant Observer: Form and Meaning in the Japanese Cinema* (Berkeley/Los Angeles, CA: University of California Press, 1979).

unknown digital "poacher,"[9] on the work of the "connected intelligences"[10] and of the "connected publics"[11] which, in one way or another, will provide information and subtitles to be attached to a digital video file. Above all, it involves a *cultural distance* as, in a time of global interconnection, Japan, or at least some of its more superficial and striking aspects, is a little closer today than it was in the 1970s, a little less "other," as people know it better, run into it more often, use its words, cook and eat its food, have metabolized its reading direction, and consume other media products which somehow converge[12] toward what they are watching. Finally, it regards also an *aesthetic distance*, as, for the same reasons, not only elements concerning contents or paratexts, but even the style, the grammar, and the iconographic patrimony of Japanese cinema may remind the viewer of something he has already seen before, in some transnational borrowing, in some restitution, in some intermedia transfer.

So, between Japanese cinema and its *digital* observer, an extraordinary lens has been interposed. It is shaped like a screen, or rather like a myriad of screens which, like many pixels, have produced a new image of this cinema: definitely more detailed and virtually more complete, yet, all things considered, equally partial and not necessarily in contradiction with more ancient and deeply rooted images of Japan and Japanese cinema. Like any other lens, it distorts the reality: even the image of Japanese cinema resulting from Burch's laborious analog research returned an incomplete picture, by his own admission conditioned by chance and arbitrariness,[13] but for the farsighted digital observer the factors which shape and deform that image are different, based

---

[9] Michel de Certeau, *The Practice of Everyday Life* (Berkeley, CA: University of California Press, 1984), 174.

[10] Quoting the title of Derrick de Kerkhove's *Connected Intelligence: The Arrival of the Web Society* (Toronto: Somerville House Books, 1997).

[11] Mizuko Itō, "Introduction," in *Networked Publics*, ed. Kazys Varnelis (Cambridge, MA: MIT Press, 2008), 3.

[12] See the seminal works by Henry Jenkins such as *Fan, Blogger and Videogamers: Media Consumers in a Digital Age* (New York: New York University Press, 2006); Henry Jenkins, *Convergence Culture: Where Old and New Media Collide* (New York: New York University Press, 2008); Henry Jenkins, Sam Ford, and Joshua Green, *Spreadable Media. Creating Value and Meaning in a Networked Culture* (New York: New York University Press, 2013).

[13] "Chance and *arbitrariness* necessarily, therefore, inform these pages. I discovered Ishida quite by accident. … While I have tried to see at least one film by as many directors as possible from that golden age of the Japanese cinema, the 1930s, I have had to follow, in large part, a hit-or-miss approach. … Of course, the random approach is always in danger of neglecting a master or two." Burch, *To the Distant Observer*, 15-16.

on huge data streams, and involve not only "material" conditions, personal actions, and the opportunities allowed and generated by them, but equally immaterial practices and actions by many other observers which are far and close at the same time. The landscape that emerges in front of this digital telescope is dotted with more sharpened and intense areas. Focusing on a specific objective (after all, a lens is the icon par excellence of all search engines), we can find almost everything and discover precisely every single phenomenon of the varied picture of contemporary Japanese cinema. Vice versa, focusing on the big picture, just the most evident zones will emerge, which correspond to the greatest, the densest, and most populated niches of the Web. If an active search can still lead to discovering something new and unknown, it is exactly these areas, visible at a glance, that define the borders of the image of Japanese cinema that today reaches our distant screens.

This new condition of digital proximity among things (Michel Serres speaks of a "topological space of neighborhoods"[14]), not only between observer and observer or between the observer and the observed but also between the observed and other media artifacts (convergence, indeed), has given rise to fluid images which blend into each other and act on each other. In the specific case of Japanese cinema, abroad, this condition has resulted in the emergence of some of its expressions at the expense of others that influenced its overall image by varying the declinations of its "cultural odor"[15] and their intensity. The result is not necessarily a more complete and accurate image of contemporary Japanese cinema, which actually corresponds to a substantial and "plural" production (as, in a broader sense, today "cinema itself has become a plural word"[16]) that includes a great number of average films not so appealing to a distant observer. Nor is it an exact recalibration of now outdated common places and self-orientalist attitudes imbued with tradition, which still

---

[14] Michel Serres, *Thumbelina: The Culture and Technology of Millenials* (London/New York: Rowman & Littlefield, 2015), 6.

[15] The term "odorless" has been used by Iwabuchi Koichi in reference to the mitigation or the erasure of ethnic or national features, particularly in certain Japanese audiovisual products aimed at exportation. See Kōichi Iwabuchi, *Recentering Globalization: Popular Culture and Japanese Transnationalism* (Durham, NC/London: Duke University Press, 2002), 27-28.

[16] Francesco Casetti, "Novi territori. Multiplex, Home Theater, canali tematici, peer to peer e la trasformazione dell'esperienza di visione cinematografica," in *Terre incognite: Lo spettatore italiano e le nuove forme dell'esperienza di visione dei film*, ed. Francesco Casetti and Mariagrazia Fanchi (Rome: Carocci, 2006), 12. My translation.

survive in some culturally performative films aimed at exportation.[17] It is actually the simple juxtaposition of *other* images which of course enrich our previous idea of Japanese cinema as we see it *from here*, but, on closer inspection, seeing them as a whole, they by no means contradict longstanding stereotypes, namely the ones which depict Japan itself as a land of contradictions, as a paradoxical and upside-down nation.[18]

The Relocation of Japanese Cinema

Stepping back toward the origin of these processes, with the aim of contextualizing briefly the relationship between digital revolution, Japanese cinema, and its contemporary image in "the West," firstly, we should notice, just as scholars like Mitsuyo Wada-Marciano have already done in-depth, especially in reference to J-horror, how the technological convergence of different resources that share the same digital matrix should be included among the main factors that allowed the worldwide spread of certain expressions of Japanese cinema. During the 1990s, a low-cost digital optical format, the VCD, spread especially in Eastern Asia, followed by the DVD.[19] This happened in parallel with the definitive mass access to the Internet, with the consequent onset of practices like *online* international commerce, piracy and sharing, and of new ways of communicating, reviewing films, and producing information on the critics and fandom sides as well. The resulting development of circulation and cinephile practices that had already taken root with the advent of home video, further strengthened by the liberation of the movies from the round plastic containers they were enchained to by their dematerialization as digital files, together with the relocation on the Web of the cinephile communities and the critical discourses which enlivened them, formed an environment of prior knowledge that turned out to be a crucial element for subsequent adoptions and more institutional takeovers. That knowledge served in fact as a reassuring

---

[17] Dorman, *Paradoxical Japaneseness*, chapter five. See also Giacomo Calorio, "Vecchi e nuovi luoghi comuni del e sul cinema giapponese contemporaneo, tra esotismo e autorappresentazioni," *Lingue Culture Mediazioni* 3, no. 2 (2016): 55-71.

[18] Endymion Wilkinson, *Japan Versus Europe: A History of Misunderstanding* (London/New York: Penguin Books, 1980).

[19] Kelly Hu, "The Power of Circulation: Digital Technologies and the Online Chinese Fans of Japanese TV Drama," in *The Inter-Asia Cultural Studies Reader,* ed. Kuan-Hsing Chen and Chua Beng Huat (London: Routledge, 2008), 550-567. See also Darrell William Davis and Emily Yeuh-yuh Yeh, "VCD as Programmatic Technology: Japanese Television Drama in Hong Kong," in *Feeling Asian Modernities: Transnational Consumption of Japanese TV Dramas,* ed. Kōichi Iwabuchi (Hong Kong: Hong Kong University Press, 2004), 232.

pre-sold element, which facilitated, including through Hollywood appropriations, late Japanese re-appropriations, and fruitful transnational forms of cooperations,[20] the passage from the local nature of the phenomenon to a global one and from its grassroots and niche origins to the overflow toward more passive mass audiences.

As many of these processes have already been extensively analyzed in the cited texts, especially in the context of J-horror, this chapter shall be limited to noticing how one of the most evident effects of this convergence of technological and cultural processes was the surprising intrusion of cultural icons born in hyper-local contexts like the Japanese V-cinema market[21] and loaded with strictly native references (both cultural and aesthetic) in the wider Asian context, then in Hollywood and, from there, on the worldwide stage and even in capillary local contexts. Emblematic in this respect is the journey of the female ghost Sadako, the main character of Nakata Hideo's blockbuster *Ringu* (*Ring*, 1998): only partially deprived of her cultural odor after her rebirth as a US citizen named Samara in Gore Verbinski's remake *The Ring* (2002), Sadako carried with her, in her naturalization process, indelible traces of her Japaneseness through the iconographic traits of the ghosts haunting Edo stamps and *Kaidan* literature and dramas (which in turn reflected the funerary practices of that time and place), which she transplanted into the public imagination of foreign audiences who were sometimes unaware, sometimes aware, and looking exactly for that residual fragrance.

One of the consequences of the greater availability of works and the information about them, together with the configuration on the Web of new geographies no longer based on kilometers and miles but on tastes and passions, built by de-territorialized and competent international film clubs, is that today there is more and better dialogue, at least in terms of the quantity and precision of information, about "minor" or niche cultures like Japanese cinema. Still, in my opinion, the most interesting thing is that there is much more talk than before about it *outside* that niche. Today Japanese cinema is increasingly present in other places, too: adjacent spaces not necessarily of a

---

[20] Dorman, *Paradoxical Japaneseness*; Tezuka, *Japanese Cinema Goes Global.*

[21] Tom Mes, "Generation Video: Nel mondo del V-Cinema," in *Anime Perdute:Il cinema di Miike Takashi*, ed. Dario Tomasi (Turin-Milan: Museo Nazionale del Cinema-Il Castoro, 2006), 47-57; Tom Mes, "V-Cinema: How Home Video Revitalized Japanese Film and Mystified Film Historians," in *Introducing Japanese Popular Culture*, ed. Alisa Freedman and Toby Slade (London/New York: Routledge, 2018), 216-226; Zahlten, *The End of Japanese Cinema*, 152-203.

cinephilic nature that, by hosting it, contribute to guiding its overall image in a certain way, with feedback effects even at the level of official production and distribution, and secondly in terms of aesthetics and contents (consider, for example, the capacity of fans to shape this fluid and shimmering image and direct the industry's exportation policy through the preferences expressed by their discourses, their reviews, and their uploading, downloading, subbing and sharing practices on the Web).

Japanese Cinema as a Tag

The boundaries that define the niches of the Web are in fact anything but clean and impervious. For instance, at the level of cinephile passions, as early as in the twilight of the analog era, the interest for contemporary Japanese cinema was combined and intertwined with that for other "cult" kinds of cinema (horror, exploitation movies, Hong Kong action cinema, and so on). In the shift toward a digital regime, this primarily determined the birth of pan-Asian and film genre-based macro-containers on the Web within which there is a condition of proximity that helps to keep up the interest *around* Japanese cinema, preventing it from being forgotten, as happened during the 1970s and 1980s, and at the same time identifying it as a category of something else.

In parallel, outside the cinephile context, there has been a growing development of international communities of fans of animation, comics, and more generally of all Japanese pop culture. Here again, as with the cinephile practices of the home video era, the prodromes date back to a few decades before, as Lawrence Eng underlines: "in many ways, overseas [*anime* and *manga*] fans were an early prototype of peer-to-peer network culture even before the advent of the Internet."[22] Besides, if we want to – with due caution – draw a line with the past, we could even say that they were inserted in much more remote and geographically broader processes (Itō Mizuko talks about a "long-standing tradition of cultural cross-pollination between Japan and other parts of the world"[23]). However, there is no doubt that these subcultures benefited greatly from the "fortuitous timing"[24] with which the new

---

[22] Lawrence Eng, "Anime and *Manga* Fandom as Networked Culture," in *Fandom Unbound: Otaku Culture in a Connected World*, ed. Mizuko Itō, Daisuke Okabe, and Tsuji Izumi (New Haven, CT/London: Yale University Press, 2012), 163-165. See also Susan J. Napier, *From Impressionism to Anime: Japan as Fantasy and Fan Cult in the Mind of the West* (New York: Palgrave, 2007), 16.
[23] Itō, "Introduction," xii.
[24] Napier, *From Impressionism to Anime,* 136.

possibilities offered by digital technology showed up, at least as much as cinephile communities did, besides which they achieved far greater results and impact on the cultural fabric. The *manga* and *anime* fan community, not forgetting video games, card games, J-pop music, action figures, and all kinds of cultural ramification (from cosplay to neko-café), found an ideal place of expression and expansion in the Web, of which *manga* and *anime* fans were among the first and most active explorers thanks to their technophile temperament which endowed them with the "technical competence"[25] necessary for new consumers of global cultural products. The rate at which the Web allowed the retrieval of these products, together with the possibility to bring together people motivated by an interest that had once been regarded with suspicion by the surrounding society, played a key role in the development of these communities and in the worldwide spread and legitimization of Japanese pop culture. In the eyes of these "digital" observers, Japanese cinema has gradually become a sector, albeit a lateral one, of a wider fan of things dealing with pop Japan, particularly, as we will see later, if it maintains strong narrative or visual relationships with them.

So, out of this general picture, the locution "Japanese cinema" emerges as an aggregate of categories or tags which can lean more or less toward one of the two poles of the locution itself (*cinephilia* on one side, *Japanophilia* on the other) and can be found abroad, individually or in clusters, in different niches of the Web. Depending on the size and nature of those niches, the resulting image of Japanese cinema may have, besides a particular declination, a greater or lesser intensity, and therefore be more or less visible to a digital eye, more or less subject to overflows in other contexts, more or less amplified by the recommendation system algorithms and by the bubble effect they generate. Furthermore, as distorted as it is, this image generated from the bottom of the Web has also contributed to shaping the development of this national cinema at the level of production and, above all, exportation strategies. As mentioned above, one of the most evident and analyzed cases in this respect is surely J-horror and, more generally, all the extreme and weird forms of cinema which, as minor as they were, toward the end of the analog era were among the first expressions of Japanese cinema that were granted a passport to cross the borders thanks to their status as "cult" movies. In the digital environment, these

---

[25] Federica Francesca Riva, "Homecoming: Le tecnologie domestiche della visione," in *Terre incognite:Lo spettatore italiano e le nuove forme dell'esperienza di visione dei film*, ed. Francesco Casetti and Mariagrazia Fanchi (Rome: Carocci, 2006), 64-66. My translation.

particular expressions of Japanese cinema enjoyed a considerable overexposure compared to less striking and appealing ones (although prevailing in numbers), contributing to toning the image of Japanese cinema toward strong colors. And "extreme" is exactly the adjective often evoked (sometimes merely as a pretext) in reference to Japanese cinema by branding strategies that "in part rely on the Western audiences' perception of the East as weird and wonderful, sublime and grotesque."[26] For instance, this is true for the proud trash and low budget forms of cinema by some directors that are alien to the most institutional festivals and the usual distribution channels, like Iguchi Noboru and Nishimura Yoshihiro, but also for beloved and appreciated authors like Miike Takashi and Sono Sion. These directors clearly flirt with the global *downloaders*, perhaps more than with the domestic audience, tickling their taste for the bizarre and their hunger for the alien through the formulation of a grotesque and unprecedented synthesis of all the possible hyper-traditional and hyper-modern clichés about Japan, like the robotic geisha of *Robogeisha* (2009) and the zombie *sushi* of *Dead Sushi* (2012) by Iguchi, or the samurai armors of the bloodthirsty policemen of *Tokyo zankoku keisatsu* (*Tokyo Gore Police*, 2008) by Nishimura. In spite of (or better, because of) their lo-fi and ostentatiously cheesy aesthetics, films like the ones mentioned circulate much more easily than the majority of Japanese cinema, firstly because the ultra-violence which characterizes them appeals to the horror, cult, or cult fans' tastes, and secondly because they have a very intense cultural fragrance, as even that weird and paroxystic violence has become an index of Japaneseness and then a form of cultural performance. As Ian Condry states: "for a while, *Machine Girl* (*Kataude mashiin gaaru*, Iguchi Noboru, 2009) was ranked the fourth most popular download on X-Box Live in the United States. In other words, this niche film had a chance in the context of film downloads, even though competing in mainstream theater multiplexes is out of the question."[27]

If the J-horror phenomenon has already been largely discussed (even) under this perspective, this was not the case, at least from the point of view of cinema, for the relationships recently established between Japanese cinema and the sphere of J-culture, at the center of which we can find *manga* and *anime*.

---

[26] Chi-Yun Shin, "The Art of Branding: Tartan 'Asia Extreme' Films," in *Horror to the Extremes: Changing Boundaries in Asian Cinema*, ed. Jinhee Choi and Mitsuyo Wada-Marciano (Hong Kong: Hong Kong University Press, 2009), 86-87.
[27] Ian Condry, *The Soul of Anime: Collaborative Creativity and Japan's Media Success Story* (Durham, NC/London: Duke University Press, 2013), 210.

Because of the macroscopic size of this niche (Itō borrows the term "meganiche"[28] from Clay Shirky to describe the dimensions of these *pop cosmopolitans'* communities that, quoting Jenkins again, "use networked communication to scan the planet in search of diversity and communicate with others of their kind around the world"[29]) and its bearing on youngsters even at a lexical level, and therefore of the higher exposure it ensures, the effects have been even greater. Hence, I believe they deserve further investigation that, without ignoring it, goes beyond what, back at the end of the 1990s, was almost nothing more than a commonplace: the belief that Japanese contemporary cinema *generally* has something to do with *manga.*

J-Pop Cosmopolitans

As Susan J. Napier notes, *manga* and *anime* were endowed at the same time and in the right dosage with those characters of difference and universality that made them suitable not only for becoming objects of desire for the distinction and transgression (from the local cultural traits) of the fans but conversely for the identification and fading of cultural barriers as well. And that is because of their non-photographic nature combined with a kind of drawing that is mostly stylized and showing few ethnic connotations (big eyes, multicolored hair, neutral somatic features),[30] regardless of the quality of the single works, of their style and content's originality if compared to the standards of that time, and again regardless of the affinities with fantasy and its "dominance"[31] in the same years and its transmedia context.

Borrowing Iwabuchi's well-known categories again, it can be stated that, compared to live cinema, *anime, manga,* and video games have, at an almost ontological level, less cultural odor, though without being entirely devoid of it. If in the first case it may be relatively easy to erase or soften the Japaneseness of "drawn" media like *manga, anime* or video games (as their images share the

---

[28] Clay Shirky, "Tiny Slice, Big Market," *Wired,* November 1, 2006, https://www.wired.com/2006/11/meganiche.

[29] Jenkins, *Fans, Bloggers,* 162. See also Itō, "Introduction," xii.

[30] "Some commentators feel that *anime* and *manga* characters look "White," but in fact they exhibit quite a range of characteristics that are not really Caucasian or Japanese, such as the marks of the media. Unlike Bollywood or Hong Kong martial arts films, which are both live action, the viewer can easily identify with anime and *manga* characters." Napier, *From Impressionism to Anime,* 137.

[31] Colin B. Harvey, *Fantastic Transmedia Narrative, Play and Memory Across Science Fiction and Fantasy Storyworlds* (New York: Palgrave Macmillan, 2015), 38.

benefits of a "pictorial" projectuality), the same cannot be said about cinematographic images, whose photographic nature is largely anchored to the material referent. However, although distances are shortened by their elements of neutrality, which require not too complex or radical operations of concealment and domestication, by contrast, it is exactly because of their "fragrance" (a fragrance that often is not directly attributable to the real Japan as much as to an "other" Japan defined as an "*anime fantasyscape*"[32] by Napier) that they raise interest in niche communities. As Jenkins notes: "At the moment, Japanese style is marketed as a distinctive 'fragrance' to niche or cult audiences and 'deodorized' for broader publics, but this distinction is starting to break down as American consumers develop a preference for those qualities they associate with Japanese cultural productions."[33] It was this paradoxical blend of neutral and appealing elements that caused the international success of this style among the youngsters, a success so huge that it was bound to trespass the boundaries of the global *otaku* communities to become simply an important tool in the great and hybrid toolbox of contemporary pop aesthetics.

To sum up, although in the cases concerning cinema described above the technological convergence of different digital resources, together with cinephiles' ability to anticipate the initiatives coming from the industry, has led to some results that are important but, all things considered, restricted (to a genre, a niche, a transient phenomenon); in the larger and impalpable context of pop culture, the effects of the marriage between fandom and technological resources have been far more visible and widespread. So much so, as is well-known, to persuade Japan itself, not only at the level of the entertainment industry but in terms of government cultural policies as well, to rethink its cultural exportation strategies in order to regain its place in the world economy through forms of *soft power* based on pop culture expressions that, in clandestine ways, were *already* growing extremely popular (citing Toshio Miyake, "a new turn-of-the-century self-orientalism which assumes the western gaze in order to reformulate its own Japaneseness"[34]). At first glance, this does not directly affect cinema, as in fact, even after the launch of the *Cool Japan* project, and despite some positive elements,[35] it has not seen any

---

[32] Napier, *From Impressionism to Anime*, 133.

[33] Jenkins, *Fans, Bloggers, and Gamers*, 161.

[34] Toshio Miyake, "Mostri Made in Japan: Orientalismo e auto-orientalismo nell'era della globalizzazione," in *Culture del Giappone contemporaneo*, ed. Matteo Casari (Latina: Tunué, 2011), 178. My translation.

[35] Dorman, *Paradoxical Japaneseness*, 12-13.

significant increase in its scarce public support.[36] At the same time, the usual timidity and lack of interest of the Japanese exporters, despite the new elements analyzed by Wada-Marciano and Andrew Dorman, did not undergo such a really striking revolution, at least when weighed against the large number of films produced per year in Japan and for the Japanese market in a basically self-sufficient environment.[37]

Leaving aside the government announcements, one gets the impression that Japanese cinema is too narrativistic a medium, endowed with too much history and with too sharp outlines to be a testimonial suitable for the futuristic, dynamic, modular, and character-based rhetoric underlying J-culture and Cool Japan, and this may be one of the reasons behind its peripheral position within the J-culture galaxy. However, this in no way means that Japanese cinema has not tried to benefit from its cousins and from their achievements. While maintaining its identity and autonomy as a medium toward such an intangible and shifting media galaxy, thanks to its history, the density of its experience, and the "specific weight"[38] of its dispositif which has prevented it from dispersing in the J-culture digital nebula, it has by no means been excluded from the initiatives of the convergent industry, much less from the grassroots phenomena. On the contrary, on the one hand, during the 2000s, it invested more and more in that "subcultural capital,"[39] lending itself to a significant intensification of its transmedia and intermedia relationships with the other planets of that galaxy, so as to share their visibility and the financial benefit (especially at home). On the other hand, abroad, these new cultural products, whose style and contents were particularly attractive among the younger global audience, have powered by extension, other than a passion for a pop Japan often taken "in a set," an interest in Japan *per se*, or at least in a dreamed-about idealized image of it, increasing the chances that also some given expressions of live-action Japanese cinema might cross the paths of these digital Japanophiles (more than cinephiles). So it happens to come across Japanese

---

[36] Aaron Gerow, "Recent Film Policy and the Fate of Film Criticism in Japan," *Midnight Eye*, July 11, 2016, http://www.midnighteye.com/features/recent-film-policy-and-the-fate-of-film-criticism-in-japan; Terutarō Osanai, "Être indépendant au Japon," *Cahiers du Cinéma* 667 (2011): 57-59.

[37] Motion Picture Producers Association of Japan, "Statistics of Film Industry in Japan," accessed January 30, 2019, http://www.eiren.org/statistics_e/index.html.

[38] Mariagrazia Fanchi, "Cinema-Grand Master: Il film e la sua esperienza nell'epoca della convergenza," in *Il cinema della convergenza: Industria, racconto, pubblico*, ed. Federico Zecca (Milan/Udine: Mimesis 2012), 203. My translation.

[39] Napier, *From Impressionism to Anime*, 150.

film reviews, of course, especially about adaptations or works that have other textual or paratextual links with other media, on websites dealing not with cinema but with comics, animation, video games, J-pop music, and so on.

Another Fragrance of Japan, Fragrance of Another Japan

These forms of convergence, synergy, and overflowing from medium to medium are determined by several factors, which in turn end up consolidating in a kind of vicious circle, and they involve both the users and the producers. In the first case, we should obviously consider the physiologic permeability of the interests of the single users and of the communities they belong to. In this respect, the Web macro-containers reflect and encourage the users' inclination to pass from one category to an adjacent one. Regarding the production processes, conversely, this kind of dynamics is the result of definite transmedia storytelling top-down policies, namely what today has become the primary production method[40] *even* for cinema (especially, but not only, for mainstream cinema). Even though Japan has a specific term, *media-mix*,[41] to describe it, certainly this is true not only for Japan. Regardless of its particular declination[42] if compared to Jenkins' definition of transmedia storytelling, one could argue that the Japanese case needs to be analyzed further, especially taking into account the way Japanese comics and animated series pervade every aspect of the Japanese culture and how broadly this phenomenon has been implemented into contemporary Japanese cinema. Just like the superhero movies based on American comics, even in Japan,[43] the adoption of contemporary *manga* or classic Japanese comics as a *pre-sold element* has

---

[40] Manuel Hernández Perez, *Manga, anime y videojuegos: Narrativa cross-media japonesa* (Zaragoza: Prensas de la Universidad de Zaragoza, 2017).

[41] Marc Steinberg, *Anime's Media Mix: Franchising Toys and Characters in Japan* (Minneapolis/London: Minnesota University Press, 2012); Marc Steinberg, "Condensing the Media Mix: The Tatami Galaxy's Multiple Possible Worlds," in *Introducing Japanese Popular Culture*, ed. Alisa Freedman and Toby Slade (London/New York: Routledge, 2018), 252-261.

[42] Ibid.

[43] Woojeong Joo, Rayna Denison, and Hiroko Furukawa, *Manga to Movies Project Report 1: Transmedia Japanese Franchising* (University of East Anglia/Arts & Humanity Research Council, 2013); Woojeong Joo, Rayna Denison, and Hiroko Furukawa, *Manga to Movies Project Report 2: Japan's Manga, Anime and Film Industries* (University of East Anglia/Arts & Humanity Research Council, 2013); Giacomo Calorio, "Man/Ei-GA: intermedialità fumetto-cinema nel Giappone contemporaneo," *Cinergie: Il cinema e le altre arti* 5 (2014): 162-175.

taken on a leading role that has secured film adaptations a place on the podium of annual revenues next to their closest kin: *anime*. Of all Japanese movies produced between 2000 and 2016, about 8% were comic adaptations.[44] While that might not seem a significant percentage, actually it means that, with an average of 430 movies per year, at least fifteen were *manga* adaptations in 2002 and 2003, a number that went up to fifty-three in 2014. As directors, we can find both unknown novices who are trying to cut their teeth with commissioned commercial movies[45] and specialists in transpositions,[46] veterans and film craftsmen,[47] and even worldwide respected authors who have made a name for themselves in different cinematic territories.[48] The distinctiveness of the Japanese example is not only due to the impact of *manga* in all aspects of Japanese culture, communication, and design, but mainly also results from the extreme variety of genres, categories, and audiences of Japanese *manga*, which translates into a superior and much broader, compared to Hollywood "cinecomics," diversification of their adaptations. Themes, narrative schemes, situations, registers, stylistic traits, visual and sound effects, graphisms, ideographic stocks, and archetypes defined by specific iconographic traits (physiognomy, hairstyles, accessories, recurring gestures, "signature poses") as well are taken directly from the universes of *manga* and *anime* without a care for their plausibility in a photographic-like regime, thus creating a sort of macro-cinema genre which is divided into subgenres that have to do more with *manga*'s categories and audiences than with cinema's.

These intermedia interferences[49] have changed the face of a part of Japanese cinema (if not the largest, the most evident one), bringing it closer to its neighbor media, that is, making it a little more similar to them both on a visual and narrative level. This has resulted in making it particularly appealing, more than to niche cinephiles, to the foreign users of these neighbors or "ancillary

[44] Naoto Mori, *Manga + Eiga! Manga gensaku eiga no genzai-chi* (Tokyo: Yosensha, 2017), 39.
[45] Even in quite personal and successful ways, as Ninagawa Mika, Suzuki Matsuo, or One Hitoshi have done.
[46] Such as Takeuchi Hideki, Satō Shinsuke, Koizumi Norihiro, Yoshida Keisuke, Kawamura Yasuhiro, Ōtomo Keishi, and Miki Takahiro.
[47] Such as Kaneko Shūsuke, Kitamura Ryūhei, and Inudō Isshin.
[48] Such as Koreeda Hirokazu, Kumakiri Kazuyoshi, Sono Sion, Ishii Takashi, Yamashita Nobuhiro, Toyoda Toshiaki, Shiota Akihiko, Kurosawa Kiyoshi, Sabu, Ōmori Tatsushi, and of course, and especially, Miike Takashi.
[49] Federico Zecca, *Cinema e intermedialità: Modelli di traduzione* (Udine: Forum, 2013).

products,"[50] sometimes even when it has no direct links to them. In this process, digital technology has played a crucial role, too: for Japanese cinema, the digitization of the production processes has involved a further convergence toward the sphere of *manga* and *anime* compared to the past. As we all know, nowadays, different media like *manga, anime,* video games, or even pop music basically speak the same language, are made of the same substance (i.e., binary code), are contained in and consumed through the same devices, and are molded by the same tools (i.e., cut, copy, paste, filter, etc.) in similar ways. This ontological "brotherhood" surely helped to change how Japanese cinema looks today, at least in its mainstream manifestations, exactly the ones that whetted the appetite of young internauts and transmedia navigators from abroad. This concerns in particular all those films, often but not exclusively taken from a *manga*, an *anime*, or a video game, which, taking advantage of the "pictorial" possibilities offered by digital technology not only in order to obtain greater photorealistic verisimilitude but also in an anti-naturalistic and "neo-figurative"[51] fashion, have borrowed the "aesthetic of artifice"[52] that is a characteristic feature of comics, taking in their expressive codes, iconographies, and narrative structures, similarly to what had already been done elsewhere with Marvel and DC comics and graphic novels, but with a superior numerical density, naturalness of approach, and stylistic consistency with the surrounding media environment because of the pervasivity of the *manga* and *anime* aesthetics on the Japanese cultural and social fabric. Firstly, computer graphics allow the representation of fantasy worlds so common in *manga* with a *realism* that had been impossible until then, and make the adoption of science fiction and fantasy *manga* stories much easier, because their strange and wonderful universes can easily and gorgeously be "painted"[53] without challenging their plausibility. However, in *manga* with a more

---

[50] Veronica Innocenti and Guglielmo Pescatore, "Dalla cross-medialità all'ecosistema narrativo: L'architettura complessa del cinema hollywoodiano contemporaneo," in *Il cinema della convergenza,* edited by Federico Zecca (Milan/Udine: Mimesis, 2012), 135.

[51] Rino Schembri, "Stratifications, Graphems and Synchronies in (Neo-figurative) Cinema: From Greenaway's The Tulse Luper Suitcases to Miller and Rodriguez's Sin City," in *Cinema e fumetto: Cinema and Comics,* ed. Leonardo Quaresima, Federico Zecca, and Laura Ester Sangalli (Udine: Forum, 2009), 659-662.

[52] Michael Cohen, "Dick Tracy: In Pursuit of a Comic Book Aesthethic," in *Film and Comic Books,* ed. Ian Gordon, Mark Jancovich, and Matthew P. McAllister (Jackson, MS: University Press of Mississippi, 2007), 13.

[53] Lev Manovic refers to cinema in the digital age as "a sub-genre of painting." Lev Manovic, *The Language of New Media* (Cambridge, MA: MIT Press, 2001), 250.

mundane setting as well, digital graphics allow the molding of efficaciously imaginary situations in everyday life or exaggerations of reality that are also typical of the medium. Secondly, the ontological convergence of the two media has led to a rise of semiological interferences from *manga* to cinema, both in quantity and in quality, and this time in a rather anti-naturalistic fashion. It needs to be pointed out again that this does not only happen with transpositions (that often may limit themselves to the adoption of the plotline) but also in works based on original stories. For instance, one could think of some *manga*-esque films by directors like Matsumoto Hitoshi, Nakashima Tetsuya, Suzuki Matsuo, Yamashita Nobuhiro, Ishii Katsuhito, Fujita Yōsuke, Kawamura Yasuhiro, Yoshida Daihachi, and of course, Miike Takashi and Sono Sion, among others, but the list is actually endless, and it includes above all many "average" products that make use of graphisms and *manga* iconographies in a less excessive but nonetheless systemic fashion.

Perhaps, regardless of the quality of its single products but taking into account the size and the visibility of this phenomenon in its entirety, it might be worth observing this new astral configuration largely still to be explored *closely*, more carefully, by analyzing its peculiar *forms and meanings* thoroughly. This is true especially since it is precisely these films that we can find reviewed, discussed, or downloadable on a galaxy of sites and torrent trackers dealing with comics, animation, or Japanese pop culture as a whole, the ones that emerge from the niches of the Web and are then more visible to a digital observer from abroad. Consequently, they are also the ones that are beginning to be exported more frequently into movie theaters (which normally prefer art cinema, films permeated with tradition or endowed with a glocal taste well suitable for exportation[54]) or are taken up by the new digital media providers like Netflix or Amazon that have recently got into the global film production and distribution business. In one way or another, today, films like the ones cited manage to reach this part of the world on a fast-track thanks to the points of contact (whether they concern content, visual or paratextual aspects) they exhibit in relation with that universe, and this is contributing to putting Japanese cinema into a more global perspective.

To sum up, it would appear that this *proximity* (among media, among spectators from different parts of the world, among different media audiences) is changing our image of Japanese cinema and, at the same time, that Japanese cinema itself is changing, as its global appeal pushes it more and more to take into account what the world and its digital observers expect from it today.

---

[54] Calorio, *Vecchi e nuovi luoghi comuni.*

Going back to what has been discussed in the previous paragraphs, on the one hand, it can be said that this "pictorial" approach in Japanese cinema is erasing part of that cultural odor that is hard to conceal as it is closely linked to a photographic and documentary nature (even in fiction), which inevitably puts in place a national identity made of landscapes, buildings, faces, and objects, with effects that can be repelling or appealing, depending on the spectator. At the same time, even the cultural baggage of films that directly or indirectly draw inspiration from *manga* maintains, as mentioned before, traces of an odor that belongs not to the real three-dimensional Japan, but to that imaginary and two-dimensional *anime* fantasy-scape recognized and appreciated by someone as effectively Japanese (and it is), by many others as a simple aesthetic option of the visual Esperanto spoken by contemporary pop culture: in both cases, considerably appealing to many people.

That is the current situation. Until yesterday, we could say that, even if *manga* aesthetics is already a shared heritage, *manga* adaptation was a distinctly Japanese phenomenon, but now even the adoption of Japanese comics as content to translate into non-Japanese movies is becoming increasingly frequent both in Asia and in Hollywood. At the beginning of 2019, following the releases of Adam Wingard's *Death Note* (2017) on Netflix and Rupert Sanders' *Ghost in the Shell* (2017), Robert Rodriguez's long-awaited *Alita: Battle Angel* finally came to light. It is not a remake of a Japanese film but a straight-to-Hollywood adaptation of a Kishiro Yukito sci-fi *manga* classic which had never been transposed into a feature film before, even in Japan. I believe that the most interesting thing in the whole film is the digitally expanded eyes of its leading actress Rosa Salazar; indeed, a long essay could be written about this topic, starting with the question: how Japanese are those eyes?

Works Cited

Burch, Noël. *To the Distant Observer: Form and Meaning in the Japanese Cinema.* Berkeley/Los Angeles, CA: University of California Press, 1979.

Calorio, Giacomo. "Man/Ei-GA: intermedialità fumetto-cinema nel Giappone contemporaneo." *Cinergie: Il cinema e le altre arti* 5 (2014): 162-175.

———. "Vecchi e nuovi luoghi comuni del e sul cinema giapponese contemporaneo, tra esotismo e autorappresentazioni." *Lingue Culture Mediazioni* 3, no. 2 (2016): 55-71.

Casetti, Francesco. "Novi territori. Multiplex, Home Theater, canali tematici, peer to peer e la trasformazione dell'esperienza di visione cinematografica." In *Terre incognite: Lo spettatore italiano e le nuove forme dell'esperienza di visione dei film*, edited by Francesco Casetti and Mariagrazia Fanchi, 9-13. Roma: Carocci, 2006.

―――. *The Lumière Galaxy: Seven Key Words for the Cinema to Come.* New York: Columbia University Press, 2015.

Cohen, Michael. "Dick Tracy: In Pursuit of a Comic Book Aesthethic." In *Film and Comic Books*, edited by Ian Gordon, Mark Jancovich, and Matthew P. McAllister, 13-36. Jackson, MS: University Press of Mississippi, 2007.

Condry, Ian. *The Soul of Anime: Collaborative Creativity and Japan's Media Success Story.* Durham, NC/London: Duke University Press, 2013.

Darrel, William Davis, and Emily Yeuh-yuh Yeh. "VCD as Programmatic Technology: Japanese Television Drama in Hong Kong." In *Feeling Asian Modernities: Transnational Consumption of Japanese TV Dramas*, edited by Kōichi Iwabuchi, 227-248. Hong Kong: Hong Kong University Press, 2004.

De Certeau, Michel. *The Practice of Everyday Life.* Berkeley, CA: University of California Press, 1984.

De Kerkhove, Derrick. *Connected Intelligence: The Arrival of the Web Society.* Toronto: Somerville House Books, 1997.

Dorman, Andrew. *Paradoxical Japaneseness: Cultural Representation in 21st Century Japanese Cinema.* London: Palgrave Macmillan, 2016.

Eng, Lawrence. "*Anime* and *Manga* Fandom as Networked Culture." In *Fandom Unbound:Otaku Culture in a Connected World*, edited by Mizuko Itō, Daisuke Okabe, and Tsuji Izumi, 158-178. New Haven, CT/London: Yale University Press, 2012.

Fanchi, Mariagrazia. "Cinema-Grand Master: Il film e la sua esperienza nell'epoca della convergenza." In *Il cinema della convergenza: Industria, racconto, pubblico*, edited by Federico Zecca, 193-204. Milan/Udine: Mimesis 2012.

Gerow, Aaron. "Recent Film Policy and the Fate of Film Criticism in Japan." *Midnight Eye*, July 11, 2016. http://www.midnighteye.com/features/recent-film-policy-and-the-fate-of-film-criticism-in-japan.

Harvey, Colin B. *Fantastic Transmedia Narrative, Play and Memory Across Science Fiction and Fantasy Storyworlds.* New York: Palgrave Macmillan, 2015.

Hu, Kelly. "The Power of Circulation: Digital Technologies and the Online Chinese fans of Japanese TV Drama." In *The Inter-Asia Cultural Studies Reader*, edited by Kuan-Hsing Chen and Chua Beng Huat, 550-567. London: Routledge, 2008.

Innocenti, Veronica, and Guglielmo Pescatore. "Dalla cross-medialità all'ecosistema narrativo: L'architettura complessa del cinema hollywoodiano contemporaneo." In *Il cinema della convergenza: Industria, racconto, pubblico*, edited by Federico Zecca, 127-138. Milan/Udine: Mimesis, 2012.

Itō, Mizuko. "Introduction." In *Networked Publics*, edited by Kazys Varnelis, 1-14. Cambridge, MA: MIT Press, 2008.

Iwabuchi, Kōichi. *Recentering Globalization: Popular Culture and Japanese Transnationalism.* Durham, NC/London, Duke University Press, 2002.

Jenkins, Henry. *Convergence Culture: Where Old and New Media Collide.* New York: New York University Press, 2008.

————. *Fan, blogger and Videogamers: Media Consumers in a Digital Age.* New York: New York University Press, 2006.

Jenkins, Henry, Sam Ford, and Joshua Green. *Spreadable Media: Creating Value and Meaning in a Networked Culture.* New York: New York University Press, 2013.

Joo, Woojeong, Rayna Denison, and Hiroko Furukawa. *Manga to Movies Project Report 1: Transmedia Japanese Franchising.* University of East Anglia/Arts & Humanity Research Council, 2013.

————. *Manga to Movies Project Report 2: Japan's Contemporary Manga, Anime and Film Industries.* University of East Anglia/Arts & Humanity Research Council, 2013.

Le Minez, Nolween. "Histoire du cinéma asiatique en France (1950-1980): Etude d'une réception interculturelle et réflexion sur l'exotisme cinématographique." PhD diss., Université Paul Verlaine, 2009.

Manovic, Lev. *The Language of New Media.* Cambridge, MA: MIT Press, 2001.

Mes, Tom. "Generation Video: Nel mondo del V-Cinema." In *Anime Perdute: Il cinema di Miike Takashi,* edited by Dario Tomasi, 47-57. Turin/Milan: Museo Nazionale del Cinema/Il Castoro, 2006.

————. "V-Cinema: How Home Video Revitalized Japanese Film and Mystified Film Historians." In *Introducing Japanese Popular Culture,* edited by Alisa Freedman and Toby Slade, 216-226. London/New York: Routledge: 2018.

Miyake, Toshio. "Mostri made in Japan: Orientalismo e auto-orientalismo nell'era della globalizzazione." In *Culture del Giappone contemporaneo,* edited by Matteo Casari, 165-196. Latina: Tunué, 2011.

Mori, Naoto. *Manga + Eiga! Manga gensaku eiga no genzai-chi.* Tokyo: Yosensha, 2017.

Motion Picture Producers Association of Japan. "Statistics of Film Industry in Japan." Accessed January 30, 2019.
http://www.eiren.org/statistics_e/index.html.

Napier, Susan J. *From Impressionism to Anime: Japan as Fantasy and Fan Cult in the Mind of the West.* New York: Palgrave, 2007.

Osanai, Terutarō. "Être indépendant au Japon." *Cahiers du Cinéma* 5 (2011): 57-59.

Perez, Manuel Hernández. *Manga, anime y videojuegos: Narrativa cross-media japonesa.* Zaragoza: Prensas de la Universidad de Zaragoza, 2017.

Riva, Federica Francesca. "Homecoming: Le tecnologie domestiche della visione." In *Terre incognite: Lo spettatore italiano e le nuove forme dell'esperienza di visione dei film,* edited by Francesco Casetti and Mariagrazia Fanchi, 64-66. Roma: Carocci, 2006.

Schembri, Rino. "Stratifications, Graphems and Synchronies in (Neo-figurative) Cinema: From Greenaway's The Tulse Luper Suitcases to Miller and Rodriguez's Sin City." In *Cinema e fumetto: Cinema and Comics,* edited by Leonardo Quaresima, Federico Zecca, and Laura Ester Sangalli, 659-662. Udine: Forum, 2009.

Serres, Michel. *Thumbelina: The Culture and Technology of Millenials.* London/New York: Rowman & Littlefield, 2015.

Shin, Chi-Yun. "The Art of Branding: Tartan 'Asia Extreme' Films." In *Horror to the Extremes: Changing Boundaries in Asian Cinema,* edited by Jinhee Choi and Mitsuyo Wada-Marciano, 85-100. Hong Kong: Hong Kong University Press, 2009.

Shirky, Clay. "Tiny Slice, Big Market." *Wired,* November 1, 2006. https://www.wired.com/2006/11/meganiche.

Steinberg, Marc. *Anime's Media Mix: Franchising Toys and Characters in Japan.* Minneapolis, MN/London: Minnesota University Press, 2012.

———. "Condensing the Media Mix: The Tatami Galaxy's Multiple Possible Worlds." In *Introducing Japanese Popular Culture,* edited by Alisa Freedman and Toby Slade, 252-261. London/New York: Routledge: 2018.

Tezuka, Yoshiharu. *Japanese Cinema Goes Global.* Hong Kong: Hong Kong University Press, 2008.

Tsutsui, William M. "The Prehistory of Soft Power: Godzillla, Cheese, and the American Consumption of Japan." In *Introducing Japanese Popular Culture,* edited by Alisa Freedman and Toby Slade, 216-226. London/New York: Routledge: 2018.

Wada-Marciano, Mitsuyo. *Japanese Cinema in the Digital Age.* Honolulu: University of Hawai'i Press, 2012.

Wilkinson, Endymion. *Japan Versus Europe: A History of Misunderstanding.* London/New York: Penguin Books, 1980.

Zahlten, Alexander. *The End of Japanese Cinema: Industrial Genres, National Times, and Media Ecologies.* Durham, NC: Duke University Press, 2017.

Zecca, Federico. *Cinema e intermedialità: Modelli di traduzione.* Udine: Forum, 2013.

Chapter 3

The Poetry of War:
Jarmusch's *Ghost Dog* and the Reinvention of the Code of the Samurai in a Contemporary Key[1]

Remo Gramigna

University of Turin, Italy

Abstract

This study explores the image of Japan as reflected in Jarmusch's film *Ghost Dog: The Way of the Samurai*. The imaginary scenarios of ancient Japan are echoed in Jarmusch's artistic expression, whose intertextual links to the Japanese samurai Yamamoto Tsunetomo's book—the *Hagakure*—and Ryūnosuke Akutagawa's *Rashōmon and Other Stories* are interwoven in the narrative of the film. The significance of *Ghost Dog* lies in the appropriation, reinvention, and translation of an ancient code of honor—the way of the samurai—in a contemporary key. The study reveals that *Ghost Dog* presents multiple sub-universe of meanings and a host of cultural codes and texts that although interlocked, sometimes clash. Three main aspects of this cultural dynamic of appropriation, reinvention, and translation in the film are discussed: a) The poetry of war as a philosophical and spiritual motive of *Ghost Dog*, b) the clash between old and new universe of meanings, and c) the reinvention and cultural adaptation of the Japanese imagery of the warrior into the contemporary American gangster subculture.

---

[1] Research for this paper was supported by the Estonian Research Council (Grant 1481, "The Role of Imaginary Narrative Scenarios in Cultural Dynamics") and by the European Regional Development Fund (Center of Excellence in Estonian Studies).

Keywords: Jim Jarmusch, *Ghost Dog: The Way of the Samurai,* samurai, cultural codes, American gangster subculture.

* * *

Introduction: Scope of the Enquiry

Japanese culture and aesthetics had a remarkable influence on Western popular media in the 20th century. Contemporary cinema aesthetics have often drawn on the Japanese warrior philosophy and found in it a distinctive source of inspiration. Indeed, the ancient code of the samurai is a repeated theme, so much so that it became a *topos* in Western cinema. In this regard, one may think of *The Seven Samurai* (Kurosawa, 1954), *Rashōmon* (Kurosawa, 1954), *The Magnificient Seven* (Sturges, 1960), *Koroshi No Rakuin* (Suzuki, 1967), *Le Samuraï* (Melville, 1967), or *Ronin* (Frankenheimer, 1998), to mention but a few.

The subject of this chapter is *Ghost Dog: The Way of the Samurai* (1999), a film written and directed by Jim Jarmusch, a well-known independent American screenwriter and director, and which has become an iconic film presenting the Japanese warrior code, *bushidō,* to a broader Western audience.[2] The Japaneseness of the film is, however, often stereotypical and presents something Japanese in a Western setting to attract audiences who are interested in consuming a "Westernized samurai story." I have found it practical to delimit the confines of the present inquiry to this particular film because it depicts the imaginary scenario of medieval Japan in an explicit and original fashion. This film also provides a suggestive depiction of the samurai philosophy in contemporary popular culture. Therefore, Jarmusch's artistic work is an exemplary case study for exploring the image of Japan represented in American independent film aesthetics.

---

[2] The literature on Jim Jarmusch's film production is quite extensive. For a comprehensive view on the subject, see Ludvig Hertzberg, ed., *Jim Jarmusch* (Jackson, MS: University Press of Mississippi, 2001); Eric Lackey, "Arbitrary Reality: The Global Art Cinema of Jim Jarmusch" (PhD diss., University of Kansas, 2012); Patrizia Lombardo, *Memory and Imagination in Film: Scorsese, Lynch, Jarmusch, Van Sant* (New York: Palgrave Macmillan, 2014); Umberto Mosca, *Jim Jarmusch* (Milan: Il Castoro, 2000); Sara Piazza, *Jim Jarmusch: Music, Words, and Noise* (London: Reaktion Books, 2015); Chiara Renda, *Jim Jarmusch: Il fascino della malinconia* (Genoa: Le Mani, 2008); Julian Rice, *The Jarmusch Way: Spirituality and Imagination in Dead Man, Ghost Dog, and the Limits of Control* (Lanham, MD: Scarecrow Press, 2012).

References to "ancient Japan" and, more specifically, to the feudal ethics and the code of conduct of the samurai abound throughout the film. As Richardson pointed out, "Japanese culture here is not merely translated into a Western context; it also provides a kind of intermediary through which many of the film's themes are enacted."[3] In *Ghost Dog*, Jarmusch constructed a very complex thread of cultural references. However, two Japanese sources are particularly significant with respect to the subject of this chapter.

Indeed, in the film, there are repeated and explicit allusions to the 18th-century book *Hagakure* – the Japanese samurai Yamamoto Tsunetomo's (1659-1719) recorded knowledge[4] – as well as to Akutagawa Ryūnosuke's (1892-1927) book *Rashōmon and Other Stories*. As we shall see, Jarmusch selected numerous themes and motifs from these two Japanese texts. In the last analysis, the injunctions of the samurai philosophy and the images of Japan embedded in the film function as scenarios within the film's narrative structure. Sometimes, such scenarios serve as anticipations of events to take place in the immediate future. Such Japanese cultural references are interwoven in the story's narrative structure, and their uses in the film bear significance.

In what follows, I shall explore the relations that such Japanese texts have with the overall economy of the film, how the cinematic narrative intertextually refers to such sources, and how these references inform the genesis and the characterization of the film's main hero as a post-modern urban samurai. The analysis of the subject reveals that there is a sophisticated web of cultural codes, cultural texts, and scenarios of medieval Japan that are commingled, negotiated, and at times conflicting in Jarmusch's film. I would like to advance the idea that the significance of Jarmusch's *Ghost Dog* may be found in the appropriation, reinvention, and translation of a forgotten samurai code of conduct and ethics – *Hagakure*. Such a dynamic of appropriation, reinvention, and translation yields to the construction and reimagining, throughout the film, of the visual imagery of medieval Japan – in particular the image of Japanese warriorship – in a contemporary key.

Ultimately, there is an interesting amalgam of influences in Jarmusch's film. The juxtaposition of different codes, texts, cultures, and scenarios creates an original syncretism of meanings within Jarmusch's cinematic work. Three main aspects of such a cultural dynamic of appropriation, reinvention, and

---

[3] Michael Richardson, "The Phantom of Communication: Jim Jarmusch's *Ghost Dog* and the Opacity of the Message," *Third Text* 24, no. 3 (2010): 365
[4] Yamamoto Tsunetomo, *Hagakure: The Book of the Samurai*, trans. William Scott Wilson (Tokyo: Kōdansha International, 1979).

translation in the film are discussed: (a) the ethics of loyalty and the attitude toward death as philosophical and spiritual motifs of *Hagakure* re-enacted in Jarmusch's film; (b) the interplay and tension between old and new cultural codes depicted in the film; and (c) the reinvention and cultural adaptation of the Japanese image of the warrior into the contemporary American black gangster subculture.

Syncretism in Jarmusch's Work

Ghost Dog: The Way of the Samurai (1999), Jarmusch's seventh cinematic work, is a hybrid text. When I first watched the film, it struck me with its simplicity, sense of humor, and proclivity for spiritual motifs. Undoubtedly, a film as complex as *Ghost Dog* cannot be easily defined in terms of genre. Indeed, gangster films, hip-hop culture, samurai movies, and Eastern and Western influences are all well amalgamated into this film. Such an aesthetics of composition creates quite an original syncretism. It is not surprising that Jarmusch himself has referred to *Ghost Dog* as a "samurai-gangster-hip-hop-Eastern Western" film.[5]

This description is totally in alignment with the director's method of writing stories. He does not conceive of strict and categorical boundaries between genres. He often blurs them. In this regard, Jarmusch has referred to his own style of composition as a sort of jazz improvisation along a main standard. The gangster genre is the main standard in the film in question. Thus, *Ghost Dog* can be thought of as an improvisation (a series of variations) around the genre of gangster movies.[6] This is certainly not the first time that the American filmmaker ventured into the production of a work that teases out the idea of the contamination of genres and capitalizes on the cross-pollination of cultural influences within one cultural unit. This proclivity for the creative mixing up and collage of cultures stands at the axis of Jarmusch's poetics of composition. It is worth recalling that, four years prior to the release of *Ghost Dog*, Jarmusch became quite famous in the American independent film circle with a film that provided a new interpretation of the Western genre – *Dead Man* (1995).

The arrangement of different texts amalgamated into one single unit is an important aspect of Jarmusch's aesthetic of composition.[7] This proclivity is

---

[5] Quoted by Nils Meyer in *Jim Jarmusch* (Berlin: Berts-Verlag, 2001), 252.

[6] Max Stèfani, "Jim Jarmusch: Slower than Paradise," *Mucchio Selvaggio* 383 (2000): 56.

[7] On this point, see Juan A. Suarez, *Jim Jarmusch* (Urbana, IL: University of Illinois Press, 2007), 126-128.

most probably the result of Jarmusch's working method, which can be described as cumulative and progressive. In other words, the director almost never begins a project with the intent of writing a precise story from the outset. He rather builds up the film script by adding up details, notes, and stories during the same act of writing, thus accumulating materials and anecdotes along the writing process, layer after layer. In the case of *Ghost Dog*, the initial idea was to write a story about a "nice killer."[8] In fact, the concept of the samurai and the Japanese philosophy overtone that inspired the film were embedded in the script only at a later stage of writing the story. Niels Meyer and Umberto Mosca, with good reason, have referred to *Ghost Dog* as a palimpsest text.[9]

Because of the rich and systematic borrowing and citing from different cultural sources, it has been argued that Jarmusch's poetic of composition in *Ghost Dog* may be regarded as an "aesthetic of sampling."[10] However, Jarmusch has referred to his own style of composition as a "be-pop" method because it freely cites other movies and cultures. Along the same lines, Juan Suarez pointed out that "the film is possessed by a cultural memory that it seems compelled to reenact, returning to what has been filmed, written, and read."[11] In general terms, intertextuality is definitely an important aspect of *Ghost Dog* as well as a marker of Jarmusch's way of making movies.

Whilst Japanese culture provides a source of inspiration for Jarmusch's artistic expression, the film embeds an unprecedented mix of gangster culture, hip-hop and rap culture, as well as black American culture that coexists within the same text.[12] Undoubtedly, one of the most important sources of influence for Jarmusch has always been music – hip-hop in particular.[13] One of the characteristic features of the director's films is that music is often organically linked to the story. In this regard, *Ghost Dog* is no exception. The music is an

---

[8] Stèfani, "Jim Jarmusch," 56.

[9] Meyer, *Jarmusch*, 253; Mosca, *Jarmusch*, 127.

[10] Eric Gonzalez, "Jim Jarmusch's Aesthetics of Sampling in *Ghost Dog–The Way of the Samurai*," *Volume! La revue des musiques populaires* 3, no. 2 (2004): 113-116.

[11] Suarez, *Jarmusch*, 129.

[12] Throughout the paper, I use the concept of "text" in a broad and semiotic fashion, therefore not limiting the idea of text to language and written text only. The concept of text encompasses any cultural unit that has meaning for someone in a given context.

[13] Jarmusch is a musician himself and has played in a band. He also produced a documentary about the musician Neil Young. On the relation between music and narration in Jarmusch, see Benedict Feiten, *Jim Jarmusch: Musik und Narration – Transnationalität und Alternative Filmische Erzählformen* (Bielefeld: Transcript Verlag, 2017).

original composition written for the film by the composer RZA – a founding member of the hip-hop group the Wu-Tang Clan. The soundtrack plays an important role in setting the dominant narrative of the story, and it is also used for the characterization of the main protagonist, who is close, in musical taste and personal appearance, to hip-hop culture.

Ghost Dog's Microcosm

Ghost Dog's tale revolves around a fairly simple plot. Forest Whitaker plays the role of a professional assassin who is loosely associated with an Italo-American group of *mafiosi* now in decline. He works for the criminal organization as a contract killer. He lives a solitary life in a shack on the rooftop of a high building in the periphery of New Jersey and communicates through homing pigeons. He has only two friends: Pearline (Camille Winbush), a ten-year-old girl who befriended him and with whom he discusses books, and Raymond (Isaach De Bankolé), a Haitian ice-cream seller who speaks only French and with whom he plays chess. In order to perform his duties, the killer follows an ancient code of samurai conduct, as expounded in the Japanese text *Hagakure*. Because he follows the samurai code, the killer establishes a lord-retainer relationship with Louie Bonacelli (John Tormey), a local member of the mafia clan, who – according to the assassin's testimony of the event – once saved his life when the hitman was younger.

Things become more complicated when Louie commissions the assassin to murder Handsome Frank (Richard Portnow), a gangster associated with the mob who has an affair with Louise (Tricia Vessey) – the daughter of the local mafia boss, Mr. Ray Vargo (Henry Silva). This is a game-changer that will compromise the relation between the lord and the retainer. Because Louise witnesses the murder of Handsome Frank, the criminal organization indeed decides, without much elaboration, to get rid of the assassin, even though he carried out his duty effectively.[14]

The Sicilian gangsters track the assassin and seek to murder him without much success. When the gangsters find his home, they kill and torture the flock of homing pigeons that he had nurtured, destroy his books, and vandalize his living space. This action provokes the killer's vengefulness. As a reaction, he eliminates all the members of the criminal organization, except for Mr. Vargo's daughter and Louie, because the samurai code dictates full devotion to the lord.

---

[14] It is not very clear, however, why the mafia organization decided to eliminate the assassin.

Due to the loyalty vow that bonds the retainer to his lord, the killer sacrifices his own life and complicitly opts to get killed by Louie in the final shooting scene.

I should now like to make a few remarks on *Ghost Dog*'s opening scene, whose significance is worth pondering. The starting point of the film is a bird's-eye perspective that shows a post-industrial landscape in motion. The city depicted is a present-day suburban area in New Jersey, where the killer lives and where most of the action takes place. The metropolitan area remains, however, quite anonymous. Although the scene was shot from the pigeon's perspective, the scenario depicted – with buildings, harbors, trains, cars, and motorways – retains an anthropomorphic overlay. Indeed, the urban landscape represented looks very much like the panorama a man would have if he were to fly in a helicopter over the city, or if he were to look down on the world from the perspective of a hot air balloon in flight. The scene gives a sense of elevation. The soundtrack of the film composed by RZA not only sets the mood of the entire film, but magnifies the rhythm and atmosphere of this first aerial scene. The rhythm is slow, fluctuating, and immersive.

The bird depicted in the setting of the scene is not a generic bird but a homing pigeon. This aspect is worth considering. The killer, as the bearer of a traditional culture almost completely lost, holds animals in great regard.[15] Indeed, he has not lost touch with nature, and his deep, almost sacred psychic connection with the animal world is remarkable. It is not only that he lives surrounded by a flock of homing pigeons, which he breeds, with whom he communicates, and which he releases daily for exercise. Most significantly, the pigeons serve as the means of communication between Louie (the lord) and the contract killer (the retainer) by carrying short written messages from the roof of the killer's house to the headquarters of the criminal organization and back. Indeed, Louie, when interrogated by the *mafiosi* who were seeking any useful information to drive the stealthy killer out, remarked that a pigeon visited him every day. In this regard, some commentators have noted that the use of homing pigeons in the film is a subtle critique of modern technology and have argued that this is indexical of the mode of communication in the film, which is always indirect.[16]

The initial scene of the film is significant for two main reasons. Firstly, because it sets the stage for the whole film by thematizing the role of the homing pigeons in the story and the spiritual relationship that these animals bear with the killer, which is not of secondary importance. Secondly, because

---

[15] References to the animal kingdom are plenty throughout the film.
[16] Richardson, "The Phantom," 361.

the scene is a visual metaphor of the voyage – the journey of the homing pigeon from the killer to Louie and back. Such a metaphor of the voyage is symbolic both of the specific type of communication between Louie and the hitman and of the particular covenant – an established contract in the true sense of the word – that bonds the retainer to his lord.

As a corollary to this, it should be added that the aerial voyage of the homing pigeon depicted in the first sequence of the film is counterpointed to the terrestrial journey of the stealthy killer, who often travels by car when he performs his service as Louie's contract assassin. This topological opposition between the movement through the air (the voyage of the homing pigeon) and by road (the journey by car of the killer) produces an important thematic isotopy that links up together different scenes throughout the film. The loyalty that binds the retainer to the lord is at the axis of *Hagakure*. This is an aspect of the book that is selected and enacted in *Ghost Dog* through the contractual arrangement between the killer and Louie. As we shall see in what follows, the bond that ties them is predicated upon a vow of loyalty between the samurai and his lord.

Soon after the initial aerial scene, the viewer is introduced to the microcosm of the killer, the eponymous hero of the film. He is depicted as a modern-day mindful and soulful Afro-American hitman, who chose to fully adhere to the moral and applied principles of *Hagakure* to refashion his own self-image. *Hagakure* is an 18th-century treatise on the conduct of the samurai that sets out the principles that a perfect retainer should follow. The array of precepts set out by this code span from the mental attitude of the samurai to the manner of conduct in society to which a commendable retainer ought to adhere. In an interview released in 1999, Jarmusch described *Ghost Dog*'s main character as a "spiritual warrior."[17] In a similar vein, in one of the final scenes of the movie, the assassin describes himself and Louie as members of an "almost extinct tribe."

Admittedly, Jarmusch tapped into the Eastern culture of warriors as a model by which to mold the main hero of his film. Two souls are combined and united in one single character: spiritual depth – symbolizing the mental discipline and the unwavering mindset of the samurai – and physical dexterity in the use of weapons and the expertise in martial arts. Thus, the discipline of the mind is as

---

[17] Stephen Ashton, "Conversation with Jim Jarmusch: Cinematic Samurai," *MovieMaker*, February 4, 2008,
https://www.moviemaker.com/archives/moviemaking/directing/articles-directing/jim-jarmusch-ghost-dog-the-way-of-the-samurai-interview-20080204/.

important as the physical delivery of the martial art. Not surprisingly, the killer in *Ghost Dog* is depicted as a zen-like, well-built black man who lives a monastic lifestyle. This interesting characterization is also reflected in his personal appearance. Whilst he has a massive body size and an intimidating stance, the assassin is a very graceful and gentle character, has presence, is spiritually aware, and shows a specific attitude in everything he does. Forest Whitaker suits the impersonation of such a role very well. He was in fact chosen by Jarmusch for his "very soft, gentle, poignant side."[18]

The assassin's proclivity for silence is worthy of note, too. In this regard, Julian Rice pointed out that "Whitaker's vocal silence incorporates the Buddhist sense of emptiness as form into the serenity of his physical presence."[19] In line with the injunctions set forth in the practical guide to the samurai, the killer is indeed self-aware of the power of words and the importance of communication. He uses words sparingly and he delivers and receives messages cautiously. For instance, when he receives a written message from Louie, he uses the precaution of destroying the message by chewing and ingesting it.

The communication channel he selected to reach out to Louie proves to be effective, although the group of Italo-American gangsters, to which the latter belongs, regard it as obsolete and out of fashion because they lack the means to understand its function and mechanism. Much of the communication between the killer and Louie is based on the exchange of very short messages attached to one leg of a pigeon trained to carry the message to a precise destination. The form of the messages carried by the homing pigeons is always succinct. Brevity is the feature that defines them. The messages are written with blue ink on a very little piece of paper. This requires the ability to write in very small letters.

We do not know much about the main character's past, except that Louie once saved his life. Yet the first depiction of the character is very topical, and a great amount of information may be gleaned from it. The killer is shown in his home setting, at night, immersed in reading. He holds in his hands *Hagakure: The Book of the Samurai* by Yamamoto Tsnunetomo. From this initial depiction of the killer's microcosm, we can infer that he is an avid reader. The camera gives a tracking shot of a series of books arranged in an orderly manner on a shelf in the killer's humble home. Undoubtedly, he has quite a sophisticated

[18] Herzberg, *Jarmusch*, 1.
[19] Rice, "The Jarmusch Way," 100.

background and is well-read in numerous areas of knowledge, spanning from American literary classics to texts on spirituality, Buddhism, and Japanese and Tibetan culture. The intellectual side of the killer is quite prominent. Indeed, among his favorite readings, we find homing pigeon manuals, *Akhnaton: The Extraterrestrial King* (Daniel Blair Stewart), *The Mayan Factor: Path Beyond Technology* (José Argüelles), *The Wild Palms* (William Faulkner), *The Tibetan Book of the Dead* (Bardo Thodol), *The Autobiography of Malcolm X*, *Indignant Heart* (Charles Denby), *Darkness at Noon* (Arthur Koestler), *Bury My Heart at Wounded Knee* (Dee Brown), *Soul on Ice* (Eldridge Cleaver), *The Wretched of the Earth* (Frantz Fanon), *The Killer* (Wade Miller), *The Chinese Room* (Vivian Connell), and others.

Not only is he depicted as an avid reader, but in his idle time, he often engages in literary discussions with one of his two friends, the ten-year-old Pearline. Like the killer, Pearline likes books that she carries around in a small briefcase. *The Wind in the Willows* by Kenneth Grahame, *The Souls of Black Folk* by W. E. B. Du Bois (which was assigned to her for reading by her school teacher), *Night Nurse* by Fern Shepard (which she has not read but liked the cover), and *Frankenstein* by Mary Shelley, which the killer has read and praised as a "good book," are among her favorite texts.

In the credits of the film, Jarmusch indirectly invites the audience to get acquainted with the books referenced in the film. The killer and Pearline are not the only characters that show a proclivity for books. Mr. Vargo is often portrayed with a book in his hands, his daughter, Louise, in her first appearance holds the book *Rashōmon* and then hands it to the killer, and even the Haitian ice cream vendor, Raymond, shows the latter a book called *L'ours*, pointing out the similarity between the appearance of the killer and the bear, the subject of the book.

Undoubtedly, books play a significant role in the film's narrative and are used as a medium of communication and exchange among the main characters. I will come back to this point in due course. Discussing and unpacking the relations between all such texts and *Ghost Dog* would definitely be an interesting endeavor, yet it would exceed the limits of the present study. Within the plethora of interwoven cultural references the movie is immeshed in, there are two which I found to be especially relevant to the present study. For this reason, in what follows, I will mainly focus on *Hagakure* and *Rashōmon* as the most prominent Japanese textual sources Jarmusch drew on for shaping the story and molding the untraceable modern samurai.

Loyalty and Attitude Toward Death in *Hagakure*

Undoubtedly, *Hagakure* had a profound influence on Jarmusch. I contend that his depiction of the black contract killer as a spiritual and modern urban *bushi* can be thought of as a contemporary filmic adaptation of the essence of the spirit of the perfect retainer, as outlined in detail in Yamamoto's book. As noted earlier, the killer literally lives by the book. The behaviors and attitudes he pursued down to the last detail are *bushidō* as laid down in *Hagakure*. Thus, the book stands as a manifesto for the retainer. He takes the book as the basis for regulating his daily routine and shaping his lifestyle. He strictly adheres to the principles of the way of the samurai to perform his duties as Louie's retainer.

In the morning, he addresses the gods, practices martial arts, and burns incense. The mental discipline and determination, the loyalty and self-reliance, the proclivity for compassion, the acute awareness of speech, the laying of a disciplinary structure upon himself, the psychological and spiritual acumen, the absolute devotion toward the lord, and the attitude toward death are all totally in alignment with the injunctions set out in *Hagakure*. The evidence that this is the case is overwhelming. However, there is probably one exception to this general pattern. It should be noted from the outset that the killer's proclivity for books and literature in general is somewhat incongruent with the principles outlined in *Hagakure*. In fact, almost no reference is found in Yamamoto's book in regard to reading and literature because the intellectual and logical skills were not meant to constitute an essential part of the training of a retainer.[20] Because *Hagakure* is key to the film narrative as a whole, it behooves us to provide some background information about such a source and its main themes.

Hagakure was penned and published in 1716, and it expounds the doctrine of *bushidō* – the way of the warrior. The Japanese word *hagakure* literally means "hidden by the shadow leaves." The book is a collection of the thoughts, aphorisms, and moral injunctions of Yamamoto Jinuemon Tsunetomo, a samurai of the Saga Domain in Hizen Province. The text was written in collaboration with Tsuramoto Tashiro (1678-1748). He was an associate of Yamamoto, and he recorded and compiled his lectures. Because it is organized as a collection of thoughts and precepts, the text does not present an overriding narrative.

---

[20] Howard Kevin Alexander, "The Essence of *Hagakure*" (PhD diss., University of Lethbridge, 1972), 24.

The scope of the book was to serve as a moral and practical guide for the samurai. The production of the book can be thought of as a reaction to the decadence of the samurai class that was rampant in Japan during the Edo period. According to Yamamoto, the samurai class had compromised its integrity and lost its true identity as a class of warriors. The ability and skills to act as warriors were downplayed by more clerical and official tasks necessary in the prolonged period of peace. Thus, the intention behind the writing of the book was to restore the strong role of the warrior in feudal Japan. For this reason, the author elaborated and laid out a set of ethical principles of various nature in order to regulate the behavior of the samurai down to the last detail. Thus, the function of *Hagakure* was to serve as a code of ethical conduct for the perfect retainer.

The book presents a variety of relevant themes woven into its pages, some of which were embedded into *Ghost Dog*'s narrative. The injunctions found in *Hagakure* span from the personal appearance of the samurai to the etiquette and ethics of speech, loyalty to the lord, the attitude toward death, the training of mental discipline, and many other aspects. The feature that distinguishes *Hagakure* from other similar historical sources is that the book was specifically designed to instruct the individual samurai rather than the high commanders and, for this reason, its injunctions focused on fostering the mental discipline of the *bushi* rather than the physical training.[21]

At the kernel of *Hagakure* lies the injunction of duty of loyalty to one's lord. This is a prominent aspect of the book, both qualitatively and quantitatively. The loyalty to one's lord is predicated on the concept of absolute devotion to service, which is a cornerstone of the entire philosophy underlying the work. It is worth noting that there are four vows between the lord and the retainer, one of which clearly states that "one must be of service to the lord."[22] As Yasuko Mitamura points out, "one of the important aspects of *Hagakure* is concealed loyalty or hidden virtue, which is implied in the word *Hagakure*, for things in the shade are hidden."[23] Thus, the loyalty of the retainer to their lord is the primary goal that the perfect retainer should strive to accomplish. According to the way of the samurai, the commitment of absolute loyalty to the lord cannot be compromised in any circumstances, and a samurai must be ready to sacrifice even his own life in order to adhere to such a principle.

---

[21] Ibid., 34.

[22] Ibid., 25.

[23] Yasuko Mitamura, "A Retrospect on the Spirit of *bushidō* as Exemplified in *Hagakure*" (PhD diss., University of Southern California, 1969), 3.

As is apparent, the lord-retainer relation is of a peculiar nature. The abovementioned vow that "one must be of service to the lord" establishes a tight covenant between the retainer and the lord. This contract is based on the service and devotion of the retainer to the lord. There are numerous passages in *Hagakure* that expound the duty of loyalty to the lord that a retainer must always pursue. Jarmusch selected one of these excerpts and encapsulated it in the narrative of his film: "If one were to say in a word what the condition of being a samurai is, its basis lies first in seriously devoting one's body and soul to his master. Not to forget one's master is the most fundamental thing for a retainer."

Furthermore, *Hagakure* is a meditation on death and on the attitude toward it. This is definitely one of the central themes of the book. The orientation one should have toward death is intertwined with the injunction of loyalty to one's lord. In fact, one presupposes the other. The vow of loyalty that bonds the retainer to his lord predicates that a samurai must always be ready to sacrifice his own life for the sake of the lord. Thus, the mental attitude of the samurai should be established on unwavering determination and attuned with the immediacy of action and resolution. Such a mental attitude is the result of coming to terms with the fear of death. Facing death and overcoming the fear of dying is key to *bushidō*.

According to the precepts of *Hagakure*, a commendable retainer must be prepared to die for his lord. As a result of this attitude toward death, the samurai's state of mind is geared on fearlessness. As Howard K. Alexander pointed out, the root of the idea of fearlessness and readiness for death can be traced back to Sun Tzu (*The Art of War*), who had a remarkable influence on *Hagakure*.[24] Sun Tzu had in fact noted that when soldiers on a battlefield experienced a situation of no escape because they were surrounded by enemies, their willingness and strength to fight to the death would exponentially increase.[25] Numerous illustrations of such a philosophy are found in *Hagakure*. The attitude toward death is epitomized in the following passage:

> The way of the warrior amounts to being resigned to death. In a situation of two choices. Life or death, there is nothing but to decide upon death immediately. It is as simple as that. It is to make up one's mind and proceed. The statement, "to die without attaining one's goal is a useless

[24] Alexander, "Essence," 56.
[25] Alexander, "Essence," 56.

death," must surely be the conceited Kyoto version of *bushidō*. In a situation of two choices it is not necessary to act so as to always achieve one's goal. We all prefer to live. Our preference would seem to prevail. It is cowardice if one lives without attaining one's goal. This point is critical. If one misses the goal and dies, it simply proves that he was fanatically determined to die in vain. But this is no disgrace. On the contrary, this is heroic behavior. Every morning and every evening, when one repeatedly thinks of dying and dying, and is always as a dead body, he should be able to acquire mastery in the martial way, live a life free of faults, and fulfil his occupation in life.[26]

The image of the samurai that may be gleaned from reading the passages of *Hagakure* is that of a man of great determination, fearless and self-reliant, with immense willpower, strong self-discipline, and, above all, extreme loyalty. The idea of immediacy and determination of action as a characteristic of the perfect retainer is also very much accentuated. The *bushi* must be able to perform his action in a resolute way, without hesitation or wavering. In a very poetic and suggestive fashion, the book in fact remarks that one should make up his mind within the timespan of seven breaths. From the cursory discussion on the main principles of *Hagakure* it can be concluded that some of the injunctions set out in the book were selected by Jarmusch and encapsulated in the film as main themes of the narrative.

Loyalty and Attitudes Toward Death as Enacted in *Ghost Dog*

As pointed out in the introduction, Jarmusch introduced *Hagakure* as a theme in the film only in the second stage of the writing of the script. The book assumes several levels of significance within the film, and it exists at multiple levels of resolution. At the first level of analysis, the Japanese samurai philosophy is an undercurrent theme of the film. It informs both the narrative and the characterization of the main character as a modern spiritual killer who sticks to the feudal code of behavior of the samurai. The influence of *Hagakure* is apparent because of the numerous references to this source. The film's title in fact explicitly hints at "The Way of the Samurai." The book is evoked as both a physical and a symbolic object in the film. Not only is the killer depicted while reading this particular book in the first scene in which he is represented, but there are also direct and repeated allusions to the text throughout the film.

---

[26] Yamamoto, *Hagakure*, cited in ibid., 58.

On the second level, it should be noted that the primary device through which *Hagakure* is embedded in the film structure is through direct quotations of excerpts of the book. The quotations are encapsulated on two levels of expression: they are voiced by Forest Whitaker and displayed as written text on the screen. Indeed, in numerous passages of the film, Whitaker's voice-over recites passages from the book – except for the last quote, which is instead read by Pearline. The same quote is reported as a caption on the screen. Thus, the modality through which the injunctions of *Hagakure* are embedded in the film is twofold: graphically – as written words projected onto the screen – and orally – as spoken words conveyed through Whitaker's voice-over. Through such a device, *Hagakure* takes on an explicit role of "text within the text" in *Ghost Dog*.[27]

On the graphic level, *Hagakure* is structured in short paragraphs. In the English translation of the book by William Scott Wilson, each paragraph is separated by a symbol. Such a symbol depicts three stylized and interlocking cranes. It is worth noting that, in the film, Jarmusch maintains the same design of the book. Indeed, the selected paragraphs from *Hagakure* appear in the film as stand-alone quotes penned in white ink on a black background. After each paragraph, the same graphic symbol used in the book to separate the passages is included. Moreover, the stealthy killer always wears a golden chain with a big locket reproducing a similar symbol. Exactly the same symbol is reproduced on the back of Ghost Dog's black jacket. In this regard, it could be said that Jarmusch reveres the book not only as a literary object, but also as an aesthetic artifact, whose main features are somewhat reproduced and reiterated in the film.

Up to this point, one can infer that *Ghost Dog* is literally punctuated by citations from *Hagakure*. On a third level of resolution, it can be argued that that the quotations function as interstices within the narrative structure of the film. As Jarmusch pointed out, "I used quotes from the Hagakure as little separations in the film itself, like breathing spaces, like – almost like a little running commentary on what informs Ghost Dog as a samurai."[28] Although *Hagakure* is comprised of over a thousand passages, Jarmusch selected only some excerpts, embedded them into the film, and linked them to situations and

---

[27] Juri Lotman, "The Text Within the Text," *Publication of the Modern Language Association of America (PMLA)* 109, no. 3 (1994): 377.

[28] Jim Jarmusch, "Jim Jarmusch on Iggy Pop, Hip-Hop and Finding Poetry in Mundane Things," *NPR*, January 31, 2017, https://www.npr.org/2017/01/31/512622404/jim-jarmusch-on-iggy-pop-hip-hop-and-finding-poetry-in-mundane-things?t=1536603169577.

people portrayed in the film. The progression in which the paragraphs are reported in the film is not the same order as the arrangement of the text. In total, Jarmusch selected 14 quotations from the book. It is hard to make a final assessment as to what the relation is between the content of the quotations and the narrative structure and to what extent the injunctions of *Hagakure* inform the plot. However, a case can be made that the quotes provide the mood and set the stage and the atmosphere of the scenes, thus functioning as scenarios within the film. In other words, they function as a sort of anticipatory device for what is yet to happen. It would also be fair to say that there are certain recurrent themes that are evoked in these passages and that permeate the film.

Undoubtedly, the injunction of loyalty to one's lord as expounded in *Hagakure* informs the lord-retainer relation between the killer and Louie represented in *Ghost Dog*. Thus, the contractual relation between the killer and Louie is an adaptation of one of the main themes of Japanese samurai philosophy. The way in which the film justifies and rationalizes such a relation is twofold. Firstly, as said before, the contract that bonds a retainer to his lord in feudal Japan is predicated upon the vow of the loyalty of a retainer to his superior. Because the hitman genuinely adheres to the code of the samurai, he feels obliged to serve Louie in all respects. Each time that he does something that may hurt Louie, he repeats the following mantras: "I'm your retainer. I follow a code. I've always given you my respect. Forgive me, I don't mean no disrespect." However, there is definitely more to it.

The lord-retainer relation, as represented in *Ghost Dog*, is somewhat asymmetrical. It would seem that the retainer has taken a unilateral decision to serve, commit, and respect his lord, without Louie being fully cognizant of his role in such a relation. According to Rice, "[a]s the story unfolds it becomes clear that Ghost Dog knows Louie's limitations and realizes that his decision to serve the man who saved his life may be physically beneficial to his master but is spiritually beneficial only to himself."[29] One may wonder whether serving a lord without the lord being fully cognizant of it would still count as adherence to the samurai code. Some have criticized such an idea in the film, thus portraying a situation that is, in the ultimate analysis, asymmetrical. *Hagakure*, however, is quite clear about this. As the title of the book – "hidden by the shadow leaves" – suggests, loyalty to one's lord is a hidden virtue. I argue that the covert alliance and secret covenant between the hitman and the mafia boss is an original adaptation of the theme of loyalty as hidden virtue described in

---

[29] Rice, "*The Jarmusch Way*," 108.

Hagakure. Thus, the representation given by Jarmusch is congruous with the underlying philosophy of the book.

Another point that deserves consideration is the clash of cultural codes within the film. In *Ghost Dog*, there is an undercurrent of nostalgia for an ancient worldview that has been gradually lost. The clash between old and new cultural codes is apparent in the dynamic between the main hero's worldview and the gangsters' culture. Indeed, Louie does not fully understand the cultural code to which the killer chose to adhere. Such a system of rules is foreign to Louie and to the other associates of the mafia clan. As such, it remains obscure and incomprehensible to them. From the viewpoint of the present Western world, as well as from the perspective of Louie's worldview, the code of conduct of the samurai is void of meaning and is, therefore, undecipherable.

Despite the enormous differences that divide Louie and his retainer, they nonetheless share a common ground. They are both the bearers of a traditional culture – sticking to an old way of handling things – that has been forgotten. Indeed, in a world of accelerated changes, both Louie and the hitman chose to adhere to a code of conduct: the way of the samurai for the killer and the mafia code of honor for Louie. However, not only are both codes regarded as obsolete and out of fashion in the timeline when the story unfolds, but these codes are also incommensurable with respect to one another. In other words, there is an incongruity between the cultural codes adopted by the characters of the films and the contemporary American (or other) cultural codes that the viewer is embedded in, as well as an inconsistency between the codes themselves chosen by each character.

This is particularly evident in the interpretation of the mafia gangsters in regards to the killer's daily rituals and behaviors. Indeed, from the point of view of the gangsters' culture, the killer's conduct is outside of their value system and horizons and is, therefore, incomprehensible. However, in comparison to the other associates of the mafia clan, Mr. Vargo is probably an exception. He is definitely more aware than the others and his cultural encyclopedia is wider than that of his subordinates. Indeed, Mr. Vargo is able to interpret and correctly decode the hitman's mysterious message extracted from *Hagakure* as "poetry of war."

The assassin's behavior and attitude toward Louie, his commitment, respect, and loyalty, find their moral foundations and rational justification in one aspect of the killer's past. Louie provides the first rational explanation of the retainer's commitment to the lord. Once the criminal organization took the decision to eliminate the stealthy killer, the mobsters try to extort background information about him from Louie. At this juncture, Louie realizes that he knows very little indeed about the killer's life, except for a few facts. Louie does not pay him by the job but once a year, always on the first day of autumn. The killer contacts Louie through a bird that comes to visit him every single day. The hitman is "a big black guy." Louie is very fond of him. Louie says that for the past four years, the killer has done twelve perfect contracts, performing his hits efficiently as a ghost, totally untraceable. Thus, Louie regards him as a very valuable ally. In addition, Louie says that once he saved the killer's life. This last detail is of pivotal importance. Louie tells the following story: "Maybe about eight years ago I saw a guy, this guy, he was more of a kid really, in a bad situation. So, I straighten things out. Anyway, then about four years ago this big guy comes to my door, this big black guy he's got a fucking pigeon on his shoulder. Fuck him, I don't know how he found me, but he said he owed me. I only saw him once after that and, well, he made this arrangement."

When Louie reports his own account as a witness of the event of the mysterious killer's past, the audience is shown the following scenario. In Louie's story, there are three men beating the killer, who is lying on the ground, to death. After Louie asked what was going on, we see one of those three men pointing a gun at Louie. Next, we see Louie killing the man who pointed the gun at him. Louie's account, however, does not coincide with the story told by the killer. The two perspectives about the past event are convergent to a certain extent, yet there are some important inconsistencies about how the events unfold. The killer dives into the "original scene" twice during the film: the first time through a dream, the second by recounting the story orally, as Louie did.

Whilst Louie was writing down a short message to his retainer to warn him about the decision to kill him – "Received your message. We have a big problem." – the killer has a dream. In this scene, he is lying down in his shack, surrounded by pigeons. He is depicted sleeping with an open book on his chest. The book is Akutagawa's *Rashōmon and Other Stories.*[30] The vision shown in the dream depicts a man with a gun. This man is pointing the gun at the killer, who is lying on the ground, his face covered with blood, and is trying to protect himself by raising his hands. Next, we see Louie pointing the gun at the aggressor and shooting him. At the end of the film, the killer narrates the story based on his own recollection of the event. He is talking to his friend Raymond and says:

---

[30] Akutagawa Ryūnosuke, *Rashōmon and Other Stories*, translated by Takashi Koijma (New York: Liveright, 1999).

Ghost Dog: Everything happens for a reason. You know that guy that was here before, with his arm in a sling?

Raymond: Yeah, the guy with his arm in a sling, what?

Ghost Dog: I know that guy. His name's Louie. I'm his retainer. See, once, a long time ago, he helped me out and I owe him for that. See, a samurai must always stay loyal to his boss. No matter what happens.

While he tells this story, the screen shows a man pointing a gun at the killer, and then Louie kills the assailant, as portrayed in the dream.

In the final analysis, there are conflicting opinions on the same event. Indeed, there is a mismatch between Louie's recollection of having saved the hitman's life and the killer's own re-enactment of the same event in the form of a dream, first, and as a story, after. The fact that the two versions of the same event present some inconsistencies sheds light on the subjective nature of memory, the mutability of truth, the simultaneous existence of different perspectives and interpretations on the same fact, and, ultimately, on the intricate and difficult relations between fact, opinion, fiction, and truth. There is a basic distinction between facts and opinions.

In general terms, "fact" is that which falls under the experience of a natural or artificial event or as a result of an action or process. A fact is an event or a situation that appears endowed with its own truth, tangible reality, and accountability, and can be reported. Ultimately, facts can be verified, and they refer to events or situations that have already occurred. In a nutshell, "the past is the domain of facts."[31] In contrast, an "opinion" is a subjective belief, often different from person to person with regard to specific facts, situations, or future events, without objective evidence of absolute certainty to establish the undoubted truth. An opinion is, therefore, the personal version of a fact, and, as such, can be more or less acceptable or accurate

This point leads us to the second Japanese literary source that is central to *Ghost Dog*: *Rashōmon* by Ryūnosuke Akutagawa. Like *Hagakure*, *Rashōmon* takes on different levels of significance within the film. On a thematic level, this book sheds light on the plurality of interpretations. Indeed, the short story *Yabu no Naka* ("In a grove"), considered by the killer and Pearline the best story of the collection, narrates three contrasting stories of a particular event: the

---

[31] Bertrand de Jouvenel, *The Art of Conjecture* (London: Weidenfeld and Nicolson, 1967), 4.

murder of a samurai, Kanazawa no Takehiro. The three accounts do not overlap, each of them recounting a subjective account of the murder. *Yabu no Naka* challenges the idea of objective truth by showing that testimonies are always subjective. Two or more people can witness the same event or read the same story and yet give an interpretation that is different from the other's. Therefore, it is apparent that the plurality of stories about the killer's past echoes *Rashōmon*'s theme and the division between subjective and objective truth.

However, *Rashōmon* is also important for other reasons. If we consider the book from a technological standpoint, it can be argued that it is quite a peculiar artifact. A book can be used in different ways, and it serves numerous functions. Indeed, the book is portable technology; it is easily transported and can be carried around. Moreover, a book can be physically passed around from person to person, whether borrowed or given as a gift. Of course, books can also be the subject of discussion because we read them and talk about them, express and exchange different opinions about their content. All these aspects of the book as technology are present in *Ghost Dog*. The director is very clear about this point.[32]

Rashōmon makes its first appearance in the film during the murder of Handsome Frank. He is with Louise in the bedroom of a villa belonging to a gangster called Alighieri. He talks on the telephone with Uncle Joe, who warns him not to mess around with Mr. Vargo's daughter, or he will be killed. In this scene, Louise sits on a sofa and reads *Rashōmon* while watching cartoons on television. Next, she throws the book on the floor. The camera gives a close-up of the text so that its cover and title can be glimpsed. At this juncture, the killer arrives and kills Handsome Frank by shooting him repeatedly with a gun with a silencer. The killer immediately notices Louise's presence in the room. He is surprised. He also notices the book on the floor and picks it up. Louise comments on the book by saying, "It's a good book. Ancient Japan was a pretty strange place. You can have it. I'm finished with it." Thus, *Rashōmon* passes from Louise to the killer. The latter carries *Rashōmon* in the left pocket of his jacket. As pointed out before, the book is on his chest when the killer had the dream. Next, the book, in turn, passes from the killer to Pearline. She is very intrigued by the book and says, misreading the title of the book, "Rashōmor. What's this about?" The killer answers, "You can borrow that, you know. Just you gotta promise that when you read it, you come and tell me what you think, all right?" When the killer lends a book to someone, not only does he ask that the book will be returned to him, but he also expects to receive a commentary

---

[32] Stèfani, "Jim Jarmusch," 58.

about it. This way of operating yields to a twofold modality of exchange through books. The book is at one and the same time, the object and subject of exchange. It is the circulating physical object that goes from hand to hand as well as the subject of discussion between subjects.

Just before the final shoot-out scene, Pearline returns *Rashōmon* to the killer, thus fulfilling her promise. In this way, the book returns to the killer, who carries it around in the pocket of his jacket. During the final shoot-out scene, after Louie has shot his retainer numerous times, the killer asks him for one last favor before dying. The killer takes *Rashōmon* out of his pocket, hands it to Louie, and says to him, "You take this book. Read it sometime. Then later on you can tell me what you think." Louie accepts the gift and complies with the killer's final request without, however, having much certainty in his promise to read and comment on the book. The killer dies after this final gesture. Louie runs away and gets into a limousine, where Louise and a driver are waiting for him. Louise takes *Rashōmon* back and says, "This is my book. Takes place in ancient Japan. You should read it," and then passes it over once again to Louie.

We now come full circle. Before his death, the killer passes *Hagakure* into Pearline's hands, who knows she has a duty to read the book sometime and to treasure it. The passing of two books – *Hagakure* and *Rashōmon* – through the hands of two women – Pearline and Louise – marks their future role as the feminine heirs of two distinct and opposing cultural traditions. In the very last scene of the film, we see Pearline sitting with crossed legs on the floor of her mother's kitchen, immersed in reading *Hagakure*. This last scene echoes the first one in which the killer is reading the book in his home space. Pearline reads a paragraph from the book and remembers her beloved friend, Ghost Dog: "In the Kamigata area they have a sort of tiered lunch box they use for a single day when flower viewing. Upon returning, they throw them away, trampling them underfoot. The end is important in all things." With his habit of exchanging books, the killer seems to put into practice one of the maxims of *Hagakure*: "Nothing should please one more than to pass on to others that which one possesses, if it is in the best interests of the lord."

Conclusion

My original intention in undertaking the present inquiry was to explore the image of Japan, as reflected in American independent film aesthetics. For this purpose, I selected Jim Jarmusch's *Ghost Dog: The Way of the Samurai* as the empirical material for the study. It is apparent that the director drew on Japanese sources for writing *Ghost Dog*. I identified some of the most relevant works that dealt with the subject of the code of conduct of the samurai. The two most important Japanese literary sources for *Ghost Dog* are *Hagakure* and *Rashōmon*. Both sources are embedded in the film narrative at various levels and play a significant role.

In the final analysis, *Ghost Dog* presents multiple sub-universes of meaning. The world of the samurai constitutes one of these sub-universes. This province of meaning is governed by certain rules and organizes its values according to a specific text. *Hagakure* is the book designed for the samurai that provides instructions for social action in all compartments of life. By subscribing to the code of the samurai, the stealthy killer depicted by Jim Jarmusch refashions his own self-image as a modern urban samurai. He goes through a process of self-transformation. This transformation involves the interpretation, appropriation, and reinvention of a forgotten code of conduct. Through this process of self-transformation and re-fashioning of the self, the killer finds meaning and integrity in his life. The assassin juxtaposes the Japanese code of the samurai with other codes (hip-hop, rap, and American black culture). The result is a unique blend of influences that converges in one powerful image: the contemporary urban samurai.

However, the relations between the simultaneous sub-universes embedded in *Ghost Dog* is complex. Ultimately, the killer's sub-universe clashes with the provinces of meaning of the gangsters' culture as embodied by Louie – the hitman's retainer. The friction between the two interpretations of reality is striking. The personal sub-universe of the killer – based on the code of the samurai, which establishes the full devotion of the retainer to the lord – and Louie's interpretation of reality – based on the rules of the mafia – are incommensurable.

Works Cited

Alexander, Howard Kevin. "The Essence of *Hagakure*." PhD diss., University of Lethbridge, 1972.

Akutagawa, Ryūnosuke. *Rashōmon and Other Stories*. Translated by Takashi Koijma. New York: Liveright, 1999.

Ashton, Stephen. "Conversation with Jim Jarmusch: Cinematic Samurai." *MovieMaker*, February 4, 2008. https://www.moviemaker.com/archives/moviemaking/directing/articles-directing/jim-jarmusch-ghost-dog-the-way-of-the-samurai-interview-20080204/.

De Jouvenel, Bertrand. *The Art of Conjecture*. London: Weidenfeld and Nicolson, 1967.

Feiten, Benedict. *Jim Jarmusch: Musik und Narration – Transnationalität und Alternative Filmische Erzählformen*. Bielefeld: Transcript Verlag, 2017.

Herzberg, Ludvig, ed. *Jim Jarmusch: Interviews*. Jackson, MS: University Press of Mississippi, 2001.

Gonzalez, Eric. "Jim Jarmusch's Aesthetics of Sampling in *Ghost Dog–The Way of the Samurai*." *Volume! La revue des musiques populaires* 3, no. 2 (2004): 109-121.

Jarmusch, Jim, dir. *Ghost Dog: The Way of the Samurai*. 2000; Artisan Entertainment.

———. "Jim Jarmusch on Iggy Pop, Hip-Hop and Finding Poetry in Mundane Things." *NPR*, January 31, 2017. https://www.npr.org/2017/01/31/512622404/jim-jarmusch-on-iggy-pop-hip-hop-and-finding-poetry-in-mundane-things?t=1536603169577.

Lackey, Eric. "Arbitrary Reality: The Global Art Cinema of Jim Jarmusch." PhD diss., University of Kansas, 2012.

Lombardo, Patrizia. *Memory and Imagination in Film: Scorsese, Lynch, Jarmusch, Van Sant*. New York: Palgrave Macmillan, 2014.

Lotman, Juri. "The Text Within the Text." *Publication of the Modern Language Association of America (PMLA)* 109, no. 3 (1994): 377-384.

Meyer, Nils. *Jim Jarmusch*. Berlin: Bertz-Verlag, 2001.

Mitamura, Yasuko. "A Retrospect on the Spirit of *bushidō* as Exemplified in *Hagakure*." PhD diss., University of Southern California, 1969.

Mosca, Umberto. *Jim Jarmusch*. Milan: Il Castoro, 2000.

Piazza, Sara. *Jim Jarmusch: Music, Words, and Noise*. London: Reaktion Books, 2015.

Renda, Chiara. *Jim Jarmusch: Il fascino della malinconia*. Genoa: Le mani, 2008.

Rice, Julian. *The Jarmusch Way: Spirituality and Imagination in Dead Man, Ghost Dog, and The Limits of Control*. Lanham, MD: The Scarecrow, 2012.

Richardson, Michael. "The Phantom of Communication: Jim Jarmusch's *Ghost Dog* and the Opacity of the Message." *Third Text* 2, no. 3 (2010): 361-371.

Stèfani, Max. "Jim Jarmusch: Slower than Paradise." *Mucchio Selvaggio* 383 (2000): 54-58.

Suarez, Juan A. *Jim Jarmusch*. Urbana, IL: University of Illinois Press, 2007.

Tsunetomo, Yamamoto. *Hagakure: The Book of the Samurai*. Translated by William Scott Wilson. Tokyo: Kōdansha International, 1979.

Chapter 4

San Francisco, Japan:
Urban Cultural Hybridizations in *Big Hero 6* and *The Man in the High Castle*

Mattia Thibault

Tampere University, Finland

Abstract

This chapter engages two fictional representations of a Japanese-like version of the city of San Francisco. Maybe because of its large Japanese community, Frisco has been reimagined and portrayed as a city occupied by Imperial Japan—after its counterfactual victory in World War II—in the TV series adaptation of *The Man in The High Castle* by Frank Spotniz (2015), and as the hybrid city "San Fransokyo" in the film adaptation of superhero comic *Big Hero 6* (Hall & Williams 2014). In order to analyze these two representations, the chapter offers some background on urban semiotics and on its methods, outlining how meaning-making and cultural changes influence the urban fabric. Subsequently, both fictional representations of Japanese San Francisco are analyzed, highlighting how the rich imaginary around Japaneseness present in the Western semiosphere has been used to produce a militaristic and colonial version of Japanese culture in *The Man in the High Castle*, and a completely different version, kawaii, technophile and nerdy, of the same culture in *Big Hero 6*. In the conclusions, the chapter proposes that these case studies can shed some light on the different and partial representations of Japan in the West, as well as on the different ways to represent cultural dynamic in an urban form.

Keywords: *The Man in The High Castle, Big Hero 6,* San Francisco, urban semiotics.

* * *

Introduction

San Francisco is host to the largest and oldest Japanese enclave in the United States, gathered around *Nihonmachi* or Japantown. Maybe it was this already existing Nippon flavor that led several artists to imagine and portray an even more Japanese-like version of the city, or what they considered to be Japanese. Philip K. Dick's (1928-1982) *The Man in The High Castle*[1] described a Frisco occupied by Imperial Japan after its counterfactual victory in World War II and therefore represents a Western imagination of a possibly "Japanized" city on the US West Coast. Its visual representation in the homonymous series (2015-2018) created by Frank Spotnitz is probably the most interesting part of the whole show. Similarly, the film adaptation of superhero comic *Big Hero 6* (Hall & Williams, 2014) moves the setting from Tokyo to the imagined city of "San Fransokyo," an alternative version of Frisco rebuilt with the help of the Japanese after the 1906 earthquake.

In these cases, the Californian city becomes a sort of subtext upon which is applied a layer of "nipponicity." The many elements of Japanese culture already imported into the Western semiosphere provide a deposit of semiotic elements available to be employed for any "Japanization."

The most evident part of this urban hybridization takes place on the surfaces of the city: a canvas available to multiple signs such as Kanji writings and advertisements. The city, then, becomes a palimpsest where new layers of writing are superimposed on previous ones and end up adding their own meanings to the preexisting signs. Cultural mash-ups, however, go deeper and involve notable structures – the re-imagined Golden Gate Bridge in *Big Hero 6* – and public spaces – San Francisco's Zen gardens in *The Man in the High Castle* – along with transportation, shops, markets, interior design, and so on. In this chapter, I aim to analyze how the film and the TV series exploit urban elements as meaningful examples of an overlapping of semiospheres, investigating both the semiotic properties of the urban landscape and the cultural tropes involved.

The City as a Text

Cities are complex semiotic mechanisms: they are multi-layered meaning-making engines, composed and brought to life by countless objects – buildings, avenues, monuments, street signs, billboards, graffiti, shop windows, vehicles,

---

[1] Philip K. Dick, *The Man in the High Castle* (New York: G. P. Putnam's Sons, 1962).

passers-by, clothes, etc. – which, in turn, project their own meanings side by side, reinforcing each other or competing for attention. All these objects are woven into a fabric – the "urban fabric" – which immediately recognizably appears as a single entity, the city.

The city, therefore, is a *text* (from *textus*, Latin for fabric), as suggested by Michel de Certeau (1925-1986) in *L'invention du quotidien*.[2] De Certeau considers the city as a text constantly actualized (and transformed) by the practices of interaction and of movement of their inhabitants which, through their journey across the urban space, *enunciate* the city by introducing in it their own subjectivity.

De Certeau's idea of a textual city has been the source of a specific research direction in semiotics, that of *urban semiotics*. In a seminal work, Ugo Volli[3] describes the city as a *discourse*: an expressive reality that is renewed and continually redefines itself which, however, at all times, projects behind itself a text: "The city is alive, it changes materially and in the meaning that it projects; but in every time it is stable and legible as a book."[4]

According to urban semiotics, the city, just like a text, is both an organic whole – that can be understood and labeled as a unique thing – and characterized by an irreducible structural heterogeneity. The city encompasses numerous texts of a smaller scale, interconnected by their simultaneous presence within the city, thus becoming a web of meaningful elements connected to each other.[5]

The city's twofold nature, of homogeneous text and of container of textualities of a smaller scale, leads to a fundamental disappearance of the distinction between text and context.[6] If, on the one hand, the elements of larger size can become the context for those of a smaller size they incorporate (a neighborhood becomes the context of a building, a square of a monument, etc.), the relationship between text and context is not limited to a simple

---

[2] Michel de Certeau, *L'invention du quotidien: 1. Arts de faire* (Paris: Union générale d'éditions, 1980), 91-110.

[3] Ugo Volli, *Laboratorio di semiotica* (Bari/Rome: Laterza, 2005), 5-36.

[4] Ibid. My translation.

[5] Ibid.

[6] Juri Lotman, "L'architettura nel contesto della cultura," in *Il girotondo delle muse: Saggi sulla semiotica delle arti e della rappresentazione*, ed. Silvia Burini (Bergamo: Moretti & Vitali Editori, 1998), 38-50; Pierluigi Cervelli and Franciscu Sedda, "Zone, frontiere, confini: la città come spazio culturale," in *Senso e metropoli: Per una semiotica posturbana*, ed. Gianfranco Marrone and Isabella Pezzini (Rome: Meltemi, 2006), 171-192.

relationship of incorporation: it is possible that the smaller size objects, but with greater symbolic efficacy, can become the context for larger-scale objects ("iconic" buildings and monuments are able to lessen the meaning of all that is around them, creating a semiotic void that allows them to "shine").

The Meaning of the City

Because of its heterogeneity, cities are inevitably *polyphonic* texts, eluding any attempt of standardization by political, economic, or religious powers. The textual appearance of the city is the product of the work and will of countless authors across several eras, guided by different conceptions of urban spaces. The city is the result of the encounter – and sometimes of the clash – of a great number of different writing strategies whose products meet, collide, mingle, and overwrite each other in the urban space.

The kaleidoscopic web of meaningful elements within the urban space also features its own hierarchy: an ideological stratification that gives greater emphasis and meaning to the buildings of political and religious power, to monuments and "landmarks" and, instead, relegating to a marginal role the communicative traces of most of the inhabitants: billboards, street art, graffiti.

Urban areas, then, are places pervaded by an antagonistic tension: buildings, streets, and neighborhoods compete to obtain dominant positions (centrality, verticality, connections), attention (traffic), and prestige. This tension, however, is *petrified*, frozen in a quasi-static spatial arrangement. This incessant internal tension of urban spaces, at the same time, entails a constant transformation: the city is a variable text, alive, never identical to itself, a text that retains elements of its past (text as *testis*, Latin for witness) and interweaves them with those of the present (text as *textus*, fabric) in a set that is often heavily layered and ontologically complex.[7]

This polyphonic and evolving text is made of an unstable and uncertain mingling, whose metamorphoses follow different times and rhythms, from the slow construction of new neighborhoods to the quick work of street-writers and the ephemeral presence of advertising posters. Some elements of the city can last for thousands of years (the topography, the orientation of the street map), others for centuries (buildings, streets, and monuments), others for years (signs and elements of street furniture) or for weeks (posters and display cases),

---

[7] Ugo Volli, "Il testo della città: Problemi metodologici e teorici," *Lexia* 1-2 (2008): 9-12.

down to the ephemeral presence of the inhabitants themselves: every look at the city essentially captures its section.[8]

The City as Producer of Culture

If every city is clearly the product of a specific culture, cities themselves are also important *producers* of culture. The city can be enunciated, as de Certeau claimed, but it is also an enunciator: producing meaning and showcasing its society and inhabitants.

Juri Lotman (1922-1993) points out that the opposition between city space (transformed by man and made habitable for humans) and the space exterior to it (the "wilderness") becomes the basis for *homeomorphisms* of global reach, such as the opposition "nature/culture."[9] The city is not limited to being a part of the cultural universe but proposes itself to symbolically enclose the whole universe.[10] The features that a culture gives to its creations reflect the overall structure of its interpretation of the world.[11]

The isomorphism between city and culture allows us to consider a fundamental aspect of urban space, namely that the city represents its culture, not only because it is a symptom of the latter, but also because it produces it. The city is made to communicate a range of ideologies, systems of belief, and identity strategies; it can be considered a "communication or recording device that intervenes in social relations through symbolic efficacy, a feature which is typical of signs. The texts are relevant in social life not only for what they are materially but for their ability to recall something else, according to Augustine's famous definition of the sign as *aliquid stat pro aliquo*."[12]

Reading and Writing the City

In the previous section, we saw that the city is a complex communicative machine, which works like a text. To live and move through the city, then, means having to read and to interpret it. As the city is an overabundant, rich text, it is necessary, first, to choose some saliences – i.e., which items are significant and which are trivial for us – and then to draw isotopies between

---

[8] Ibid.

[9] Juri Lotman, "Vmesto zakliucheniia: O roli sluchainyi faktorov v istorii kul'tury," *Izbrannye stat'i* 1 (1992): 472-479.

[10] See also Cervelli and Sedda "Zone, frontiere, confini," 171-192.

[11] Lotman, "Vmesto zakliucheniia," 472-479.

[12] Volli, "Il testo della città," 13. My translation.

them in order to give a unique and organic meaning to the heterogeneous whole in which these diverse elements are immersed. In other words, a pedestrian will cross the city ignoring most of the vehicle-related street signs as they will not be particularly meaningful for them. On the other hand, a disabled person will pay attention to parking spaces reserved for the handicapped, which will be relevant to her, and so on.

Selecting the saliences, however, is not enough to be able to move consciously within the city: the same objects may even be used in many ways. The selection of a specific use from among many possibilities is guided by what Volli defines the "urban semiotic competence,"[13] i.e., the ability to correctly interpret what the city tells. It is our urban semiotic competence that allows us to distinguish between the entrances of public and private spaces, even when no sign indicates it. It is this competence, based on our encyclopedia, our previous knowledge, that directs us through the city. This becomes particularly evident when we move in a foreign city. A European citizen in a US city will be disoriented: much of his urban competence will prove useless because of the profound differences between the European way of organizing a "city center" and the American one. Finally, the city itself can hinder or facilitate the use of the urban semiotic competence in virtue of its *legibility*,[14] i.e., the features of a city that assist people in creating their mental maps and in their activities of *wayfinding*.

As for the ways of writing the city, they are strongly dependent on the power held by the perspective authors. In history, the political and religious powers have often been charged with shaping urban spaces, erecting buildings, fortifications and temples, outlining ghettoes, tracing infrastructure, etc. In modern times the economic powers have probably gained the most influence, with shopping centers attracting traffic and wealth, real estate determining gentrification effects, and so on.

It would be incorrect, however, to assume that common citizens are not entitled to any authorship within the city space. There are many ways the citizens themselves can design their city, from putting plants on a balcony and street art to their strategic choices about how to move through the city (including their choice to leave the predetermined track to climb a fence, cross the street where it is forbidden, ignore a traffic light, etc.). Either way, due to the density of the urban text, most forms of writing the city assume a character of

---

[13] Ibid.
[14] Kevin A. Lynch, *The Image of the City* (Cambridge, MA: MIT Press, 1960), 2-5.

*re*writing, of superimposing new writing on an existing text. Writing the city means adding layers of meaning, removing and filling gaps, rectifying what already exists in an environment that is then continuously modified. It is a sort of *bricolage* activity that re-works already existing elements and materials. The city, then, is formed by a material substrate produced by the superposition of multiple inscriptions which, in turn, become the substrate and support of new writings, whether they are strategic or simply the traces of the human activities that take place in the urban space.

We can distinguish two polarities of city writing: one close to the idea of palimpsest (involving the removal, at least partial, of the pre-existing substrate and the construction of something new) and one characterized by a kind of *maquillage,* in the name of recovery, based on the transformation or resemantization of existing urban objects. This second form of rewriting is more common, as it requires a more limited kind of intervention in the city. It is exercised both by the power – for example, the transforming of a convent into a hospital or an ancient palace into a town hall – and by peripheral social actors, who occupy buildings, become squatters, camp in parks, write on the walls, and in general reappropriate and refunctionalize urban spaces according to their needs. Marginal actors can also claim the power of *erasing* something from the city: this is the case for several forms of vandalism and, more importantly, of terrorism: the 9/11 attacks on the World Trade Center were partly so effective due to erasing an iconic landmark of New York City from its urban landscape.

These rewritings, even when with practical purposes, cannot be regarded as exclusively functional: instead, they always have a highly communicative character. On the one hand, they affect the general meaning of resemantized text, and, on the other, it is a way for individuals and social, political, or religious groups to engrave themselves *within* the text, to leave a trace, to represent their existence within the universe that the city represents.

Fictional Cities and Possible Worlds

The semiotic wealth of the cities, their being complex meaning-making machines, at the same time symptoms and producers of cultures, explains the frequency of their representations. Cities are the setting for innumerable narratives, the irreplaceable backgrounds of countless works of art, they are sung in songs, praised in poems, digitally reconstructed in video games. They offer their streets to artist *flaneurs* and set apart their inhabitants according to how they use the *metro*,[15] attract tourists, and become tracks for runners. Cities enter in the collective imagination with their own "personalities," impossible to ascribe specific characteristics to, but still crystal clear in the minds of many, so that Paris and New York, Tokyo and Hanoi become archetypes of lifestyles, tastes, philosophies.

From a semiotic perspective, it is interesting to note that Umberto Eco's (1932-2016) theory of possible worlds is explained by using the city of Paris as a starting point. In *Sei passeggiate nei boschi narrativi*[16] he tells of his attempt to reconstruct the toponymy of the Parisian neighborhood in which Alexandre Dumas' three musketeers lived and of the impossibility of doing so. The names of two roads that in the book are presented as distinct have, in reality, been born by the same street at different times. Dumas' Paris, then, must be different from the real Paris, not by the author's intention, but due to an accident. In *Lector in Fabula*,[17] Eco describes how the possible worlds of narrative, or W_N, are generally assumed as homologs of the real world, or W_0: if a novel is set in Paris, the readers will assume that the city is identical to the *real* Paris based on their encyclopedia (i.e., their previous knowledge about the city). Nonetheless, many elements of W_N are not "anchored" to elements of W_0, but only to other elements of W_N, in a symmetrical relationship that Eco calls "structurally necessary properties": this is the case of Raoul and Marguerite in *Un drame bien parisien*, two characters who are defined by their reciprocal relation, not by a relation with any meaningful portion of W_0. Following Eco's theory, therefore, every city represented in a narrative is fictional. It may be inspired by a real city such as Paris and anchored to the reader's encyclopedia, but the author will be allowed to modify it and the reader will be ready to adjust her inferences and tone her suspension of disbelief according to what the text tells her.

Furthermore, the city, as mentioned, often becomes the cultural representation of the whole cultural universe,[18] and so Augustine of Hippo (354-430), in order to defend Christianity from the accusation of bringing about the decline of Rome, uses the image of the holy City of God, or *Civitate Dei*, juxtaposed to the corrupt *Civitate Terrena*. Before him, Plato (c.427-c.348 BC), also used two cities to embody his ideal state – ancient Athens – and its enemy

---

[15] Jean Marie Floch, *Sémiotique, marketing et communication: Sous les signes, les stratégies* (Paris: PUF, 1990).
[16] Umberto Eco, *Sei passeggiate nei boschi narrativi* (Milan: Bompiani, 1994).
[17] Umberto Eco, *Lector in fabula* (Milan: Bompiani, 1979).
[18] Lotman, "Vmesto zakliucheniia," 472-479.

– Atlantis. The modeling power of the representation of cities is strong throughout history, and we can find many contemporary examples, from Gabriel García Márquez's (1927-2014) Macondo to Italo Calvino's (1923-1985) *Invisible Cities*, where fictional cities become the framework to represent life, humanity, and their contradictions. Narrative representations of cities, then, will not only offer the propositions for inferring a possible world, but will also cast behind them a *possible cultural universe*. The organization of the city, its tensions, its structure, dynamics, hierarchies, all are isomorphic with a symbolic universe and with a cultural organization of society.

When an author represents a city, he or she enunciates it and will be entitled to invent new cities, or to change (slightly or profoundly) the nature and appearance of cities existing in W_0. In this case, the author will have the power to write and rewrite anything she wishes, a power that is rarely granted to anyone in respect of real cities. However, the artificial city will lose its nature of choral text, and it will be the duty of and a challenge for the author to imitate effectively the tensions that make the city alive and to recreate them *in vitro*. An analysis of the representation of the city – which is obviously strongly related to the medium used to portray it – is then a way to investigate the possible cultural universe implemented by the author and the ideologies that it subsumes. Especially when the importance of the urban setting and its features coexist with a narrative oriented to cultural problematics. This is the case both for the series *The Man in the High Castle*, portraying a Japanese San Francisco and a Nazi New York, and for the animated film *Big Hero 6*, set in the hybrid city of San Fransokyo. The opportunity to approach two different versions of a Japanese San Francisco is rather interesting, as it will allow us to compare the two possible worlds and their cultural universes and to reconstruct, from them, the ideologies they subsume.

San Francisco, Japanese Pacific States[19]

The Man in the High Castle is a 1962 novel by prolific sci-fi author Philip K. Dick. In the novel, the author presents an alternative history in which the Axis powers won the Second World War and the United States of America have been divided into three areas: the German-controlled Eastern United States, the Japanese-controlled Pacific States of America in the West, and a Neutral Zone in between. In 2015, Amazon released a homonymous TV series based on Dick's novel and

---

[19] Some screenshots of the case studies of this section and the next can be found at: http://bit.ly/FriscoJapan

created by Frank Spotnitz. The series maintains the same setting with some alterations – the occupied territories are now called the Greater Nazi Reich and the Japanese Pacific States – and makes deep changes to the plot and most of the characters. These changes, however, are not relevant to our analysis. The TV series portrays two cities under occupation: New York and Frisco. The Nazi version of New York is the most frequently used in the promotional materials, probably due to the great impact entailed in seeing the Statue of Liberty making the fascist salute or a menacing Nazi building in downtown Manhattan.

Nevertheless, the city that is portrayed with more accuracy and that gets the most screen time is San Francisco. Most of the main characters' storylines take place there (especially in the first season), and the audience becomes familiar with many of its spaces and buildings. If the mixture between the Japanese and American cultures appears less menacing than that in the German-occupied territories, it is still the one that is portrayed more in detail, especially with regard to the daily life of the inhabitants. While the encounter between these two cultures is also portrayed through practices, linguistic habits, media products and so on, the morphology of the city of San Francisco is certainly the most prominent symptom of their clash and mingling. Let us consider this in more detail.

We stated, in the second section, that the ephemeral presence of the inhabitants, their clothes, and their activities are all part of the complex semiotic mechanism of the city. The inhabitants of the San Francisco in *The Man in the High Castle* are particularly interesting from this perspective. First of all, the portion of Asiatic-looking people is rather high. We can assume that most of them are Japanese, even if some of them are said to be Chinese in the series. Most of these people, but also a share of Westerners, do clothe according to Eastern fashion, and several people wearing Japanese Kempeitai[20] uniforms can be seen in the city. The behavior of the inhabitants also mirrors the adoption of Japanese etiquette, as many of them bow to each other with courtesy, especially if at least one native Japanese is involved.

The sounds that can be heard in the city are symptomatic of the adoption of several aspects of Japanese culture by the inhabitants of San Francisco. Japanese people tend to speak to each other in Japanese in public (with the exception of several of the main characters, undoubtedly for extra-diegetic reasons), but many Americans have also adopted some Japanese lexicon. In addition, Japanese music can be heard in most public places, even those that

---

[20] Japan's military police.

do not show any other Eastern influence, such as the pub attended by some of the protagonists. The most striking characteristic of this version of Frisco, however, is the massive work of overwriting the city went through. Most of the buildings are literally covered by posters, billboards, and signs mostly written in Japanese and in the Japanese alphabet. This, on the one hand, mirrors the baroque approach that Japan has to advertising, and, on the other, continuously recalls the fact that San Francisco is occupied and, in some measure, stranger (if not to the inhabitants, who may have learned to read Japanese, then at least to most of the viewers). Side by side with these writings, flags of the Japanese Pacific States can also be found on most surfaces, a constant reminder of the conquest of the city, of its ownership. Flags are not only placed on most buildings but can also be found glued to the walls of side alleys, making it difficult to ignore them at any time. Less militaristically, but equally colonially, several oriental lamps can also be seen hanging in the streets and between windows, alongside hanging clothes.

The city's skyline, on the other hand, is mostly similar to that of the real San Francisco. There are few new landmarks; instead, we face more of an appropriation of existing buildings. Nevertheless, there are several buildings with traditional Japanese interiors that are shown throughout the series. In the first episode of the first season, the first shot of San Francisco is inside a dojo during a lesson of aikido. The dojo's furniture and interior are typically Japanese, and there are no hints to the fact that it is on American soil. Other Japanese interiors include that of a wealthy Japanese family's house, the office of the Trade Minister, the Kempeitai headquarters, and a nightclub near the docks owned by the Yakuza.

Two buildings stand out as specific to the situation. The first one is the Nazi Embassy, a big palace with a large garden. The second, more interesting, is an Americana antique store. Owned by one of the main characters, it displays objects of an idealized pre-war America that will be purchased by wealthy Japanese. The latter mostly live in new, rich neighborhoods, built completely in the Japanese style and set rather apart from the rest of the city. Besides those quarters, the largest intervention made upon the city by its conquerors is a large "Zen garden" in the city center.

It is interesting to notice that the second season of the series also includes a struggle around the power of writing the city. A resistance group places a bomb under the Kempeitai headquarters in order to blow up one of the symbols of the Japanese occupation. In the second-last episode of the season, the bomb detonates and destroys a large part of the building, killing many of its occupants. One shot from afar shows a San Francisco suddenly devoid of any sign of the occupation, while a column of smoke testifies the erasure of one of the symbols of the oppression.

We have seen several ways in which the Japanese occupation is represented, engraved in a city that, otherwise, maintains its typical look. It is interesting to note that also the cinematography of the series is used to reaffirm and reinforce this duplicity. Several shots are aesthetically consistent with the traditional representations of the city: long avenues going downhill with the ocean and the Golden Gate in the background, where all the buildings are covered in Japanese writings, or dark shots typical of the *noir* genre, where the police are substituted with the Kempeitai. It is easy to see that the relation between cultures that is portrayed by the city is not a symmetric one. Japanese culture is depicted as a conquering culture that tends to overwrite the previous strata to show its dominance. In order to do so, several aspects of Japanese culture (or, better, of its Western perception) are selected and magnified.

First of all, the rigidness of etiquette and of behavior is made clear by the interactions between the inhabitants, by the general lack of evident fun, the seriousness and conformity of the buildings, and the signs. Japanese culture is portrayed, throughout the city, as extremely controlled and repressive. Second, the militaristic aspects of Japanese culture are continually underlined. The presence of soldiers and policemen from the Kempeitai is frequent and uninterrupted, the use of violence steady, the surveillance uninterrupted. The quantity of flags confirms the will of dominance and of possession of the occupants.

This is also linked to the ravenousness of Imperial Japan, here engraved in the city with countless writings that almost suffocate the buildings underneath, and contrasted with the nostalgic but colonialist approach to American culture, exemplified by the Americana antique shop. All these aspects are, of course, reinforced by the narrative told in the series, but what is relevant to us is that the representation of the city alone already makes them very clear.

Many other aspects of Japaneseness, generally appreciated in its Western perceptions, are completely disregarded and absent from the representation of San Francisco: those that have been chosen are functional for the creation of a possible cultural universe where the mixing of American and Japanese cultures is almost impossible, where Japaneseness is in itself dominant and colonialist and, despite the goodwill of several characters, the tensions deeply inscribed within the city can lead only to violence in the attempt to physically remove the presence of the other.

San Fransokyo

San Fransokyo (a portmanteau of San Francisco and Tokyo) is a fictional city introduced in Disney's 2014 animation film *Big Hero 6*, directed by Don Hall and Chris Williams. While the homonymous comics that (rather loosely) inspired the film were set in Tokyo, a new environment was developed for the animated film and the TV series that followed it (2017-, directed by Stephen Heneveld, Ben Juwono, Kathleen Good, and Kenji Ono). Although it is not explicated in the film, the city is an evolution of San Francisco. The official Facebook page of Walt Disney Animation Studios shared a quote by *Big Hero 6* art director Scott Watanabe claiming that "Don [Hall] wanted to figure out a logical explanation for how a mash-up city like this could exist. I came up with the idea that, after the 1906 earthquake in San Francisco, Japanese immigrants rebuilt the place using techniques that allow movement and flexibility in a seismic event."[21]

The fact that the city is featured in a computer-generated animation film allowed its creators to proceed with this "mash-up" in a much deeper way than a live-action film would probably have allowed. The hi-tech sci-fi setting of the film, in addition, had a strong impact on the representation of the city, which is not only a mixing of Frisco and Tokyo – as the name suggests – but also a futuristic evolution of the two. Like in *The Man in the High Castle*, the percentage of inhabitants with Japanese looks and/or names in San Fransokyo is rather elevated, even if their clothing and behavior are typically modern Western ones. The only important exception, although barely noticeable, is that of the police. A single policeman is shown in the film, but his uniform and floral symbols are those of the Keisatsu-chō, the Japanese National Police Agency.

Sound is much less important than in *The Man in the High Castle*: there is no Japanese music and Japanese words are very rare, limited to a character nickname ("Wasabi") and some names as well as a few other occurrences. Japanese writings are still an important part of the cityscape and an obvious strategy for creating a certain mood, but their presence is certainly more discrete, and it is often accompanied by English writings. The morphology of the buildings, on the other hand, is probably the most interesting feature of San Fransokyo. Dojos appear to be inevitable, and in *Big Hero 6*, after a brief

---

[21] Walt Disney Animation Studios, " Don wanted to figure out a logical explanation for how a mash-up city like this could exist," Facebook, February 17, 2015, https://www.facebook.com/DisneyAnimation/photos/pb.23245476854.-2207520000. 1424332542./10152980421081855/?type=1&theater.

panoramic of the city, the opening scene is set in one, albeit one devoted to hi-tech robot fights. Most of San Fransokyo's buildings are clearly a mash-up between American and Japanese cultures, both in the exterior and in the interior. The mixing proceeds on many levels, from architecture to food preparation (where American donuts can be seen side by side with Japanese tea kettles), from different styles of family pictures hanging on the walls to ever-present pop culture references based on American superhero comics and Japanese *manga*.

The buildings of San Fransokyo also encompass several temples, giving the city a spiritual dimension (completely absent from the cityscape of the San Francisco of *The Man in the High Castle*), and a huge presence of vegetation, which is not limited to the University's Zen garden but is also portrayed by a large presence of trees inside the city – mainly very culturally charged cherry trees, which appear to blossom all year long. Several of these buildings work as landmarks and are the result of the hybridization of existing monuments. A small copy of the Tokyo Tower, for example, is positioned at the top of a skyscraper, the Port of San Fransokyo is a clear revisiting of the actual Port of San Francisco, and even the house of the main character is a Japanese-like version of a famous building from Frisco. Some of the buildings that are modified in order to look more Japanese are also taken from other Californian cities, such as the main building of the San Fransokyo Institute of Technology, which appears to be a reworked Royce Hall from Los Angeles' University of California.

Interestingly enough, in *Big Hero 6*, we can also witness some actions of city writing: a university building is burned to the ground in the first half of the film, while a research lab is sucked into a portal toward the end. Both buildings are destroyed by the main villain, but while the first one is destroyed to cover up a crime, the second one is intentionally erased from the city in order to get revenge on its owner. The portal device used to this end dismantles the building through an invisible force and makes it completely disappear, leaving nothing behind. The struggle for control of the city, then, is not political anymore, but scientific: both the villain and its victim are brilliant scientists, the building is a brand new, incredibly advanced research lab, and the method for erasing it is also based on sci-fi.

That of clean, endless technological advancement is certainly the first ideology outlined by our analysis of the city of San Fransokyo: it is a modern city, full of technology-related buildings, its sky dotted by flying wind turbines visually similar to Japanese kites, where, however, the artificial is equally balanced by the natural (the large presence of trees and parks) and the spiritual (the temples). This technological utopia goes side by side with a cultural utopia, the latter organized around an ideology of perfect cultural hybridization. Every aspect of the city, and of the culture it produces, seems to be a blend of Western and Japanese elements. Monuments and buildings, transportation, food, religious practices, gadgets: all seem to be equidistant from both cultures, while neither one ever prevails.

If in *The Man in the High Castle* flags were omnipresent, in San Fransokyo there are hardly any flags: we can see just two outside the police stations, but they are unrecognizable. From the little that we are able to see, they neither resemble the flag of San Francisco, nor the symbol for Tokyo, nor that of their respective regions/states or nation states. In fact, if it was not for Scott Watanabe's claim, it would be impossible to determine which country the city is located in, even if it appears rather clear that the substratum is San Francisco that was later made-up to look more and more Japanese. This layer of Japaneseness, however, goes rather deep in the city; it changes the shape of its buildings, the spiritual life and dietary habits of its inhabitants, and so on. To realize this hybridization, several aspects of the Western perception of Japanese culture have been selected and magnified.

The idea of a tech-friendly Japan, where ordinary life is embedded with hi-tech devices, is the obvious basis upon which one of the main ideologies of this possible cultural universe is built. Japanese culture is here portrayed in its friendliest examples: playful, nerdy, and *kawaii* (cute). The city is full of figurines and drawings of cute fishes and *manga* robots, robot fighting is an illegal but highly popular practice, research labs are full of flying cats and fun projects, and so on. The aesthetic element, finally, is very important. Most of the things retrieved from Japanese culture and engraved in San Fransokyo are beautiful and graceful: cherry trees, kites, temples, architecture, decorations. Japaneseness is eye-candy; it is used to make the city look more beautiful, to create awe.

Conclusion

The two different approaches to the idea of a Japanese San Francisco that we have analyzed can be summarized by their representations of the Golden Gate Bridge. The iconic symbol of Frisco plays an important role in the popular image of the city, and both the narratives we have approached dedicate their attention to it. In *The Man in the High Castle*, the Golden Gate is identical to the real one, with one important difference: on its top, there are now some flags of the Japanese Pacific States. The monument is untouched in its iconic appearance, but its ownership is made clear: it might have been the product of American talent, but it is now part of the spoils of war and belongs to the victors.

On the other hand, the Golden Gate Bridge in San Fransokyo is rather different from the real one. Though it is immediately recognizable, at the same time, its appearance is now a hybrid with the aesthetic of *torii*, the traditional Japanese gates generally situated at the entrance of a Shinto shrine. The new bridge, then, is a beautiful-looking cultural mix with spiritual undertones. The two narratives that we have approached, then, feature diametrically opposed depictions of Japanese culture engraved in the cities they portray: a cold, disciplined, militaristic culture on the one hand and a friendly, nerdy, eye-candy culture on the other. Both their possible cultural universes are created by making a selection from the vast entries in the Western encyclopedia that is Japanese culture. Among the many prejudices, stereotypes, fashions, and influences that the West has of Japanese culture, the authors have chosen those that better fit their narrative and discarded the others: the cities that they have created, after all, are not made to be an academic study of cross-cultural influences, but to be the setting of the story they wanted to tell.

These selections, however, are particularly interesting because their elements seem to be rather coherent with different historical takes on Japan. Without indulging too much in the analysis, it appears that we have two faces of Japan that we could describe as an "old" Japan and a "new" Japan. On the one hand, with these terms, we refer to the cultural changes that operated in the country after its defeat in World War II, where the militaristic past of the Japanese Empire was replaced by a mostly pacifist attitude toward foreign relationships. On the other hand, however, we refer to the American and Western perception of this change, also related to a change in the status of the country from war enemy to ally. The portrayal of Japanese culture in *The Man in the High Castle* is clearly influenced by a certain idea of Japan built in the wartime propaganda, and the main traits of this representation are all present in its narrative. In *Big Hero 6*, on the other hand, the representation of Japan is based on its cultural influences build on *manga* and *anime*, on video games, and on the importing of tech gadgets that started to grow strong in the 1980s.

These representations are, of course, partial, both because they are functional for the entertainment-oriented narrative of their authors and because they are based on strongly partial historical perceptions of Japanese culture. In this paper, however, we are not interested in moralistic arguments about the representation of foreign cultures. What we have been more interested in is how the cityscape and its subtexts can be used in a variety of ways to represent a wide array of cultural aspects. Our two Japanese versions of San Francisco, although based on similar procedures, end up being completely different cities according to the ideologies that they are charged to represent, being dystopic and full of dangerous tensions or utopic and harmonious.

Works Cited

De Certeau, Michel. *L'invention du quotidien: 1. Arts de faire*. Paris: Union générale d'éditions, 1980.

Cervelli, Pierluigi, and Franciscu Sedda. "Zone, frontiere, confini: La città come spazio culturale." In *Senso e metropoli. Per una semiotica posturbana*, edited by Marrone Gianfranco and Isabella Pezzini, 171-192. Rome: Meltemi, 2006.

Dick, Philip K. *The Man in the High Castle*. New York: G. P. Putnam's Sons, 1962.

Eco, Umberto. *Lector in fabula*. Milan: Bompiani, 1979.

———. *Sei passeggiate nei boschi narrativi*. Milan: Bompiani, 1994.

Floch, Jean Marie. *Sémiotique, marketing et communication: Sous les signes, les strategies*. Paris: PUF, 1990.

Lotman, Juri. "Vmesto zakliucheniia: O roli sluchainyi faktorov v istorii kul'tury." *Izbrannye stat'i* 1 (1992): 472-479.

———. "L'architettura nel contesto della cultura." In *Il girotondo delle muse: Saggi sulla semiotica delle arti e della rappresentazione*, edited by Silvia Burini, 38-50. Bergamo: Moretti & Vitali Editori, 1998.

Lynch, Kevin A. *The Image of the City*. Cambridge, MA: MIT Press, 1960.

Volli, Ugo. *Laboratorio di semiotica*. Bari/Rome: Laterza, 2005.

———. "Il testo della città: Problemi metodologici e teorici." *Lexia* 1-2 (2008): 9-12.

Walt Disney Animation Studios. "Don wanted to figure out a logical explanation for how a mash-up city like this could exist." Facebook, February 17, 2015. https://www.facebook.com/DisneyAnimation/photos/pb.23245476854.-2207520000.1424332542./10152980421081855/?type=1&theater.

Chapter 5

The "Occidental American" Ninja: *The Master* (1984) and the Display of Japanese Martial Arts

Frank Jacob

Nord University, Norway

Abstract

The chapter offers a close reading of the short-lived TV series *The Master* (1984) starring Lee Van Cleef as an American, who became a ninja in Japan and is now looking for his daughter in the United States. Together with Max, who becomes a Ninja-apprentice, the two travel through the country and help people in need against villains, gangsters, and organized crime. As an expression of the American interest in martial arts, the series, however, represented many stereotypes about Japan in general, and the ninja in particular. A close examination of these cultural stereotypes, representing a form of "Western Japaneseness" is provided by the chapter.

Keywords: ninja, The Master, martial arts, US television.

* * *

Considering the things that are usually affiliated with Japan, the ninja, next to sushi, yakuza, or Godzilla,[1] is probably one of the most well-known from the field of action and martial arts entertainment of the 1980s. Many feature films about the mysterious Japanese warriors were shown on Western cinema screens in that decade, often showing a form of "white exoticism" by casting

---

[1] On Godzilla as a global icon of Japanese descent, see Frank Jacob, "From Tokyo's Destroyer to International Icon: Godzilla and Japanese Monstrosity in the Postwar Age," in *All Around Monstrous: Monster Media in Their Historical Contexts*, ed. Verena Bernardi and Frank Jacob (Wilmington, DE: Vernon Press, 2019), 211-244.

non-Asian actors in the starring role. The "American ninja" was Michael Dudikoff, who starred in the movie series of the same name. Film posters for *American Ninja* (1985) emphasized that "The deadliest art of the Orient is now in the hands of an American" who, in this cult martial arts film, would use it to fight the Black Star Order of ninjas on the Philippines.[2] Dudikoff's casting, as well as Lee Van Cleef's in the television series *The Master* (1984) that will be discussed in more detail in the present chapter, in the leading role continued the casting of white men in the role of the male hero familiar with foreign martial arts, which was quite common in Hollywood both before and after the "ninja hype" of the 1980s. David Carradine (1936-2009), not Bruce Lee (1940-1973),[3] starred in the television series *Kung Fu* (1972-1975),[4] and the 1990s were dominated by Steven Seagal, Jean-Claude Van Damme, and Chuck Norris, whose career in martial arts films spanned the years from the late 1970s to the early 1990s and who is especially well-known to television audiences due to playing the title role in *Walker, Texas Ranger* (1993-2001).

Many of these films and series addressed the audience's interest in foreign martial arts and *The Master* (1984) was no exception, yet it was not as successful as other formats. Only 13 episodes were broadcast in 1984 and no second season was produced. One could therefore consider the TV series a flop, maybe because it was produced relatively cheaply and followed a similar narrative in every episode. Nevertheless, it would use and display existent stereotypes about Japanese martial arts in general and the ninja in particular. In a way, and to stress Reinhart Koselleck's (1923-2006) theoretical work on *Erfahrungsraum* and *Erwartungshorizont*,[5] the series addressed the horizon of expectation (*Erwartungshorizont*) of an audience that was already familiar with some of the

---

[2] By 1993 five *American Ninja* films had been shot, although Dudikoff only starred in the first four. Although the first film in 1985 is still considered a classic martial arts movie today, Dudikoff remained a B-movie star, as his recent films, e.g. *Navy Seals vs. Zombies* (2015) or *Fury of the Fist and the Golden Fleece* (2018), prove.

[3] SCMP, "Bruce Lee: How His Chinese Race Counted Against Him in Hollywood with Its History of Negative Asian Stereotypes in Films," *South China Morning Post*, July 30, 2018, https://www.scmp.com/culture/film-tv/article/2157471/did-bruce-lee-suffer-racism-hollywood-studio-executives-were.

[4] The 1970s were considered the "kung fu decade," while the 1980s saw a higher interest in ninjutsu. Terence Allen, "Which Martial Art Will Be the Fad of the '90s?" *Black Belt* 10 (1994): 48-49 and 52-55.

[5] Reinhart Koselleck, "'Erfahrungsraum' und 'Erwartungshorizont': Zwei historische Kategorien," in *Vergangene Zukunft: Zur Semantik geschichtlicher Zeiten* (Berlin: Suhrkamp Verlag, 2010), 349-375.

things being displayed due to their own intellectual space of experience (*Erfahrungsraum*). It thereby also helped to strengthen existent stereotypes about these aspects in the United States. In the present chapter, a short analysis of the plot of *The Master* shall be provided before the display of Japanese martial arts and the use of stereotypes are discussed.

The Master (1984)

The plot of the NBC series can generally be described in just one sentence. John Peter McAllister (Lee Van Cleef) – probably the whitest possible American name for a ninja master –, the "only *occidental American* ever to become a ninja,"[6] is searching for his daughter in the United States and teams up with the young drifter Max Keller (Timothy Van Patten), and together they experience numerous adventures that are usually related to a young woman in need for some heroes to help her with some problems that tend to involve all kinds of evil characters, such as rogue police officers (Episode 13), criminal businessmen (Episode 3), or even terrorists (Episode 4). The series starts with McAllister's decision to leave his ninja sect to search for his daughter. Due to his decision, he turns into an outcast, hunted by his former ninja student Okasa (Shō Kosugi), who follows him to the US and will appear from time to time to confront and try to kill his former master. After his arrival, however, McAllister meets Max, who is a young drifter traveling in his GMC van with his hamster Henry, who resided in a spinning wheel in the car. Max, who had lost his mother and elder brother in a plane crash,[7] looks like a troublemaker and somebody who usually leaves a bar by being thrown out of a window. He is short of temper and often gets into trouble, especially when he is defending pretty young women. Max and McAllister meet in the fictional town of Ellerston, where Holly Trumbull (Demi Moore) is being chased by a corrupt sheriff (Bill McKinney), who tried to rape her. Max helps her to escape, but is later confronted by the sheriff in the town's bar. McAllister is also present and wants to gather information about his daughter, but his suitcase is then thrown around and the sheriff finds all kinds of weapons inside, including a ninja sword and a *shuriken* (ninja star).[8] While Max, who wanted to help McAllister, is thrown out through

---

[6] *The Master*, episode 1, "Max," directed by Robert Clouse, written by Michael Sloan, aired January 20, 1984. My emphasis.

[7] *The Master*, episode 5, "High Rollers," directed by Peter Crane, written by Susan Woollen, aired March 2, 1984.

[8] On *shuriken* – generally all kinds of short thrown weapons – and their use, see Markus Bär, *Shuriken: Sicherer Umgang mit Wurfsternen*, 5th ed. (Berlin: Weinmann, 2004);

the window again, the old ninja master provides a show of his skills when he destroys game machines, glasses, and other stuff, before snapping a billard stick with his neck. McAllister tells Max his story, i.e., about how he spent time in the air force during the Second World War and the Korean War before settling in Japan and becoming a ninja. Max offers to help to find McAllister's daughter in exchange for some ninja training. The master, however, declines, since the young man seems to lack "discipline and commitment."

In the meantime, Holly's father (Claude Akins) is asked to sell his airfield to the businessman Mr. Christensen (Clu Gulager), but he refuses to do so. The wounded McAllister, who is still suffering from a *shuriken* wound caused by Okasa, and Max find shelter at the airfield, and when the sheriff and his thugs set fire to the hangar and the planes, McAllister saves Holly from being burnt alive at the last minute when he drives a plane through the hangar's wall. Max confronts Christensen about the events at a dinner party hosted by the businessman, but he is thrown out. Consequently, McAllister, referencing *Rocky* (1976), a film he supposedly saw on the plane from Japan to the US, tells Max to prepare for a confrontation. He eventually agrees to teach Max enough ninjutsu "to stay in one piece." Using a rope, Max has to train to obtain perfect balance, while he also needs "speed and courage," abilities the young new disciple already has. The two men eventually go for a final confrontation with Christensen in his office on the top floor of a skyscraper. McAllister climbs up the building's facade while Max takes the elevator. The latter confronts Christensen and kills him with a *shuriken*, while McAllister has to fight against Okasa again. The former student wants to take revenge for McAllister's betrayal: "A ninja does not betray his destiny." It turns out in later episodes that Okasa had killed for money, while McAllister did not want to train killers anymore. The master catches two arrows with his bare hands and eventually defeats his former student by separating an artery with his bare fingers. However, McAllister does not want to kill Okasa and leaves him alone. This is in a way necessary, as the other ninja will have to show up again and again, thereby allowing new action scenes to be included in the plot at any time, sometimes in moments that just seem too constructed and consequently a bit weird (e.g., Episode 11). At the end of the first episode, McAllister agrees to teach Max in the future: "What good is a ninja teacher without a student?"

That the writers of *The Master* were not too interested in historical or cultural accuracy becomes visible as early as the second episode, during which Max and

---

Wolfgang Ettig, *Shuriken-jutsu* (Bad Homburg: Ettig, 1991); Kubota Takayuki, *The Ninja Shuriken Manual* (Carson, CA: I & I Sports Supply Co., 1985).

McAllister get into trouble with the Chinese triads.[9] In San Francisco, McAllister's daughter supposedly worked in a dance club, and Kelly Patterson (Shanna Reed), a dancer and the daughter of the club's owner, seems to know her. As Max is getting into trouble with the club's bouncer while asking questions in the changing rooms, McAllister witnesses a visit by Jonathan Chan (Brian Tochi), a triad boss, and Mr. Lika (Soon-Tek Oh), his security guard. It turns out that Lika is a ninja of another clan, indicated by a dragon symbol on his ring. He seems to acknowledge McAllister's heraldic animal, a butterfly, which the master is wearing as a necklace – and which is also prominently printed on his ninja mask – and he indicates the existence of an old feud between two ninja clans. However, Japanese ninjas, who were mostly active in Japan's medieval and early modern periods,[10] probably never worked for Chinese triads,[11] which were founded in the 18th century. Regardless of such considerations, the episode continues to mix things Asian as long as they serve the storyline. Lika consequently tries to kill Max and McAllister, leading the former to complain about the master drawing them into conflicts: "Can't you just shake hands?" Chan decides to kidnap Kelly and requests a $20,000 ransom from her father, who then would have to be indebted and allow a triad takeover of his dance club. McAllister suggests a "smokescreen illusion" in this situation and rescues Kelly together with Max, balancing on a rope to get out of the triad headquarters to a neighboring roof. There, Lika is waiting for a showdown with the master, already dressed in his own ninja outfit. During the fight, however, McAllister puts his own suit onto a power connection, and when Lika hits it with his sword, he dies from the electric shock. It eventually turns out that Kelly

---

[9] *The Master*, episode 2, "Out-of-Time-Step," directed by Ray Austin, written by Michael Sloan and Susan Woollen, aired January 27, 1984.

[10] Wang Peng, *The Chinese Mafia: Organized Crime, Corruption, and Extra-Legal Protection* (Oxford: Oxford University Press, 2017). The triads as criminal organizations go back to traditional Chinese secret societies. Frank Jacob, *Geheimgesellschaften: Geschichte und Gegenwart verborgener Macht* (Stuttgart: Kohlhammer, 2015), 69-79; Frank Jacob, "Social Organization, Secrecy, and Rebellion – Secret Societies in China and Ireland," *Comparative Studies of China and the West* 1 (2013): 53-57. For the role of the triads within organized crime in the US, see "Asian Organized Crime," Hearing Before the Permanent Subcommittee on Governmental Affairs United States Senate, One Hundred Second Conngress, First Session, October 3, November 5-6, 1991, accessed March 20, 2020, https://www.ncjrs.gov/pdffiles1/Digitization/147409NCJRS.pdf. On San Francisco in particular, see 131-153.

[11] An introduction to the history of the ninja can be found in Stephen Turnbull, *Ninja AD 1460–1650* (Oxford: Osprey, 2003).

did not know the master's daughter, which is why the journey of Max and McAllister continues after a birthday party is held for Patterson in his club.

The duo continue the search for McAllister's daughter during the series, and while sometimes they are summoned by some old friend or former girlfriend for help, the two get often drawn into local conflicts where they take the side of the weaker party, often represented by a young and beautiful woman in need. In Episode 3, they help the young female union organizer Carrie Brown (Crystal Bernard) in her fight against a cannery owner, although she is resistant to Max's initial attempts at flirting, something McAllister comments upon by saying: "I've never seen one walk away from you."[12] The factory owner Chad Webster (Cotter Smith) tries to kill anyone who threatens to unionize his facility, and therefore he also attacks the heroic duo. McAllister, however, lowers his heartbeat, something he had done earlier in this episode and explained to Max as well as the audience. Max commented on this technique, saying: "I sometimes wonder if being a ninja is going to agree with my health." Not knowing this ninja trick, the bad guys consider him dead and bring his body, Carrie, and Max to the graveyard, where they had already killed Carrie's brother. McAllister seems to reawaken from death, and he and Max are able to overwhelm Webster and his thugs.

In Episode 4, a Freedom Fighter terrorist called Castile (David McCallum) highjacks a party held by Senator Clayton (Robert Dowell) and kidnaps some people. Among them is the daughter of the senator, Alicia (Jennifer Runyon), whom Max had saved before with a motor glider after the brakes of her car had been tampered with. McAllister, after the kidnapping, is forced by the head of the CIA (Monte Markham) to team up with a British agent, Mallory (George Lazenby), whom he knew from his previous spying and ninja activities. They are able to free the hostages from the terrorist organization. In Episode 5, Max and McAllister are on a short trip to Las Vegas when their car is forced off the road by John Craig (Edward Edwards), who is on the way to a casino heist at the Grand Palace Casino. There, Max meets his former girlfriend Tracey (Andrea Gray) and her daughter Suzie (Angela Lee). The former is blackmailed into getting the manager's key for the robbers, who are led by Randy Blake (Art Hindle) and who are eventually successful. They get away with $2 million and retreat to an old Western film set, where Max and McAllister deal with the bad guys and save the day. The heroic journey of the two is continued in New Orleans during Mardi Gras in Episode 6. There they support the reporter Eve

---

[12] *The Master*, episode 3, "State of the Union," directed by Alan Myerson, written by Susan Woollen, aired February 3, 1984.

Michaels (Connie Marie Brazelton), who had used the name of McAllister's daughter for a source she made up to bring down Beaumont (Robert Pine), a rich guy who wants to steal weapons from the US military base and sell them to Arab terrorists.

The plots become relatively boring the more episodes one watches, as they always have a similar structure. The duo support the weak and McAllister's ninja skills save the day, while Max can always test the new abilities he trained in at the beginning of the episode. In Episode 7, a mother and daughter, Maggie (Diana Muldaur) and Cat Sinclair (Tara Buckman), are in need and are attracted by McAllister and Max, respectively. The duo help them to deal with Cat's father, Hellman (Stuart Whitman), who wants to force the farmers to use his Intercontinental Company's trucks for the transportation of their goods. The conflict is a consequence of jealousy, because Maggie had left Hellman and took his daughter with her. Nevertheless, McAllister proposes forming a juggernaut, a convoy, and getting the crops to the sellers. In the end, Cat comes with the duo, but only reappears in the next episode in New York, where Simon Garrett (George Maharis) wants to steal the Crown Jewels while they are exhibited there. Garrett also owns a model agency, which McAllister's daughter had worked for before. Knowing this, Gina (Janine Turner), who works for an insurance company investigating Garrett, pretends to be the daughter the duo are looking for. She asks McAllister to help her to prove that Garrett was involved in several heists and to find out about his current plans. The latter eventually kidnaps Gina and forces McAllister and Max to steal the Crown Jewels from the Manhattan Museum of Modern Art. They do so, but eventually save Gina and bring the criminals to justice.

Afterward, the duo are in Washington, DC upon the request of a high government official, Brian Elkwood (Jack Kelly), who had been a POW together with McAllister. However, the whole reunion was an intrigue planned by Okasa, who wanted to kill Elkwood to protect the position of a double agent called the Hawk. Okasa has trained his own female pupil, Allison Grant (Kelly Harmon), who is, however, not successful in killing Elkwood, since Max and McAllister are able to stop her. Having prevented an assassination and saved the US government from a foreign spy, the team travel to Hawaii to help McAllister's old friend Leo Fairchild (Dick O'Neill) and his daughter Shelly (Cynthia Cypert) with a treasure hunt for a priceless statue known as the Java Tiger on one of Hawaii's small islands. Episode 11 deals with the fractured relationship between Max and his father, Patrick Keller (Doug McClure). Again, two young women, Kathy Hunter (Ashley Ferrare) and Laura Crane (Rebecca Holden), are kidnapped and rescued by the duo and Max's father during the episode.

Eventually, the father and son reconcile before the latter continues his journey with the ninja master.

In the final two episodes, Max and McAllister support the former's old high school girlfriend Talia Donovan (Cindy Harrell) and her brother Jerry (Paul Tulley), a police officer, in their investigation of a group of rogue police officers led by Lieutenant Loring (Kaz Garas). They had robbed numerous luxury stores and were trying to get away with it by silencing Jerry, who had started to look into the cases more closely. In the final episode, the duo do not find McAllister's daughter, whose fate is never revealed, but help a missionary, Kim Anderson (Susan Woollen), to defend her orphanage against Mark Richards (Jock Mahoney), who wants to get into possession of the mission's land to mine uranium from an old Native American cemetery. McAllister and Max help them to resist and gain the respect of the community, whose members initially wanted to get rid of the children.

As mentioned before, the series' plot concept was probably repeated too fast and too often to attract the steady interest of a TV audience, especially since the concept had copied the plots of other, more successful TV series like *The A-Team* (1983-1987).[13] The model of the superhero duo, which was common in previous years, like the Green Hornet (Van Williams) and Kato (Bruce Lee) (1966-1967), Batman (Adam West) and Robin (Burt Ward) (1966-1968), etc., was outdated, and more complex superhero teams like the A-Team were popular in the 1980s. Such teams were also able to better reflect the diversity of US society, and minority characters like B. A. Baracus (Mr. T) became relatively popular. An all-white ninja team was probably also outdated, and the cheap production – Shō Kosugi also performed Lee Van Cleef's fighting scenes, to name just one example – was not suitable for a television hit at this time. In addition, the stereotypes used to highlight the ninja aspect of the story, which became more like a side narrative that was only used to explain McAllister's superhero moves, were not enough to keep the audience following the series. These existent stereotypes shall therefore be taken into consideration in the next section.

The Occidental Ninja in Action

The casting of Lee Van Cleef, who was rather better known for his role in Western films like Sergio Leone's *For a Few Dollars More* (1965), in which he starred alongside Clint Eastwood, has already been emphasized. *The Master* even references this, for example, in Episode 11. When the blind Laura touched

---

[13] Sally Bedell, "How TV Hit 'The A-Team' Was Born," *New York Times*, April 28, 1983.

McAllister's face, the latter asks the young woman about her impression of him. Her reply is a reference to Van Cleef's former career: "A Western movie actor. Clint Eastwood." McAllister answers: "Close."[14] The whiteness of the ninja seems to have been created to attract the audience to some kind of reversed exoticism, as the protagonist is of Western origin and can therefore provide an insight into martial arts and a hidden knowledge that would otherwise not be accessible, especially since Okasa is hunting the former master due to his betrayal of his order/sect and his assumption that McAllister is sharing secret knowledge, in particular with his new non-Japanese student Max.

Regardless of such assumptions, the stereotypes related to ninjas are clearly displayed, and McAllister always has to wear his black silk suit, even when he is in broad daylight next to Max, who mostly wears regular clothes. McAllister's appearance often therefore looks strange, as his identity as a ninja needs to be constantly displayed. Only once, in Episode 7, does he use another disguise, when he is brought to jail as a drunkard, to help Max to escape. The latter comments on this tactic when he claims ninjas to be "the first masters of disguise,"[15] but this ability to hide in the open is never really stressed in other episodes.[16]

The Japaneseness of the ninja's abilities is only emphasized in the introduction of the series, when two ninja warriors fight in front of a screen that resembles the Japanese flag, although the circle is yellow and the surrounding space red. A red *shuriken* is also shown at the beginning and some "oriental sounding electronic music"[17] is played during the introductory sequence, which also plays at the end of each episode, over a short summary of McAllister's story, which shows him fighting against three other ninjas before leaving in a small plane for the US, hunted by Okasa. All in all, references to

---

[14] *The Master*, episode 11, "Failure to Communicate," directed by Sidney Hayers, written by Michael Sloan, aired May 4, 1984.

[15] *The Master*, episode 7, "Juggernaut," directed by Gordon Hessler, written by Chris Bunch, Allan Cole, Michael Sloan, and Susan Woollen, aired March 16, 1984.

[16] The idea of the ninja as master of camouflage is very close to another stereotype related to Asia, namely that of the oriental magician (Chinese and Japanese), who has very iconic features (long mustache, suit of iridescent colors, etc.) and who was shown in performances when disappearing in smoke screens or changing suits. Such stories go way back and some references can be found in Kenneth J. DeWoskin, trans., *Doctors Diviners and Magicians of Ancient China: Biographies of Fang-shih* (New York: Columbia University Press, 1983).

[17] The theme tune, composed by Bill Conti, is actually the same as in the Firebird computer game *Ninja Master*.

Japan are relatively few during the whole series. A few stories about old ninja masters and their abilities are interwoven in the teaching-related dialogues between Max and McAllister, but nothing else about Japan is actually referenced in the episodes. The series simply offered the audience too little, especially when compared to other sources of entertainment that also based their story on the relationship between an old martial arts master and a younger student, who needed, besides training in martial arts, guidance, and wisdom from a teacher. *Karate Kid* (1984) told the story of Daniel LaRusso (Ralph Macchio), who was successfully trained by Kesuke Miyagi (Pat Morita), leading to three sequels (1986, 1989, and 1994) and a remake with Jackie Chan and Jaden Smith in 2010. These films offered more than stereotypes but also, due to the casting of Asian or Asian-American co-stars, a better insight into the stories of Asian-American immigrants in the United States as well. The films also highlighted the history between the two countries and thereby offered more than just a display of martial arts. Important philosophical questions of growing up and finding a place were highlighted, instead of the simple hero narratives that were provided by *The Master*. The TV series was trying to serve too many different audiences at the same time and failed to use the hype for ninjutsu in an effective way, and, due to its boring plot and storylines, also lost those TV audiences that were already favoring new formats and new heroic team structures, such as those provided by *The A-Team*. While ninja and martial arts films attracted many visitors to watch them in the cinema and became box office hits and cult films, *The Master* was not able to replicate such successes. The series' approach was too old-fashioned and too superficial with its stereotypes, which did not really say anything about Japan besides the fact that ninjas had once existed there and obviously still existed.

The series disappeared from TV screens as quickly as it had appeared, almost imitating McAllister's disappearance in a smoke bomb. It left unresolved issues for those who had hoped to find out if Max would become the second occidental American ninja, if McAllister would be able to find his daughter, and how he and his former student Okasa would settle their conflict. These questions, however, obviously did not spark the interest of the audience enough to keep the series in production. Ultimately, the story of a ninja operating in broad daylight was probably not sufficiently attractive after all, especially since it is the mysterious aspect of their character that tends to make the ninja an interesting film subject.[18]

---

[18] Budnik names many such films from the 1980s. See Daniel R. Budnik, *'80s Action Movies on the Cheap: 284 Low Budget, High Impact* (Jefferson, NC: McFarland 2017).

Conclusion

Coming back to Koselleck's theoretical work on *Erfahrungsraum* and *Erwartungshorizont*, the TV series *The Master* does not seem to have offered anything beyond the actual space of experience that it shared with the audience. It never opened an *Erwartungshorizont* to tell the spectators more about Japan, the origin of the ninja, or why it still existed in Japan. It rather only used superficial stereotypes, and therefore remained in the existent *Erfahrungsraum*. Without anything new to offer the audience, it lost its attraction because it did almost nothing more than resemble old-fashioned narratives. McAllister's appearances in his black suit were not surprising at all, nor were the attacks by Okasa, who challenged his master every now and then.

Regardless of its shortcomings, *The Master* is a good example to show how the TV industry worked and still works today. NBC has started multiple series but only continued those that attracted an audience, and the history of McAllister and Max thus shows how far audiences reacted to mere stereotypes on the screen. Instead of falling for them, they got bored, and the series was eventually buried. Like many other TV series, *The Master* is nothing more than evidence highlighting how Hollywood and TV producers worked with Japanese stereotypes on the screen. It also highlights that making a few quick dollars was responsible for the rapid speed of productions, whose aim was not to introduce knowledge about a foreign culture to US living rooms but rather to extract some money from these living rooms for semi-cooked and halfhearted stories, sewn and cemented together with a sprinkle of orientalism.[19]

Television productions are supposed to entertain, and therefore they need and want to address the expectations of the audience. Naturally, stereotypes, which in a way resemble common sense, are therefore included to reproduce existent semiotics. According to Marshall McLuhan's media theory,[20] stereotypes are consequently part of the message, i.e., the media, and consequently tend to be reproduced until society changes their semiotic value and replaces them with new demands, which are probably related to new ninja images of the time. In our days, other images, stimulated by the success of post-

---

[19] Edward Said, *Orientalism* (New York: Pantheon Books, 1978).
[20] Marshall McLuhan, *Understanding Media: The Extensions of Man* (London/New York: McGraw-Hill, 1964).

modern ninjas like Naruto[21] in Japan and abroad, have already begun to replace the images that dominated the 1980s.

Works Cited

Allen, Terence. "Which Martial Art Will Be the Fad of the '90s?" *Black Belt* 10 (1994): 48-49, 52-55.

"Asian Organized Crime," Hearing Before the Permanent Subcommittee on Governmental Affairs United States Senate, One Hundred Second Conngress, First Session, October 3, November 5-6, 1991. Accessed March 20, 2020. https://www.ncjrs.gov/pdffiles1/Digitization/147409NCJRS.pdf

Bär, Markus. *Shuriken: Sicherer Umgang mit Wurfsternen.* 5th ed. Berlin: Weinmann, 2004.

Bedell, Sally. "How TV Hit 'The A-Team' Was Born." *New York Times*, April 28, 1983.

Budnik, Daniel R. *'80s Action Movies on the Cheap: 284 Low Budget, High Impact.* Jefferson, NC: McFarland 2017.

DeWoskin, Kenneth J., trans. *Doctors, Diviners, and Magicians of Ancient China: Biographies of Fang-shih.* New York: Columbia University Press, 1983.

Ettig, Wolfgang. *Shuriken-jutsu.* Bad Homburg: Ettig, 1991.

Jacob, Frank. "From Tokyo's Destroyer to International Icon: Godzilla and Japanese Monstrosity in the Postwar Age." In *All Around Monstrous: Monster Media in Their Historical Contexts*, edited by Verena Bernardi and Frank Jacob, 211-244. Wilmington, DE: Vernon Press, 2019.

———. *Geheimgesellschaften: Geschichte und Gegenwart verborgener Macht.* Stuttgart: Kohlhammer, 2015.

———. "Japanese Mythology in Manga: Naruto as a Case Study." Paper presented at the I Love Pop Conference, CUNY Graduate Center, New York, 2016. https://cunypop.files.wordpress.com/2016/08/panels-final7.pdf.

———. "Social Organization, Secrecy, and Rebellion – Secret Societies in China and Ireland." *Comparative Studies of China and the West* 1 (2013): 53-57.

Koselleck, Reinhart. "'Erfahrungsraum' und 'Erwartungshorizont': Zwei historische Kategorien." In *Vergangene Zukunft: Zur Semantik geschichtlicher Zeiten*, 349-375. Berlin: Suhrkamp Verlag, 2010.

McLuhan, Marshall. *Understanding Media: The Extensions of Man.* London/New York: McGraw-Hill, 1964.

---

[21] The manga *Naruto* (1999-2014) by Kishimoto Masashi in a way redefined the semiotics of the ninja in Japan, although he used traditional Japanese semiotics as a point of reference as well. See: Frank Jacob, "Japanese Mythology in Manga: Naruto as a Case Study" (paper presented at the I Love Pop Conference, CUNY Graduate Center, New York, 2016), https://cunypop.files.wordpress.com/2016/08/panels-final7.pdf.

Peng, Wang. *The Chinese Mafia: Organized Crime, Corruption, and Extra-Legal Protection.* Oxford: Oxford University Press, 2017.

Said, Edward. *Orientalism.* New York: Pantheon Books, 1978.

SCMP. "Bruce Lee: How His Chinese Race Counted Against Him in Hollywood with Its History of Negative Asian Stereotypes in Films." *South China Morning Post*, July 30, 2018. https://www.scmp.com/culture/film-tv/article/2157471/did-bruce-lee-suffer-racism-hollywood-studio-executives-were.

Takayuki, Kubota. *The Ninja Shuriken Manual.* Carson, CA: I & I Sports Supply Co., 1985.

Turnbull, Stephen. *Ninja AD 1460–1650.* Oxford: Osprey, 2003.

Chapter 6

Japanese Memory and Ideology in Western-Inspired *Shōnen* Animes

Gianmarco Thierry Giuliana

University of Turin, Italy

Abstract

This chapter is a semiotic inquiry on the notion of "Japaneseness." The reflection starts from the debate about the adoption and disappearance of Japanese culture in both Western countries and in Japan. The debate is a starting point to highlight the fallacy of both arguments, which are grounded on a simplistic notion of identity and culture. Therefore, both contemporary semiotics and anthropology are applied to propose an alternative perspective that conceives identity as a particular and dynamic way of including the alterity through mechanisms such as the one of translation. Indeed, the chapter claims that Japaneseness is a particular process and rule of translation. Afterwards, a concrete example of these theoretical claims are given by analyzing four apparently very different shōnen anime: *Naruto* (1999-2014), *Saint Seiya: The Lost Canvas – The Myth of Hades* (2009-2011), *Rage of Bahamut: Genesis* (2014), and *Baccano!* (2007). All these texts will highlight the presence of references to Japan's culture and the recurrence of underlying values belonging to the Edo period (1600-1867). However, the chapter will also highlight how these iconic elements of "Japaneseness" are transformed and blended with Western culture and Japan's contemporary history.

Keywords: anime, shōnen manga, cultural translation, Edo period.

* * *

Introduction

In today's global culture, Japaneseness is an interesting and somehow contradictory concept. On the one hand, it seems to be everywhere in most Western countries: we eat sushi every week as something not extraordinary (while in 1975, Luciano Salce's movie *Fantozzi* still represented Japanese restaurants as terrifying places), we grow up reading mangas and watching animes (which are even aired on national TV channels), we use Japanese emojis in chats, we can laugh with our friends talking about the weirdness of Japanese pornography, we can randomly learn on the internet of very specific Japanese practices like *kintsugi*,[1] we watch travel guides about Japan and know about Japanese game shows (such as *Takeshi's Castle*), we read novels written by famous Japanese writers (think about Kazuo Ishiguro), we play video games often produced by Japanese companies and with many cultural references to Japan (*Persona 5*, 2016), we recognize and love Japanese-like aesthetics in Western-produced movies (such as Quentin Tarantino's *Kill Bill*, 2003), we have city fairs with cosplayers (a Japanese-invented term that makes us forget about the Western origin of fan costuming or masquerade[2]) and maid cafés, we have specific studies called "Nihonjinron" about the Japanese culture and mentality, and so on. Therefore, at first glance, we could almost speak of an Eastern "cultural colonization" of the West thanks to which Japanese people are unquestionably no longer "alien"[3] to us. However, on the other hand, *authentic Japaneseness* seems to be nowhere to be found: we eat Westernized sushi,[4] we watch censored animes (often without knowing it), and many studies about Japan actually create a Westernized vision of it through artificial resemblances[5] that invented Japaneseness. More generally speaking, we still think of Japan mainly through stereotypes and *known languages*[6] ("crazy" or "weird" are the etiquettes of almost anything Japanese on the web), we usually know very little of the past of Japan before the 16th century, we care little for understanding Japanese customs, and all we know about Japan did not really change the values we live by. Japan is still *untranslatable* for us (as in Sofia Coppola's movie *Lost in Translation*, 2003).

---

[1] A traditional method to repair broken ceramics.
[2] Brian Ashcraft and Luke Plunkett, *Cosplay World* (New York: Prestel, 2014), 10-20.
[3] Ruth Benedict, *The Chrysanthemum and the Sword* (London: Secker & Warburg, 1947), 1.
[4] Simona Stano, *Eating the Other* (Newcastle upon Tyne: Cambridge Scholars Publishing, 2015), 88; Imai Shoko, "Nobu and After: Westernized Japanese Food and Globalization," in *Food and Social Identities in the Asia Pacific Region*, ed. James Farrer (Tokyo: Sophia University Institute of Comparative Culture, 2010), 4.
[5] Urs App, *The Cult of Emptiness: The Eastern Discovery of Buddhist Thought and the Invention of Oriental Philosophy* (Kyoto: University Media, 2012), 11.
[6] Roland Barthes, *L'Impero dei Segni*, trans. Marco Vallora (Turin: Einaudi, 1984), 6.

But there is even more. In fact, Japaneseness seems to be absent even in Japan: Japanese cities are full of Western signs and citations,[7] Japanese people undergo eyelid surgery, English words are constantly used in the Japanese language, and all Japanese cultural productions are influenced by the need to spread globally and so often repeat a simplified and stereotyped vision of Japan itself. So, it is also possible to think that Japan has been permanently disfigured by Western countries and globalization and is slowly but constantly disappearing, thus reminding us of Yukio Mishima's (1925-1970) words: "I cannot have much hope for the future of Japan. As days pass, I feel more and more deeply that if things should proceed this way, 'Japan' might end up disappearing."[8]

The aim of this chapter, though, is precisely to demonstrate that neither of these two impressions are right about Japaneseness. First of all, the idea of a "nationality-ness" as a set of "local" and "pure" unique cultural elements that have belonged and will belong forever only and exclusively to a certain group of humans born in a particular space of the earth, and that have never been influenced by other cultures, is in many cases ideological. As the semiotician Juri Lotman (1922-1993) pointed out in his works, cultures are dynamic[9] structures and are constantly in dialogue with every cultural element outside of their "sphere," endlessly "translating" and integrating the not-known and the unknown. Furthermore, cultures also endlessly reorganize their own elements so that something from the "periphery" can become central and vice versa. A similar perspective is shared by the Italian anthropologist Francesco Remotti, who writes that both in nature and in culture, all the stabilized forms are born from the flux of the everchanging[10] and continually disappear within this flux. And that, consequently, *identities are constructions*: a matter of names, of decisions, of cuts, of both arbitrary separations and assimilations, the result of an inevitable fictional and representational need.[11] More importantly, identities are always born from an alterity and are always struggling to hide the endless operations that create the two sides of identity and alterity.[12]

---

[7] Rolf J. Goebel, "Japanese Urban Space and the Citation of Western Signs," *Comparative Literature Studies* 35, no. 2 (1998): 93.

[8] Joseph Verbovszky, "Overcoming Modernity in Yukio Mishima," *Discussions* 9, no. 2 (2013): 2.

[9] Juri Lotman and Boris Uspenskij, *Tipologia della Cultura* (Milan: Bompiani, 1995), 60.

[10] Francesco Remotti, *Contro L'Identità* (Rome: Laterza, 1996), 3.

[11] Ibid., 97.

[12] Ibid.

So, while it is undeniable that some elements are iconic of a culture and can be "unique" (such as the Japanese phenomena of the *ways*[13]), "nationality-ness" is a kind of identity that can vary from time to time, and that is the result of a selection and interpretation of some cultural elements and historical facts, of the "translation" of "external" elements, and of the creation of a collective imaginary[14] and cultural memory.[15]

Nationality-ness is, therefore, outside of the rhetorical speeches and, ironically, the everchanging product of alterity in many ways. This is especially easy to see in the case of Japan that, before the Heian period, first borrowed almost anything from the Chinese culture and then later claimed ownership of the adaptations of what had been borrowed for three centuries.[16] Japan, as a consequence of the Second World War and of the petrol crisis in 1973,[17] transformed once again during the twentieth century to become the over-civilized, polite, and peaceful[18] democratic country of technological and economic progress. This is why Japan is famous for having a "double identity": "Japan is often seen both as the ultimate embodiment of post-modernity and as a country that remains linked to its centuries-old traditions but has always shown a great ability to integrate allogenous cultural elements, making them then become part of its own tradition."[19]

This is especially due to its modern cities being "the tangible, concrete materiality of these phenomena that metonymically reveals the larger underlying mechanisms of Japan's self-definition as an eclectic plurality of cultural traditions from the East and the West."[20] Secondly, and as a consequence of the previous point, Japaneseness can be thought of in two ways. Firstly, as an invisible and delicate resistance to the alterity, like when "all

---

[13] Aldo Tollini, *L'ideale della Via: Samurai, Monaci e Poeti nel Giappone Medievale* (Turin: Einaudi, 2017).

[14] Maurice Halbwachs, *La Mémoire Collective* (Paris: Presse Universitaire de France, 1950); Juri Lotman, *Tesi per una Semiotica delle Culture*, ed. Franciscu Sedda (Rome: Meltemi, 2006), 153.

[15] Jan Assmann, *La Memoria Culturale: Scrittura, Ricordo e Identità Politica nelle Grandi Civiltà Antiche*, trans. Francesco De Angelis (Turin: Einaudi, 1997).

[16] Edwin O. Reischauer, *Storia del Giappone dalle Origini ai Giorni Nostri* (Milan: Bompiani, 2013), 13-15.

[17] Guido Tavassi, *Storia dell'Animazione Giapponese* (Latina: Tunué, 2012), 105.

[18] Jean-Marie Bouissou, *Il Manga*, trans. Gianluca Di Fratta (Latina: Tunué, 2009), 190.

[19] Marcello Ghilardi, "Da Sabi a Cyber: Un Immaginario in Trasformazione," in *Culture del Giappone Contemporaneo*, ed. Matteo Casari (Latina: Tunué, 2011), 143.

[20] Goebel, "Japanese Urban Space," 94.

the industrial and scientific influences during the Meiji period from the West, Hearn argues, have left the emotional, aesthetic, and spiritual life of Japan basically untouched."[21]

Secondly, and this will be our approach, as the result of *a particular interpretative rule of translation* and as *mediated speech* where the specific identity of the speaker is determined by his speaking *through something else*, as in Umberto Eco's (1932-2016) enunciative and encyclopedic theory.[22] Japaneseness will therefore be not only an opposite term grounding its identity in difference (between East and West, between Japan and non-Japan) but will also be considered as a complex and inclusive concept grounding its meaning in a *participatory* way.[23]

In this particular case, Japaneseness will be the rule for which, in the apparently most diverse animes, we will find some central underlying ideas[24] and values that are characteristic both of when these texts are produced and of a certain symbolic period of Japan's history and culture. A period in which the cultural identity of Japaneseness has been forged by externalizing the memories[25] of this nation and by creating a new memory-culture[26] to be remembered and defended in the future. Different periods during which Japanese culture flourished could be chosen, such as the Heian period (794-1185) or the Muromachi period (1336-1573), however, we will claim here that this period is undoubtedly the Edo period (1600-1867), which is, paradoxically, not the time when most of what we usually consider iconic of Japan was born. In fact, much of what is usually considered "traditional" (ikebana, tea ceremony, martial arts, kimono, *shodō*, etc.) dates to before 1600. For example, though many elements of the samurai code (today known as *bushidō*) were transcribed during the Edo era in Yamamoto Tsunetomo's (1659-1719) *Hakagure*,[27] it was during that same period that the samurai's decline began.[28] The Edo era is therefore not a historical period in which all the Japanese tradition is born, but it is that period in which Japanese society "cultivated its

[21] Ibid.

[22] Claudio Paolucci, *Strutturalismo e Interpretazione* (Milan: Bompiani, 2010), 480.

[23] Ibid., 35-48

[24] Paolo Fabbri, *La Svolta Semiotica* (Rome: Laterza, 1998), 27.

[25] Patrizia Violi, *Paesaggi della Memoria* (Milan: Bompiani, 2014), 28.

[26] Lotman and Uspenskij, *Tipologia della Cultura*, 44.

[27] Yamamoto Tsunetomo, *Hakagure: Il Libro Segreto dei Samurai* (Milan: Mondadori, 2009).

[28] Reischauer, *Storia del Giappone*, 76.

own culture," codified it, interpreted it, elaborated its past, and consequently created its own *image* through which society could represent itself.[29] It was a historic moment of peace and the reunification of Japan, after hundreds of years of struggle, which would last for over two hundred years.

At that time, there was an almost complete closure of Japan to any other state, and this situation allowed the citizens of Japan to represent themselves as a "unique" people and to resume ancient traditions or invent new ones such as *ukiyo-e, haiku,* or *kabuki* theater. The Edo period is thus the period of memory *par excellence*: at the same time, the period both of the reminiscence and of the creation of a euphoric imaginary through which Japan would characterize itself in the future. That is why we can consider the Edo period as the "structural backbone" (what is *continuous in discontinuity*[30]) of the Japanese semiosphere and of what gave birth to interpretative rules that are meant to guide not *what* Japan *must keep being* but *how* Japan *should keep changing.*

So, while katanas or kimonos are usually seen as icons of Japaneseness, in our perspective, Tokyo's skyscrapers (with greeters at the entrance who frenetically bow to greet the employees) and tanegashima (matchlocks copied from those used by Portuguese adventurers and then modified[31]) are even more Japanese. Similarly, while the emperor is usually seen as something characteristic, for us, the particular variety[32] of Japanese capitalism is even more distinctive. Accordingly, in this work, I will try to show how some central values of Japaneseness can be at the same time contradictory (i.e., the rhetoric of the peace and idealization of a *shōgun* state) and coexistent in *shōnen* animes that are a great example of the complexity and fusion behind Japaneseness.

Why Animes?

There are five main reasons for the choice of *shōnen* animes to carry out such an inquiry. First, animes are something iconic of Japan, both because of their origin, their visual language,[33] and all the references to Japan that are both explicit (cities, habits, food, history, names, mythology) and implicit (the head of many *mecha* that looks like the *kabuto* helmet of samurai). They are so iconic that *Doraemon* was officially appointed as the "Cultural Ambassador of Anime"

---

[29] Lotman, *Tesi*, 149.

[30] Ghilardi, "Da Sabi a Cyber," 144.

[31] Reischauer, *Storia del Giappone*, 60.

[32] David Hundt and Jitendra Uttam, *Varieties of Capitalism in Asia: Beyond the Developmental State* (London: Palgrave Macmillan, 2017), 39-76.

[33] Bouissou, *Il Manga*, 7.

by the Ministry of Foreign Affairs[34] and anime art was used in the teaser video[35] for the upcoming 2021 Summer Olympics in Tokyo.

Second, animes are also perceived as a strange mix of East and West: let us think of adaptations like *Heidi*, of the not-Japanese faces, of the use of English words, of the global production of animes, of the presence of a Mount Rushmore even in a "traditional" anime like *Naruto*, but also of the Superflat artistic movement that uses animes to critique today's Japanese consumer culture[36] and of the word *anime* itself, which derives from the English word animation.[37] Third, many scholars have already shown the strong presence of Japaneseness inside animes, focusing especially on the multiple levels of narration and interpretation that are present.[38] Fourth, animes are strongly "ideologic" by definition: let us think about the cynical ending of *Hiroshima Gen* that is cut in the anime version (significantly transforming the message[39]) or of the *yaoi-hentai Enzai* that ends by celebrating the value of friendship, community, and truth. Lastly, the animes of the last ten years seem profoundly different from the ones we were used to seeing in the past; in particular, the references to Japan (with Japanese heroes and cities) are far less common than they used to be, and this could easily be mistakenly read as another proof of the disappearance of Japaneseness.

Consequently, in this paper, we will start by looking at a famous and very traditional anime such as *Naruto* (2002) to find some examples of this translation process that we defined as Japaneseness. Then, we will look for the underlying values and ideas of these different examples and regroup them in broad categories that can be applied to other animes. Finally, we will look into three recent Western-inspired animes to see how Japaneseness is still strongly present even in these products, even though it is *disguised* and invisible. Hopefully, through this specific analysis, we will be able to prove the usefulness

---

[34] Toshio Miyake, "Mostri Made in Japan," in *Culture del Giappone Contemporaneo*, ed. Matteo Casari (Latina: Tunué, 2011), 167.

[35] Al Jazeera Turk, "Tokyo 2020'ye hazır," YouTube Video, 2:13, August 22, 2016, https://www.youtube.com/watch?v=FNuqKVG781I. Thanks to Bruno Surace for this suggestion.

[36] Francesco Bonami, *Lo Potevo Fare Anch'Io: Perché l'Arte Contemporanea è Davvero Arte* (Milan: Mondadori, 2009), 95.

[37] Tavassi, *Storia dell'Animazione Giapponese*, 19.

[38] Ibid., 98.

[39] Bouissou, *Il Manga*, 191.

of our semiotic perspective on identity to better understand Japaneseness both as a concept and as an issue.

Naruto: Japaneseness Inside a Western Jumpsuit

Naruto is a Japanese *shōnen* manga written and illustrated by Kishimoto Masashi, which was first published in 1999 and then adapted into an anime in 2002. Set in an alternative and fantastic "ninja world" similar to feudal Japan, it tells the story of a reckless young orphan boy called Naruto who is marginalized by others because of a demon that was "sealed" and lives inside of him. He is a typical childish *shōnen* protagonist with a very Japanese name (an ingredient of ramen), and at the beginning of the story, he is not particularly skillful (he is the worst student in his class) or smart. Despite his name, he also has a Western-pop look (explicitly created to be liked by the Western audience[40]) with an orange jumpsuit and blond hair. Thanks to his willpower ("Believe it!" is his catchphrase), his determination, and his good heart (his motto is "I won't go back on my word... that is my ninja way!"), and thanks to the guidance of his masters (especially Jiraiya, who is called the "perverted sage"), Naruto will manage to become strong and wise enough to save both his village and the world. By doing so, he will succeed in being accepted, respected, and loved by everyone, and he will also fulfill his dream of becoming "*Hokage*" (a political leader considered the strongest ninja of all) and even find a wife and have a child. However, Naruto is not the only protagonist of this anime. There is another main character who also grew up alone and who will save the world: Uchiha Sasuke. This character is Naruto's best friend and rival by being in many ways his exact opposite: he has a Japanese look with dark hair, he is smart, he is loved by the girl (Sakura) that Naruto loves, he has the opposite magical affinities (lightning and fire versus wind), he is cynical, etc. Although following a different path and having different objectives, Sasuke too, in the end, will have his family and will protect the same village where he and Naruto grew up.

The story will explain that Sasuke and Naruto are the "reincarnations" of two ancient brothers (Indra and Asura, a tacit mythological reference) who fought against each other in the past and who are fated to an eternal struggle because they represent *two opposite forces*. Indeed, while they both have a very dark and tragic past, they will choose different paths. Naruto will follow the *way* to become a ninja by trusting the adults of his village, guided by the hope to be loved by everyone and to bring peace to the world. Sasuke is instead guided by

---

[40] Masashi Kishimoto, *Uzumaki: The Art of Naruto* (San Francisco: Viz Media, 2007).

hatred and will abandon his village, betray his friends, become the pupil of an evil character, and even take part in a criminal organization; all this to become strong enough to kill his brother (Itachi) who slaughtered his clan and family. And it is exactly this fight between brothers that takes place over four episodes (135, 136, 137, and 138) of the second part of the series (*Shippūden*) that will be analyzed to find some of the main elements of Japaneseness inside this anime.

The first thing to note is that episode 135 begins with a flashback: a return to the past which opens the battle that must still begin. Flashback is one of the most frequent mechanisms in animes and somehow connects what happens (and is about to happen) to something that has already happened. Differently from Western cartoons,[41] flashbacks in animes often happen during fights and constantly interrupt the action. While, of course, it is undeniable that the non-conclusive episodes of animes are well-suited for such a narrative mechanic, it should not be understood as a simple expedient among others. In fact, the sense that springs from these continuous references to the past is related to the impossibility of affirming a present reality without referring to a past one. Indeed, in *Naruto*, characters remember constantly, passing almost more time in doing so than in accomplishing their own actions. Furthermore, many solutions are found by discovering the past, with knowledge and memory often being the real key to new problems, such as when Itachi tells Sasuke that in order to defeat him, he must read *an ancient secret scroll.*

During the flashbacks, we see many explicit figurative elements of traditional Japan on which there is no need to dwell. But what is far more interesting is looking at the training scene between Sasuke and Itachi. Indeed, after an impeccable launch of *kunai*,[42] Itachi opens his eyes that reveal a *sharingan* (lit. copy circle eye, special eyes of the Uchiha clan that allow members to copy other ninjas' techniques). The eyes of the character are red and contain three commas within the iris. These signs are not random signs but *tomoe*, a recurring form in Japanese logos and connected to the Shinto religion. We are interested here in noting that for the "average" Western viewer these symbols are random and are not explained or related to something "real."

Yet, soon after, we witness a significant scene: Itachi's *sharingan* changes, as the three commas merge together and form something new, a more powerful eye that can be used by him in different ways (e.g., to create a black fire). This is

---

[41] A quick search on YouTube about cartoon fights of Western heroes like Spiderman, Batman, etc. can show this very easily.

[42] Serge Mol, *Classical Weaponry of Japan: Special Weapons and Tactics of the Martial Arts* (Tokyo: Kodansha, 2003), 123.

not only a matter of aesthetics but one of the fundamental traits of the ideology: *change as a way to improvement.* However, we can note how the change in question starts from a symbol of tradition, something that happens punctually throughout the anime and especially with reference to the skills of the protagonists. Not only is the *sharingan* more capable of transforming and the ninja more powerful, but both Naruto and Sasuke become very powerful because they can invent variations of the *jutsu* (ninja techniques) they have learned. Thus, the power of the past is exactly expressed by not being static.

Thus, we see here a second very interesting element: the creation of an "artificial" sign system that tacitly evokes a very precise historical and cultural reality. The same also happens when Sasuke and Itachi perform a series of hand gestures before using a special technique. These gestures are narratively explained in the anime as "seals," but in fact, they correspond to the animals of the Chinese zodiac (never explicitly mentioned). A last example can be found in the explanation of the "magic" that exists in this world that is based on the "*chakra*" (chakura).

Even more interestingly, a few minutes later, we see Itachi using a power on Sasuke, and to do so, he pronounces a name. While this *nomination* is often derided by the Western public (who have never seen Superman giving a name to his punches and shouting it), this feature is in reality profoundly meaningful. A first explanation can come from the martial arts culture where there is a particular shout, called *kiai*, that is used when performing an attacking move and has a spiritual dimension.[43] However, there is far more. Indeed, in *Naruto* these names are almost always references to Japanese mythology. So, what actually happens is that naming an action consists of evoking a double narrative dimension: on the one hand, the myth of the attack is created internally (intratextual value), but on the other hand, it also means referring to something else (intertextual value) that links this specific anime to the whole Japanese culture and that also creates some sort of causality between the power of the past and the power of the present.

There are countless examples of this, like when Itachi uses a technique named *Tsukuyomi*: the name of a central character in Japanese mythology. So, while the strength and the sense of the move for the unaware spectator is determined only by its figurative and narrative consistency, for a more "educated" spectator, there is another strong cultural dimension.

---

[43] Werner Lind, *Budo: La Via Spirituale delle Arti Marziali*, trans. Antonio Manco (Rome: Edizioni Mediterranee, 2012), 101.

These mythological references happen many other times during the three episodes, with and without nominations: when we see black-eyed ravens coming out of a false Itachi body (a reference to *Yatagarasu*), or when the "Nine-Tailed Fox" appears (a central figure in the anime as well as in Japanese mythology and culture). Yet probably the greatest example is at the end of the fight (episode 138) when, exactly as in Shinto mythology,[44] Itachi uses the *Susanoo* (a technique granting him a spiritual armory) to fight against the eight-headed snake summoned by Orochimaru and defeats it with the *Totsuka* sword. Thus, we can easily see how the *Naruto* anime is a text that, through many mythological references and through nominations, both repeats ancient stories and creates a new one from the past ones. Not surprisingly, this kind of relation between nomination and myth has also been studied by Lotman and is a fundamental aspect of his theory: "In the mythological world, as we have described it, there is a sufficiently specific type of semiosis that can be traced, in general, to the process of nomination: the sign of mythological consciousness is analogous to the proper name [...]. The myth and the name are by their nature connected by a direct link. In a certain sense, they mutually determine their self...."[45]

Looking further, just before the beginning of the fight (episode 135), we can see Sasuke walking toward Itachi and a series of close-ups on the protagonists with another visual element worthy of interest: the resemblance between the characters. Japanese animes often have a bad reputation of having characters with all the same faces, but this is obviously a prejudice. Yet, in *Naruto*, this distinction can sometimes be difficult. Why? The extreme resemblance between Sasuke and Itachi or between Naruto and his father should not be explained only as a "realistic" (genetic) similarity. It should be enough to say that Sasuke's father, Fugaku, does not really look like his son, while Naruto and his father are almost indistinguishable in certain frames.

This resemblance brings into play another feature of *shōnen* animes: the lack of *individuality* of the various characters, with both the faces and the moves of the characters that always refer to other persons and stories.

Naruto cannot escape from the "destiny of the son of the fourth *Hokage*." As the son of an exceptional father, he develops not only the same skills and a similar fate but also a similar appearance and similar behavioral

---

[44] William George Aston, *Nihongi: Chronicles of Japan from the Earliest Times to A.D. 697* (London: Trench & Trübner, 1896), 20.
[45] Lotman and Uspenskij, *Tipologia della Cultura*, 86-89. My translation.

characteristics. Several times during the anime, we can see Naruto with a fade-out effect in which figures such as his father and teacher appear "within" him (with the most striking example in episode 163). Furthermore, Naruto also uses the techniques of his father and master. The name Naruto itself is the name of a character invented by his master in a book, and Naruto will claim this origin and try to live *as the character*. But more importantly, even the guilts that Naruto carries are not his own, but rather those of the demon that lives inside of him and is the reason of him being refused as an equal by society. In the same way, Sasuke will never follow an "independent" path but all his actions are made in the function of his brother and the clan to which he belongs (that is his personal pride and his social shame). At the end of the fight, Itachi will even symbolically give his eyes to his brother, granting him all his powers. Thus, the form of Sasuke's *sharingan* will change to include two distinct forms: his own and the one of his brother (and not an entirely new form, as it would have been possible). Whenever Sasuke opens his eyes, the figure, the memory, of Itachi will be re-evoked. Lastly, both Naruto and Sasuke must also follow the destiny of Indra and Asura. Sasuke and Naruto are consequently heroic not only for *what* they accomplish but also for *how* they change the world by keeping and transforming the past. This past is on the one hand euphorically represented as a way to overcome the difficulties of the present, but on the other, it is the enemy itself: the brothers, masters, and parents must die, the techniques of the past must be reinvented, and more importantly the final enemy is an army made of ancient resuscitated warriors (controlled against their will) led by the most powerful ninja that refused death (Madara). Finally, this lack of individuality also emerges from an enunciative point of view by noticing how the combination of internal narrators and flashbacks, and also of the intertextual and intratextual dimensions, prevent the protagonist from fully speaking *for himself*: the references to a dimension far from the *I-here-now* are incessant.

The story of *Naruto* is therefore not a story of individuals, but a story of clans, villages, fathers, brothers, masters, descendants, of ancient guilts and traumas, of traditions to keep and change, of memory, and of a community. It is the story of a present peace that must be obtained by the new generations fighting against the past (literally, as the technique of the enemy is the *Edo Tensei* which can give life to the dead) but in a fight that can be won only thanks to the past (its knowledge, teachings, values, etc.).

The heroes of this story must therefore be praised both for their actions and for having followed what their masters wanted them to follow, as the tea-master, Kobori-Enshiu (1579-1647), said: "In my young days I praised the master whose pictures I liked, but as my judgement matured I praised myself for liking what the masters had chosen to have me like."[46] Society, with its values and traumas, is therefore always at the center of the narration and is changed by *disqualified*[47] characters, "saved" by the love of their masters and families.

We can then see how in this anime *the individual is divisible* (which is exactly what happens with Naruto's iconic move "Kage Bunshin No Jutsu") and how from this it derives its strength and identity: at the end of the story, Naruto, like Tokugawa Ieyasu (1543-1616) before him, will unify the various "villages," defeating the evil and giving rise to an era of peace. And this will happen thanks to an impulsive, stupid (*baka*),[48] and demoniac *shōnen* who will fight against what binds "the world of the ninja" to the past and at the same time defends this past. And he cannot do this alone, needing especially the help of his opposite (represented by Sasuke and by the symbols they are given in the end, an empty sun and a full dark moon, both incomplete and complementary), and more generally of the whole ninja community. So, we can see here how this *non-individuality* is positively valorized and, in the end, this "ideology of the community" is the real power thanks to which the world can be saved (think of the *Genki Dama* in *Dragon Ball*). Furthermore, we can also see how the apparent "contradiction" of the Naruto character himself (a Western-like Ieyasu) is precisely related to his being Japanese, while the whole story is a huge modern-pacifist rhetoric made mostly of euphoric scenes of people fighting and killing each other to become the greatest *bushi* of all time. Lastly, it is extremely interesting to note that many narrative elements of Naruto could be read as historical metaphors related to post-World War II Japan. Let us think of the Uchiha clan (with the fan as a symbol[49]) that is characterized by the guilt of having tried to unleash a war and, more generally, by a long history of violence and the pursuit of power.

Itachi will try to remedy by killing all his clan and even his parents, who accept and understand this action. Itachi, who is nonetheless stained with many faults, must also die for Sasuke's good. On the other side, in order to succeed, Naruto will need to pacify the hated and feared demons (*bijū*) of the past, using their strength to face the threats of the present. In particular, Naruto will need

---

[46] Kakuzō Okakura, *The Book of Tea* (London: Putnam, 1906), 30.

[47] Osamu Dazai, *Lo Squalificato*, trans. Marcella Bonsanti (Milan: Feltrinelli, 2009).

[48] Naruto regularly uses this quite insulting Japanese term.

[49] William E. Deal, *Handbook to Life in Medieval and Early Modern Japan* (Oxford: Oxford University Press, 2007), 167.

to tame and befriend the demon (Kurama) that has existed inside him since he was a child and that killed his father and destroyed his village: only by "embracing" and forgiving this manifestation of hate will he be able to become an adult strong enough to change the world by putting an end to the struggle for power between the various nations of the ninja world (with a very interesting example here of a history *rewritten* to face a problematic past).[50]

Japaneseness' Key Features and the Ideological Heart of Animes

The key cultural elements of Japaneseness that we have seen in *Naruto*, which emerged from a multi-layered analysis of signification (in particular by taking into consideration the linguistic, semantic, symbolic, figurative, narrative, and intertextual levels of meaning), can now help us to list and regroup 35 main traits of Japaneseness in *shōnen* animes. However, it is important to note that these signs of Japaneseness acquire their full meaning only when combined and that these categories are strongly interconnected (i.e., there is a religious dimension in martial arts). Finally, from our perspective, it is not the presence of these traits that highlight something as uniquely Japanese, but rather it is the fact that Japaneseness consists in the many different possible *translations* of these traits.

A) <u>Aesthetic and Narrative</u>

1) An aesthetic of the invisible and fantastic (and magical realism)

2) The *wabi-sabi* aesthetic of incompleteness, imperfectness, and impermanence

3) The typical presence of "altered faces" in comical moments

4) The presence of violence (with explicit blood) typical of popular tales

5) The presence of "vulgarity" in many forms, the same that scandalized the first Westerners

6) The presence of comicality mixed with seriousness[51]

---

[50] Bouissou, *Il Manga*, 187.

[51] Donald Richie, *Sull'Estetica Giapponese*, trans. Gabriella Tonoli (Turin: Lindau, 2009), 38-45; Barthes, *L'impero dei Segni*, 52; Miyake, "Mostri Made in Japan," 165-197; Sagiyama Ikuko, "Wabi e Sabi nella Tradizione Estetica Giapponese," in *Culture del Giappone Contemporaneo*, ed. Matteo Casari (Latina: Tunué, 2011), 24; Bouissou, *Il Manga*, 140, 231 and 269-271; Atsushi Ueda, ed., *Electric Geisha: Tra Cultura Pop e Tradizione*, trans. Luca Pierecchi (Milan: Feltrinelli, 1996).

B) Religion and Philosophy

1) The need for acceptance of what is "natural," such as pain and death

2) The need for pain to shine, as in the *Genji Monogatari*

3) The influence of Taoism

4) A certain relativity of good and evil

5) A general *animism* (especially evident in Miyazaki's animes)

6) The connection between each person and the "universe" or nature

7) The cyclicity of life and destiny

8) Agreement and understanding with *yōkai*[52] (that can often be corrupted with just some rice)

9) The valorization of a certain irrationality as "only a system among others"

10) Polytheism and spiritism

11) The importance of a learned "way" (*dō*) to follow for interior and spiritual enlightenment[53]

C) Social and Political Values

1) The need for the hero to stay true to himself combined with his willingness to improve

2) A young hero that is often *baka*, impulsive, violent, cursed, resolute, perverted, and optimistic

3) The value of community with the rhetoric of the companion (*nakama*)

4) The relevance of family names and bonds

5) The themes of honor and dishonor

---

[52] Mythical creatures. For more detailed studies, see Elisabeth Scherer, ed. *Unheimlich prominent: Yōkai und yūrei in der japanischen Kulturgeschichte (DJAS 4)*. Düsseldorf: Institut für Modernes Japan, 2012.

[53] Gian Carlo Calza, *Genji: Il Principe Splendente* (Turin: Electa, 2008), 9; Shigeru Mizuki, *Enciclopedia degli Spiriti Giapponesi*, trans. Emilio Martini (Bologna: Kappa Edizioni, 2007), 42; Barthes, *L'Impero dei Segni*, 43; Tollini, *L'Ideale della Via*, xi.

6)   Self-sacrifice as a duty and a key element for victory

7)   Conformist contents and endings

8)   Martial arts as a way to reach the main goal

9)   The isotopy of *peace* through union and pacifist rhetoric

10) The final inclusion of excluded members of a society[54]

D) History, Memory, and Trauma

1)   The centrality of memory and of the past to overcome difficulties

2)   The importance of masters and ancients

3)   The presence of the collective trauma of World War II (especially in the *mecha* genre)

4)   The sacrifice of the old generation for the new one

5)   Mythological names and nominations

6)   An abundance of references to the Heian, Muromachi, and Edo periods

7)   Explicit and implicit cultural references to Japan through symbols, dresses, cities, food, customs (like *onsen* baths), weapons, fight styles, etc.

8)   The compresence of Eastern and Western contents

There are three main reasons for choosing these traits as *clues* of Japaneseness. Firstly, there is an obvious connection between them and Japanese culture and history, with many of these themes being present also in important movies of Akira Kurosawa (1910-1998) like *Rashōmon* (1950), *Yōjinbō* (1961), and *Shichinin no Samurai* (1954), and even in video games with anime aesthetics such as *Gravity Rush* (2012), *Nier: Automata* (2017) and the *Persona* (1996-2016), *Tales* (1995-2016), and *Disgaea* (2003-2017) series.

Secondly, these traits can be easily found in most *shōnen* and *kodomo* animes[55] and are mostly absent in the Western animated cartoons aimed at the same audience. Thirdly, these "underlying ideas" need a close reading to be acknowledged and have strong moral and political implications; for this

---

[54] In my undergraduate thesis, I analyzed these features in more than 160 animes. See also Bouissou, *Il Manga*, 180.

[55] Tavassi, *Storia dell'Animazione Giapponese*, 83.

reason, we can talk about these traits as an "ideology,"[56] and they deserve our attention. Lastly, there is an evident "dissonance" between some of these elements, thus perfectly showing both the complexity and the validity of our perspective to understand how today's Japaneseness can be found not only in the cross streets and temples forgotten by travel guides but also in the closeness between some red shrines and Tokyo's Sky Tree.

Saint Seiya:
Mixing-Up and Mashing-Up Without Ever Losing the Way

Saint Seiya (*Seinto Seiya*) is not only one of the most famous[57] manga (1986-1990) and anime (1986-1989) of all time, but also one of the most interesting and earliest examples of fusion between Japanese and Western cultural elements. In particular, the *Lost Canvas* series of 2009 is even more interesting because of its new aesthetics and contents.

Indeed, we can see that the opening song is now fully in English, the enemies are called by the English name "Specter," the setting has shifted from Japan and Greece to Italy and Greece, the protagonist is no longer Japanese, and of course all the classic transcultural elements that were kept such as the presence of English names of super moves, all just from the first episode (*Thunder Claw* in 1986, and *Worm's Bind* here). It is therefore very easy to think that this is another example of how Japaneseness is slowly disappearing. But things are not so simple.

Let us begin with the names of the three protagonists that are a perfect example of cultural fusion: Tenma (Pegasus), Sasha (Athena), and Aron/Alone (Hades). But we can see this also by looking at the names of other characters that range from Kagaho, Yato, Yuzuriha, and Dohko to Veronica, Pandora, Minos, and Aiacos (from the Greek "Aeacus") but also Edward, Cid, and Golem Rock. We should not, however, think of some "randomness" by looking at these names of such different origins; indeed, the names of the three young heroes (Yato, Yuzuriha, and Tenma) are, without exception, all Japanese-like (despite the kanjis of Tenma not referring to the Japanese name). Also, in episode 9, the good character "Aldebaran/Hasgard," despite his name, will try to teach good manners to an enemy by forcing it to bow. Similarly, the all-powerful Greek god

---

[56] I do not use the term ideology here with its usually negative meaning.

[57] Scott Green, "'Saint Seiya' Inspires International Live-Action Production," *crunchyroll.com*, May 18, 2017, https://www.crunchyroll.com/it/anime-news/2017/05/18/saint-seiya-inspires-international-live-action-production.

"Oneiros" is actually represented as a six-armed *Asura* that has four different souls. Furthermore, the names of attacks are coherent with the names of the characters and their identity: Pegasus will shout "*Ryūseiken*" when attacking, while the first enemy he fights will attack by shouting "*Worm's bind.*"

Looking at a different aspect, we can see that the main protagonist, Tenma/Seiya, is the classic stereotypic Japanese childish *shōnen* hero, both from a figurative point of view (his hairstyle, for instance, reminds us of heroes like Goku of *Gensōmaden Saiyuki*, Kabuto of *Mazinger*, and so on) and from a psychological and behavioral one.

Indeed, he is impulsive, violent, light-minded ("*baka Tenma*," episode 23), and is not very respectful toward traditions, but always fights with honor; he follows his *kokoro* no matter what, he will fight even if it is rationally impossible to win, and he does all this only to save his friend and protect (*mamoru*) others in danger. He will also lose a fight as early as in the second episode and will grow stronger thanks to the many older teachers who will teach him how to follow a way (in episode 22 he is told to make his heart a sword "to never lose the way"), and he must not only follow their path (episode 23) but his destiny is also to follow the path of the Pegasus armor and of all the warriors that wore this armor before. His teacher is "Doko," whose symbolic animal is a tiger and whose special attack involves dragons. Additionally, the hero's strength is not his own but derives from the "cosmos," which is a kind of connection both with people (who believe in him) and with nature (because it is said in episode 17 that each life is a precious part of a universe).

Furthermore, Tenma/Seiya does not have a strong "truth" or vision of "good," his passion and his will to succeed by any means are his truth and why he is "good."[58] Lastly, he grew up in an orphanage and his hometown has been destroyed by war. The main antagonist too, despite his name, is molded from Japaneseness: he is the orphan boy with the purest soul and has the evil god of death inside him. As a "conscient" Hades, he also wants to end the suffering that exists in the world with death and by creating a beautiful painting that will bring peace. He also follows the rule of a figurative change of hair color (from blond to black) that signifies a change not only in power but also of personality, and despite his being the opposite of Tenma, he has a strong bond with him and is his best friend.

---

[58] In episode 7 we can see something very similar to what will happen in *Naruto: Shippuden* episode 174.

Another interesting factor is the centrality of rituals, Buddhist prayers, mantras, sacred beads to defeat evil, and so on. The enemies act doing the "will of the gods," and many humans become evil because they seek immortality and freedom from suffering, even at the cost of "dirtying" the family name (and must be stopped by other members of the family, as in episode 15). Additionally, regarding the compresence of realistic and supernatural/magical elements with cultural references, there is a very interesting scene (in episode 2) in which it is explained that "the world is made of atoms created by the Big Bang" and that the power of the saints comes from the universe inside of them (think of the chakra) that can "explode" to break atoms (unbreakable as in the Western atomic philosophy of Democritus, 460-370 BC).[59]

Looking at the setting, even when the action is said to be in Italy, the characters will find themselves in a place such as the "forest of the death" that does not sound so Italian and which of course recalls the *Aokigahara* forest that is also a recurrent setting in *shōnen* animes. We also have a Western-like Hell guarded by Cerberus, but in this Hell, there is a sacred tree called *Mokurenji*.

Lastly, self-sacrifice happens in almost every fight, fights that must be fought "one-on-one" with honor and until death. In particular, in the last episode, an old samurai-like warrior (hairstyle, dress, stance) with a non-katana sword held like a katana will be the only one strong enough to fight the enemies and die to protect the younger soldiers. Finally, this same "samurai-like" warrior will also defeat the final evil god thanks to the help of the spirits of the past warriors that all merge together into a blue sphere, which is very common in animes and is called by the Japanese name of "*sekishiki tenryō ha.*"

Shingeki no Bahamut: King Arthur and the Samurais

Based not on a Japanese manga but on a Japanese card game, *Shingeki no Bahamut: Genesis* is an anime that first aired in 2014. From the title, we easily understand that we are far from the Shinto mythology, as the well-known *Bahamut* belongs to Muslim cosmology, and *Genesis* obviously refers to the Hebrew and Christian tradition. It is not surprising, therefore, that the setting of this anime (clothes, places, weapons, technology, etc.) refers both to the European Middle Ages and (more interestingly) also to the Old West (with the presence of bounty hunters, caravans, etc.). Accordingly, we will find many references to Western and Middle Eastern culture: Lucifer, Pazuzu, Zeus, Azazel, Bacco, and Jeanne d'Arc are all names of characters that are present in

---

[59] Thanks to Bruno Surace for this suggestion.

this anime. Needless to say, the protagonists here will not be Japanese, and differently from *Saint Seiya* we will have no "masters," no special moves with names, and almost no explicit reference of things related to Japanese culture. Moreover, the aesthetics are also somehow uncommon, and this can already be seen in the movie-like presentation and the Western-like font at the very beginning of episode 1.

Here again, we could reasonably think that this anime was only made in Japan, but it is clearly very different from the typical *shōnen* anime. However, the truth is that we are in front of a *trompe l'oeil*.

Indeed, in this anime, we will find:

1) A demonic protagonist (ep.1), womanizer (ep. 2), liar, traitor (ep. 2) and *baka*

2) The presence of an "opposite" co-protagonist with samurai-like haircut

3) Both protagonists being orphans who grew up facing the hardships of life

4) Joy for the "bath" and nudity without shame (from ep. 1)

5) Fights with bare hands with typical martial arts poses (from ep. 1)

6) Transformation as improvement (from ep. 1)

7) Blood and physical violence (ep. 1) up to torture (ep. 3)

8) Polytheism and almost blasphemy (ep. 3, ep. 9)

9) Victory thanks to unions of demons and angels (ep. 1, ep. 12)

10) An ancient dragon revealing the truth and giving the protagonist the weapon to defeat the main foe

11) A main good character (Amira) who is a half-demon

12) An enemy that can become a "good" travel companion (ep. 4)

13) History that repeats itself (ep. 1, ep. 9) and fights against destiny (eps. 9, 12)

14) The value of the community with people who will die trying to save Jeanne d'Arc

15) The protagonist extracting a "sword from the stone" despite being "impure" (ep. 9)

16) A graphic overlay between the protagonist and the ancient knight (ep. 12)

17) Sad moments mixed with comedy

18) The theme of disgrace (of the father and the family)

19) The recurring theme of what will "come tomorrow"

20) The compresence of realism, magic, and "technology"

21) Humans, demons, and magical beasts all living together

As we can see, these elements are a real Japanese beating heart hiding behind a Western disguise. The next case is even more interesting.

Baccano! So Happy to Be a *Camorrista*

Differently from the previous anime, *Baccano!* is not about a war to save the world, and there are no warriors, demons, gods, masters, and so on. This anime is set in America in around 1930, and the main story is apparently about a struggle between different mafia families and a train robbery. Furthermore, the whole story is structured on two different narrative levels and consists in many single sub-plots presented in a non-chronological order that eventually all fits together like a puzzle. Also, there are multiple main characters and there is no end to the story. Needless to say, most of the cultural references are based on Western culture, there are a lot of English terms used by the characters, and we will not find any signs of things like mythological names of special techniques or of Japanese-like places. Additionally, not only are the names of the characters here almost all Western-like, but already from the opening, we can clearly see aesthetics close to what we can find in Western comics and cartoons.

Baccano! could therefore be considered as a perfect example of a *shōnen* anime without any traces of Japaneseness. But, once again, this would be a big mistake. The first distinctive tract is the violence, not only linguistic but also and mostly visual; in episode 10, a ten-year-old child is first shot in the head with a shotgun (with blood all over the place) and then tortured. This is something that, in the West, we would consider really inappropriate for a *shōnen* audience. Then we can see that we also have dramatic and extremely violent moments which can immediately shift into comic ones.

A second interesting feature is the presence of a kind of magical realism. Indeed, the plot starts back in 1700 when some alchemists summon the devil and find a potion that can give immortality to men. Those immortals can then "devour" other immortals, and the study of the recipe for this elixir can also lead to the creation of a *homunculus*. Furthermore, immortality aside, all the fights between the characters are very *shōnen*-like with implausible capacities of each human character. Finally, there is an interesting scene where the "unwise" brother of Eve tells her that she is stupid because she believes in God, and in the end, the "miracle" of his brother being alive really happens.

Also, as is typical for *shōnen,* all the protagonists are very young while the main adult characters are kinds of "masters" by being the respected heads of the families. In particular, Maiza is the good one who takes care of the young hero Firo and, predictably, he will be the one to kill the evil Slizard. It is also interesting to note that the assassin Clair, a former train conductor, goes almost crazy when his train conductor "teacher" is killed and will avenge him. Besides, many of the protagonists have no family and have been adopted or have lost someone dear; belonging (or not) to one family instead of another will determine most of the characters' personalities and fates: the young psychopath killer Ladd is raised by a ruthless and unscrupulous uncle, the good-hearted Firo is raised by the good Martillo family, the disgraceful behavior of Dallas is coherent with the shameful rich family from which he came, the exceptional and fearful assassin Clair belongs to the respected Gandor family, and so on. Generally speaking, the lack of a family is a common trait and is what makes all the good characters companions, such as in episode 15, when Jacuzzi argues that Chané (a terrorist girl) is a *nakama* because she too has no family. Indeed, the rhetoric of the companions is stronger than ever and is especially easy to see in the case of Jacuzzi's band and in the ending that mostly consists in some kind of friendship between all the different families and bands of "thugs." Furthermore, the main antagonist Slizard has no friends and is "defeated" by the combination of many different characters who "casually" collaborate as in the most typical *shōnen* anime.

In regards to the lack of a "protagonist," very interestingly, we have a situation where many *actors* (the main characters) combine to create what in semiotic terms is a unique actant that owns all the traits of the stereotypical *shōnen* hero who is an orphan with a dark past (almost everyone), altruist (especially Jacuzzi and Firo), weak but courageous (Jacuzzi), who can change and become wiser (Ellis, Chané, Jacuzzi), is *baka* and impulsive (Miria and Isaac), has a dark side (Ellis, Clair, Jacuzzi), has trained to be a great fighter (Firo, Clair), uses martial arts (Firo, Clair), is optimistic (Firo, Jacuzzi, Miria, and Isaac), and is most of all childish, represented in a wonderful ending scene in episode 14 where everyone enjoys watching many dominos fall, a game that is explicitly explained as a game for little kids who do not understand the rules of dominos.

The distinction between good and evil is also very Japanese-like. Indeed, all the main characters are criminals of some sort, and there is an amazing scene in which everyone congratulates the "good-hearted" Firo, who had just become "a true *camorrista*" and is very happy about this. Even the apparently most "evil" and psychopathic ones, such as Ladd, have some kind of morals due to which he kills the arrogant thugs, and he even sacrifices himself to save the woman he "loves." Similarly, the cruel serial killer known as "Rail tracer" kills to avenge his *senpai*, defends the woman in danger, has distorted morals (episode 9) but does not kill a good journalist, fights honorably, and, in the last episode, declares his love to a female character with sincere sentiments. Likewise, the demonic *homunculus* that in the beginning is an enemy will betray his masters and tell Firo how to defeat him, and will of course became a *nakama*. Also, the terrorist girl Chané only acts as a criminal to save her "father," will betray the other terrorists, will never kill any innocent, and will become a *nakama*. Lastly, the devil itself, who gives the immortality elixir to humans, is represented as only "curious" and will keep his promise to protect Maiza, the "good" alchemist who takes care of Firo and who wonders how to use immortality for the good of humanity. "Evil" is only represented by Slizard, who does not problematize "immortality" and desire it for the whole of humanity. Indeed, Maiza will ask for forgiveness from his friends when he discovers that they are now immortal.

To conclude, while there are apparently not many references to Eastern culture, there is a noteworthy scene in episode 8 where Miria and Isaac say that this story is like *Sangokushi* (a reference to an Eastern literary classic) and that Jacuzzi is like *Yoshitsune* (a well-known hero of the Heian period).

Conclusion

We are fully aware of the many limits of this work in which we made statements about Japan and cultures that need a much more extended *corpus* and bibliography. Moreover, to further validate the claims of this paper, it would also be important to look at adaptations of Western classics of literature such as *Gankutsuou: The Count of Monte Cristo* (2005) and *Les Misérables: Shōjo Cosette* (2007). Additionally, the methodology we used could be criticized for different reasons: taking into consideration only four episodes out of 700 in *Naruto*, creating broad categories of "traits" without proper explanations, describing the Western-inspired animes too briefly, making strong interpretative decisions to sustain our ideas, generalizing a few occurrences to describe an entire genre, and so on. Lastly, because of using concepts such as "ideology," this work could also be misread as "proof" of Japan's closure to the other cultures.

However, this short essay was never meant to end the debate about complex themes such as national identity, Japanese culture, and anime's ideology; it was neither thought nor written to end the discussion about Japaneseness by proposing some kind of flawless argumentation with unquestionable empirical (textual) evidence. Our goal was to propose a new perspective on these problems by discussing and highlighting two crucial points.

First, that the "empty center" of Tokyo acknowledged by Roland Barthes (1915-1980)[60] can be thought as a *jeu*: a space of possibility[61] for *otherness*. And so that the expression dear to Nishida Kitarō (1870-1945) of "the *continuity of discontinuity*" (*hirenzoku no renzoku*)[62] can be seen as a continuous and dynamic process (and not only as an historical one) of translation that leaves *traces* and evidence in textual occurrences such as animes. It is exactly in this sense that we tried to highlight how Japaneseness can be thought of as a certain rule of translation and can be found in the different transformations of what is uniquely Japanese.

Second, on the more general level of the study of cultures, we wanted to show that Japan is the perfect example of how "[i]n virtue of the fact that culture does not live only thanks to the opposition between the internal sphere and the external sphere, but also thanks to the passage from one area to another, it is not limited to fighting with the external 'fortuity,' but at the same time it needs it, not only does not annihilate it, but constantly creates it."[63]

Indeed, this semiotic idea of identity as something not only *relational* but also continuously *incomplete* and *transforming* is precious for the study of cultures and also to avoid the *impasse* of both enclosing or negating Japaneseness. Finally, it encourages us to think that *we* (both as persons and as members of a community) are also the alterity within us and the otherness that made us, what we are constantly not knowing to be, what we are adapting to, becoming, speaking through[64] and *could be*.

Works Cited

Al Jazeera Turk. "Tokyo 2020'ye hazır." YouTube Video, 2:13. August 22, 2016. https://www.youtube.com/watch?v=FNuqKVG781I.

App, Urs. *The Cult of Emptiness: The Eastern Discovery of Buddhist Thought and the Invention of Oriental Philosophy.* Kyoto: University Media, 2012.

Ashcraft, Brian, and Luke Plunkett. *Cosplay World.* New York: Prestel, 2014.

---

[60] Barthes, *L'Impero dei Segni*, 39.

[61] Stefano Bartezzaghi, *La Ludoteca di Babele* (Turin: Utet, 2016), 58.

[62] Ghilardi, "Da Sabi a Cyber," 144. My translation.

[63] Lotman, *Tesi*, 109. My translation.

[64] Paolucci, *Strutturalismo e Interpretazione*, 500.

Assmann, Jan. *La memoria culturale: Scrittura, Ricordo e Identità Politica nelle Grandi Civiltà Antiche*. Translated by Francesco De Angelis. Turin: Einaudi, 1997.

Aston, William George. *Nihongi: Chronicles of Japan from the Earliest Times to A.D. 697*. London: Trench & Trübner, 1896.

Bartezzaghi, Stefano. *La Ludoteca di Babele*. Turin: Utet, 2016.

Barthes, Roland. *L'Impero dei Segni*. Translated by Marco Vallora. Turin: Einaudi, 1984.

Benedict, Ruth. *The Chrysanthemum and the Sword*. London: Secker & Warburg, 1947.

Bonami, Francesco. *Lo Potevo Fare Anch'Io: Perché l'Arte Contemporanea è Davvero Arte*. Milan: Mondadori, 2009.

Bouissou, Jean-Marie. *Il Manga*. Translated by Gianluca Di Fratta. Latina: Tunué, 2009.

Calza, Gian Carlo. *Genji il Principe Splendente*. Turin: Electa, 2008

Dazai, Osamu. *Lo Squalificato*. Translated by Marcella Bonsanti. Milan: Feltrinelli, 2009.

Deal, William E. *Handbook to Life in Medieval and Early Modern Japan*. Oxford: Oxford University Press, 2007

Fabbri, Paolo. *La Svolta Semiotica*. Rome: Laterza, 1998

Ghilardi, Marcello. "Da Sabi a Cyber: Un Immaginario in Trasformazione." In *Culture del Giappone Contemporaneo*, edited by Matteo Casari, 143-164. Latina: Tunuè, 2011.

Goebel, Rolf J. "Japanese Urban Space and the Citation of Western Signs." *Comparative Literature Studies* 35, no. 2 (1998): 93-106.

Green, Scott. "'Saint Seiya' Inspires International Live-Action Production." *crunchyroll.com*, May 18, 2017. https://www.crunchyroll.com/it/anime-news/2017/05/18/saint-seiya-inspires-international-live-action-production.

Halbwachs, Maurice. *La Mémoire Collective*. Paris: Presse Universitaire de France, 1950.

Hundt, David, and Jitendra Uttam. *Varieties of Capitalism in Asia: Beyond the Developmental State*. London: Palgrave Macmillan, 2017.

Ikuko, Sagiyama. "Wabi e Sabi nella Tradizione Estetica Giapponese." In *Culture del Giappone Contemporaneo*, edited by Matteo Casari, 11-24. Latina: Tunuè, 2011.

Kishimoto, Masashi. *Uzumaki: The Art of Naruto*. San Francisco: Viz Media, 2007.

Lind, Werner. *Budo: La Via Spirituale delle Arti Marziali*. Translated by Antonio Manco. Rome: Edizioni Mediterranee, 2012.

Lotman, Juri. *Tesi per una Semiotica delle Culture*, edited by Franciscu Sedda. Rome: Meltemi, 2006.

Lotman, Juri, and Boris Uspenskij. *Tipologia della Cultura*. Translated by R. Facciani and M. Marzaduri. Milan: Bompiani, 1995.

Mishima, Yukio. *Lezioni Spirituali per Giovani Samurai.* Translated by Lidia Origlia. Milan: Feltrinelli, 2010.

Miyake, Toshio. "Mostri Made in Japan." In *Culture del Giappone Contemporaneo,* edited by Matteo Casari, 165-198. Latina: Tunué, 2011.

Mizuki, Shigeru. *Enciclopedia degli Spiriti Giapponesi.* Translated by Emilio Martini. Bologna: Kappa Edizioni, 2007.

Mol, Serge. *Classical Weaponry of Japan: Special Weapons and Tactics of the Martial Arts.* Tokyo: Kodansha, 2003.

Okakura, Kakuzo. *The Book of Tea.* London: Putnam, 1906.

Paolucci, Claudio. *Strutturalismo e Interpretazione.* Milan: Bompiani, 2010.

Reischauer, Edwin O. *Storia del Giappone dalle Origini ai Giorni Nostri.* Translated by Maria Sepa. Milan: Bompiani, 2013.

Remotti, Francesco. *Contro L'Identità.* Rome: Laterza, 1996.

Richie, Donald. *Sull'Estetica Giapponese.* Translated by Gabriella Tonoli. Turin: Lindau, 2009.

Scherer, Elisabeth, ed. *Unheimlich prominent: Yōkai und yūrei in der japanischen Kulturgeschichte (DJAS 4).* Düsseldorf: Institut für Modernes Japan, 2012.

Shoko, Imai. "Nobu and After: Westernized Japanese Food and Globalization." In *Food and Social Identities in the Asia Pacific Region,* edited by James Farrer. Tokyo: Sophia University Institute of Comparative Culture, 2010.

Stano, Simona. *Eating the Other.* Newcastle upon Tyne: Cambridge Scholars Publishing, 2015.

Tavassi, Guido. *Storia dell'Animazione Giapponese.* Latina: Tunué, 2012.

Tollini, Aldo. *L'Ideale della Via: Samurai, Monaci e Poeti nel Giappone Medievale.* Turin: Einaudi, 2017.

Tsunetomo, Yamamoto. *Hakagure: Il Libro Segreto dei Samurai.* Milan: Mondadori, 2009.

Ueda, Atsushi, ed. *Electric Geisha: Tra Cultura Pop e Tradizione in Giappone.* Translated by Luca Pierecchi. Milan: Feltrinelli, 1996.

Verbovszky, Joseph. "Overcoming Modernity in Yukio Mishima." *Discussions* 9, no. 2 (2013): 1-2.

Violi, Patrizia. *Paesaggi della Memoria.* Milan: Bompiani, 2014.

Chapter 7

From Japan to the World: *Super Mario*'s World-building Across Two Continents

Juan Manuel Montoro

University of Bologna, Italy

Abstract

This chapter aims to explore how Japanese and Western cultures have simultaneously influenced a global cultural icon like Nintendo's *Super Mario* video game series and the fictional world created around it. The methodology of this study focuses on a textual analysis of the design of characters, scenarios, and resources to be found in video games as well as analysis of media outsources like an American animated series and a Japanese animated film. Firstly, this paper examines the notion of Japaneseness and identifies three aspects of Japanese culture that appear as highlighted in *Super Mario*'s fictional world, especially if considered as opposed to Western traditions. These are: 1) the limited yet persistent presence of Japanese folk figures, 2) a centripetal hierarchy of constituents in the world-building going from an embracing environment to an embedded character, and 3) a tendency to use aesthetics that favor change and passion instead of mimetic representation. Finally, the cross-cultural analysis of transmedia texts, like the Japanese animated series and the American animated film, will show how each process of inter-semiotic translation, respectively, tend to reinforce or mitigate these three aspects of Japanese/Asian tradition.

Keywords: Super Mario, Japanese video games, Nintendo.

* * *

Introduction

The aim of this chapter is to examine the narrative universe of one of the most well-known global media franchises, namely Nintendo's *Super Mario*, through the lens of transmedia semiotics and intercultural studies. The main question leading this inquiry is to what extent Japanese cultural traditions have influenced the design of a storyworld based on characters, *power-ups*,[1] and levels, among other features. In relation to this, one must consider that the universe around *Super Mario* is not only a media franchise created and developed by a Japanese company through its chief designer Shigeru Miyamoto but also that its iconography stands at the core of Nintendo's corporate imagery. Consequently, traces of Japaneseness in the world-building of the *Super Mario* series[2] are worth studying because they might show how local cultures are textually represented abroad once different media industries (different both in terms of cultural origin and in terms of format) elevate a fictional world to the category of a global icon, as in the case of the *Super Mario* franchise.[3]

The fictional universe around Mario has been approached several times in media scholarship as a milestone in the evolution of transmedia storytelling due to the combination of technological advances and groundbreaking creative decisions.[4] It is not a coincidence that Mario was the main protagonist

---

[1] In video games scholarship, a power-up is a device acquired in gameplay that temporarily gives extra abilities to the gameable characters. The best-known examples of power-ups in the *Super Mario* series are red mushrooms that make the character grow, green mushrooms that give an extra life to Mario, and fire flowers that enable the character to spit fire balls.

[2] In this paper, we understand the *Super Mario* series as the saga of video games and other media that explicitly tackles or adapts the logic of gameability of its main title, *Super Mario Bros.* (1985), that is, a platform game in which a gameable character, Mario or Luigi, has the duty to rescue the Princess. Other media dealing with isolated aspects of Mario as a character, different arrangements of the components of its iconography, or adaptations to other narrative or gameable logics will be treated as the Mario franchise or Mario's fictional world.

[3] We owe the application of the fictional world to interactive platforms such as video games to authors like Jesper Juul, according to whom they offer the player an experience that combines rules and storytelling in which, "in most cases, the incompleteness of a fictional world leaves the user with a number of choices in the imagining of the world." Jesper Juul, *Half-Real: Video Games between Real Rules and Fictional Worlds* (Cambridge, MA: MIT Press, 2005), 293.

[4] Some examples are to be found in Mary Fuller and Henry Jenkins, "Nintendo(R) and New World Travel Writing: A Dialogue," in *Cybersociety: Computer-Mediated Communication*

in the first narrative video game in history, the 1981 arcade game *Donkey Kong*, nor that it sourced pioneering experiences in adapting video games into movies, like the anime film *Super Mario Bros.: The Great Mission to Rescue Princess Peach!* (Japan, Dir: Masami Hatari) or the live-action science-fiction film *Super Mario Bros.* (United States, Dir: Rocky Morton and Annabel Jankel) in 1993. In between, Mario featured in dozens of TV shows, comics and manga publications, costumes, licensed and non-licensed merchandising, and events of varied nature, not to mention his evolution on his main platform, the video game, that led him to become even more recognizable than Mickey Mouse among American children, according to a much-publicized survey in 1990.[5]

However, Mario's universe and particularly its transmedia spreading was rarely taken into consideration from a perspective that stresses the productive exchanges of cultural texts between Japan and the West. On the contrary, authors like Koichi Iwabuchi[6] cite the *Super Mario* series as an exemplary case of *mukokuseki*[7] and, then, a sample of how Japanese cultural industries work to erase their own cultural specificity:

---

and Community, ed. Steven G. Jones (Thousand Oaks, CA: Sage, 1995), 57-72; David Sheff, *Game Over: Press Start to Continue – The Maturing of Mario* (Wilton, CT: Games Press, 1999), 37-56; Steven L. Kent, *The Ultimate History of Video Games: From Pong to Pokémon and Beyond* (New York: Three Rivers Press, 2001), 199-219; James Newman, "In Search of the Video Game Player: The Lives of Mario," *New Media & Society* 4, no. 3 (2002): 405-422; Chris Kohler, *Power Up: How Japanese Video Games Gave the World an Extra Life* (Indianapolis, IN: Brady Games, 2005), 23-76; Martin Picard, "Video Games and Their Relationship with Other Media," in *The Video Game Explosion: A History from PONG to PlayStation and Beyond*, ed. Mark J. P. Wolf (Westport, CT: Greenwood Press, 2008), 294-297; Jeff Ryan, *How Mario Conquered America* (London: Portfolio/Penguin, 2011); Bill Loguidice and Matt Barton, *Vintage Games: An Insider Look at the History of Grand Theft Auto, Super Mario, and the Most Influential Games of All Time* (Oxford: Focal Press, 2009), 271-290; Manuel Garín Boronat, *El gag visual: De Buster Keaton a Super Mario* (Madrid: Cátedra, 2014); Richard Stanton, *A Brief History Of Video Games: From Atari to Virtual Reality* (London: Robinson, 2015), 110-129; Dustin Hansen, *Game On! Video Game History from Pong and Pac-Man to Mario, Minecraft, and More* (New York: Feiwel and Friends, 2016), 34-41 and 50-55.

[5] Koichi Iwabuchi, "How Japanese is Pikachu?" in *Pikachu's Global Adventure*, ed. Joseph Tobin (Durham, NC: Duke University Press, 2010), 30.

[6] Koichi Iwabuchi, *Recentering Globalization: Popular Culture and Japanese Transnationalism* (Durham, NC: Duke University Press, 2002), 70-78; Iwabuchi, "How Japanese," 58.

[7] The term *mukokuseki* ("state-less") is largely used in Koichi Iwabuchi's argumentation as a strategic resource of Japanese cultural exports such as *manga, anime* and video games. It is related to the design of universes without distinctive traces of Japanese culture in order to appeal the Western eye, resulting in "culturally odorless" products set

Japanese media industries seem to think that the suppression of Japanese cultural odor is imperative if they are to make inroads into international markets. The producers and creators of game software intentionally make computer-game characters look non-Japanese because they are clearly conscious that the market is global. Mario, the principal character of the popular computer game, Super Mario Brothers, for example, does not invoke the image of Japan. Both his name and appearance are designed to be "Italian." Even if Japanese animators do not consciously draw mukokuseki characters with export considerations in mind, the Japanese animation industry always has the global market in mind and is aware that the non-Japaneseness of characters works to its advantage in the export market.[8]

For that reason, Iwabuchi argues, "consumers of Japanese animation and games may be aware of the Japanese origin of these commodities, but they perceive little 'Japanese bodily odor.'"[9]

Mario video games and spin-off media portray a damsel-in-distress plot in which the protagonist is an average working-class person, Mario or Luigi, who faces a series of obstacles until defeating a monstrous villain in order both to free that kidnapped damsel, Princess Peach, and to restore the peace in a fantastical place, called the Mushroom Kingdom. Though it could be said that its universe depicts a Westernized plot with Western-looking characters that differ to the ideas of Japan that many have in mind, many aspects of its world-building are still strange to Western principles of storytelling, like narrative coherence and parallelism to real-life descriptions. For instance, if he is characterized as a plumber, why are his power-ups mushrooms that make him grow or flowers that gift him with fireballs? Why is the information we have about him so scarce?

It would be understandable if cultural specificity is avoided in texts that demand simple storylines and few details in characterization, however, Japanese specificity would appear in other formats, like movies or TV shows, in

---

in magical kingdoms far from any cultural experience. Cases like this could be most of Nintendo's fictional universes like *Pokémon* and particularly those created or co-created by Shigeru Miyamoto like *The Legend of Zelda, Donkey Kong, Star Fox, Kirby* or *Super Mario* proper. For a more detailed discussion see Iwabuchi, *Recentering Globalization* and Iwabuchi, "How Japanese."

[8] Iwabuchi, *Recentering Globalization*, 94.

[9] Iwabuchi, "How Japanese," 58.

which plots have to be filled with more accurate information. Considering Mario as a transmedia phenomenon, exploring the relation between cultural specificity and textual representation would put into the spotlight the question of how certain media platforms would ease the presence of cultural traces.

Therefore, the focus of this article will be to retrieve some aspects of Japanese culture, identified by a series of classical intercultural studies, that might have a relation with deeper aspects of the video game's world-building, on the one hand, and in narratively extended media platforms, on the other. The latter will be integrated by comparing Japanese and American animated versions of the video game in order to track which aspects of the video game have been stressed, which ones have been added to the original, and which ones have been avoided. The corpus to be analyzed will be *Super Mario 3* as an exemplary video game in which Mario's universe proved to be already consolidated, and the aforementioned anime film *Super Mario Bros.: The Great Mission to Rescue Princess Peach!* from Japan and the TV show *The Adventures of Super Mario 3* from the United States.

Before moving deeper into the analysis, it is important to question how Japanese culture is going to be assessed and which criteria are used to differentiate Japanese (or Asian) models from American (or Western) ones.

What is Japaneseness?

To start with, it is important to note that, in this case, Asia and the West appear not merely as qualitatively opposed terms in a semantic category of global icons but most clearly like the title of a celebrated book by intercultural psychologist Richard Nisbett, two different *geographies of thought*.[10] Therefore, their differences should not be taken as cultural determinisms according to which every Asian or Westerner thinks in one way or another, but as underlying trends that might help us to understand complexities beyond superficial clichés.

When speaking of media production, it is difficult to set cultural borderlines between Japan and the United States, to cite just a prototypical token of each term, and it is even harder if that involves so globalized a cultural export like the *Super Mario* franchise. To make things more complicated, Japanese national uniqueness has continuously been emphasized by an intellectual current called *nihonjinron* (literally, "theories/discussions about Japan") that

---

[10] Richard E. Nisbett, *The Geography of Thought: How Asians and Westerners Think and Why* (New York: The Free Press, 2003).

emerged in the miraculous recuperation of the nation after World War II once its society left behind the trauma.

For post-war Japanese society, *nihonjinron* represented what the Russian Tartu-based cultural semiotician Juri Lotman (1922-1993) understood as mechanisms of stabilization of a culture because it worked through meta-descriptions of cultural norms that constituted the basis for creating new texts, stimulating the circulation of existing texts, and forbidding the appearance of texts of a certain kind. It established a canon that, at the same time, was not an objective description of its own culture but one of its competing poles.[11] For this reason, correspondence to values proposed in *nihonjinron* authors cannot be taken as solid criteria to examine the Japanese influence of cultural texts.

I propose, then, three patterns that could be related to the Japanese influence over *Super Mario*'s world-building: (1) the presence of folk figures and contemporary pop culture, (2) a centripetal hierarchy of constituents in the world-building going from an embracing environment to an embedded character, and (3) a tendency to use aesthetics that favor change and passion instead of mimetic representation. The risk of oversimplifying such a cultural tradition in these three patterns is of course big but, as in any cultural description, I consider it should lead us to further discussions.

In order to develop the first pattern, it is important to remember that, as in any cultural export, folktales and ancient myths are sources of contemporary world-building. It is understandable, then, that an authentic Japanese fictional world ought to present patterns from both Shintō and Buddhist traditions. On the other hand, contemporary icons in media culture may contribute to assigning cultural values to a certain world because such portrayals would

---

[11] Juri Lotman, *La Semiosfera I: Semiótica de la cultura y del texto* (Valencia: Frónesis, 1996), 29 and 50. Despite its claim of being a coherent and authentic set of ideas dealing exclusively with Japanese identity, *nihonjinron* is sometimes conceived as a fierce opposition to Western values in Japanese society. As Kosaku Yoshino proposes, *ninhonjinron* is different to other auto-descriptions in the sense that the distinctive element is not 'theirs' but 'ours' in relation to Westerners. Kosaku Yoshino, *Cultural Nationalism in Contemporary Japan* (London: Routledge, 1992), 8. Complementarily, Harumi Befu understands that such reflections of its own culture were needed as a way to fill a 'vacuum' once previous symbols such as the anthem and the flag were avoided as they addressed Imperial Japan. Harumi Befu, *Hegemony of Homogeneity: An Anthropological Analysis of Nihonjinron* (Melbourne: Trans Pacific Press, 2001). In any case, *nihonjinron* proposed a proactive search and discussion of Japanese identity that appear imprinted in texts and social practices and also an auto-conscience, following Lotmanian terms, of Japanese uniqueness.

contribute to the idea of a shared community: a video game about Spiderman, Superman, or Batman would reasonably sound more American than one inspired by Ultraman, Godzilla, or Ōgon Bat that would reveal its Japanese influence because each of them is themed according to its respective popular culture.

Secondly, centripetal models of hierarchy differ from centrifugal ones in which, following Trompenaars and Hampden-Turner's model of cultural differences,[12] the United States among several other Western national cultures are placed. This classic study proposes that while the West prefers individualistic and internally-controlled dimensions, Japan and other Asian cultures tend to stimulate collectivist and externally-controlled dimensions. Therefore, in Asia, conceiving the individual as a member belonging to a given group is more common. This would lead to a cultural *ethos* in which the placement of the subject changes from culture to culture. While in Japan, it tends to be seen just as a part of a wider environment, in America, it is placed in a more protagonistic role that enables the subject to manipulate the surrounding environment by managing the resources at its disposal.

According to Nisbett,[13] this difference emerged as the result of two different kinds of philosophy: ancient Greece as the cradle of the West and Confucius as the ideological father of Asian cultures. At the same time, each school of thought derived from different surviving practices: hunter-gatherer societies in mountainous Greece and agricultural societies on the plains of ancient China. While the latter needed to share and conceive society as a unity, the former stimulated more individual behaviors.

As a result, notable differences in the hierarchical relations among characters, resources, and spaces are expected. We could consider the *Super Mario* series as being "more Japanese" if it presented a schema in which characters are defined by the resources used, resources that similarly depend on the previous space design. On the contrary, Western world-building rules show the prevalence of a heroic biography that sets a series of tools and resources which are thus relevant to a particular context.

This is a cultural difference if we oppose American-like *bio-transformation* and Japanese-like *mecha-transformation*, as shown in a study on cross-cultural

---

[12] Fons Trompenaars and Charles Hampden-Turner, *Riding the Waves of Culture: Understanding Cultural Diversity in Business* (London: N. Brealy, 1997).
[13] Nisbett, *Geography of Thought*, 8-20.

popular heroes.[14] According to this typology, heroes activate bio-transformation if superpowers are already present in their biography and if they derive from an individual characterization that was previously affirmed. In mecha-transformations, on the other hand, superpowers are assigned externally regardless of characters' biographies, and thus subjects get related to them fortuitously: they are an attachment that is activated "mechanically," while in Western storytelling they are enacted "biologically," and everyone who finds one is in a condition to use it. This study analyzes how this difference is textually enacted by Superman and Ultraman, prototypes of the respective Western bio- and Japanese mecha-transformation models.

Another good example of how bio-transformation works in Western storytelling could be Spiderman. The tipping point in Peter Parker's biography is when he gets bitten by a spider because, from that moment on, he gets a series of superpowers derived from biological changes in his organism, and afterward, he discovers that those superpowers gift him with incredible advantages in a city packed with skyscrapers like New York. That is, at some point in the biography of the subject, something happened that bodily affects him/her and provides him/her with a new identity. This new identity is narratively coherent with the brand-new superpowers he/she gets (if he is Spiderman, then they are related to what spiders do) and, finally, mastering these superpowers enable him/her to have proper control of the space, and thus meet his/her duties. It is therefore clear that human agency prevails over the environment in defining how the fictional world is being built.

Differently to this, a Japanese-like centripetal hierarchy of components would assume a logic in which the individual needs to get identified with the group of belonging, and the environment defines individual characteristics. If this structure is organized centrifugally, for instance, with a hero whose biography arranges a series of relations with power-ups, villains, and levels, we can assume that it is more oriented toward Western or American storytelling.

The third pattern is related to how Japanese and American cultures link fictional worlds to real-life experiences. Japanese culture, like Asian ones, tend to present more tolerance for ambiguity[15] with a higher predisposition to

---

[14] Tom Gill, "Transformational Magic: Some Japanese Super-Heroes and Monsters," in *The Worlds of Japanese Popular Culture: Gender, Shifting Boundaries and Global Cultures*, ed. Dolores P. Martinez (Cambridge: Cambridge University Press, 1998), 33-55.

[15] We owe the idea of "tolerance for ambiguity" to Geert Hofstede's cultural dimension theory and, in particular, the dimension called *uncertainty avoidance*. According to Hofstede, the dimension "is related to the level of stress in a society in the face of an

metaphors or, as Edward T. Hall (1914-2009) coined it, they belong to "high-context cultures."[16] In them, less is required to release the message because all the information needed is already shaped through pragmatic implicatures in social interactions, so members can dispense with explicit markers. Consequently, statements tend to be not universal and get meaningless once the reader takes them out of the specific pragmatic situation in which they were produced. Conversely, Western cultures tend to be less dependent on context because written language historically prevailed in them, so utterances are expected to be meaningful in almost any conceived context. Thus, redundancy is considered the key to clarify messages, and this is usually developed through interactions centered on literality and the importance of so-called plain speaking.

This could explain why, in Western tradition, fictional worlds usually rely on a series of concessions that the model reader interprets from the real world.[17] Just to take one mainstream case in Western fiction, the Netflix-produced series *House of Cards* sets the fictitious 2012 presidential elections as the starting point of the plot and avoids explicit mentions of political figures from recent years (mainly from Bill Clinton's administration onward), but it poses its characters and storyline as a continuation of the American political tradition: the main character, Frank Underwood, makes constant references to Ronald Reagan's presidency (1981-1989), and George H. W. Bush's term (1989-1993) is mentioned at least once in Season 3. If the work of the historian begins when

---

unknown future." Geert Hofstede, *Culture's Consequences: Comparing Values, Behaviors, Institutions and Organizations Across Nations* (Thousand Oaks, CA: Sage, 2001), 141. In this case I do not take the concept of Hofstede literally but in some regard similarly: tolerance for ambiguity would show how much a culture can produce figures in an unattached text whose overt meanings are not given by the storyline. In the case of the *Super Mario* series, this would be, for example, why the character is powered-up by strange and disconnected items such as a star, red and green mushrooms, or a fire flower.

[16] Edward T. Hall, *Beyond Culture* (New York: Anchor Books, 1989), 115.

[17] The notion of the model reader derives from Umberto Eco's semiotics. According to Eco, a model reader "*is a textually established set of felicity conditions to be met in order to have a macro-speech act (such as a text is) fully actualized.*" Umberto Eco, *The Role of the Reader: Explorations in the Semiotics of Texts* (Bloomington, IN: Indiana University Press, 1981), 11. In other words, the model reader coincides with the interpretation needed for a given sender to consider that his/her message has been successfully conveyed. In simple messages this does not seem to imply a difficult task, but when speaking on works of arts, literature or, like in this case, intercultural texts, what a reader can interpret from a text can greatly differ to the intentioned interpretation that was once planned.

the past is no longer "inhabited" in the present,[18] we can suggest that, at least in Western world-building, fiction begins when the real is no longer discussed because fictional worlds need agreed perceptions over the historical reality to support its narrative world. Otherwise, we would be exploring specific genres such as alternate history or science-fiction, whose tags prove that they are exceptions in Western tradition. This is why Western storytelling across ages, platforms, and languages has been characterized as being *mimetic*.

According to Western tradition, representations must have a concrete correlate in the empirical world: the painting must resemble the historical figure or landscape depicted, events evoked in the novel have to be plausible in our everyday accounts, the actor on stage ought to show a range of reactions that we can identify from some of our previous experiences, and so on. What ancient Greeks called *mimesis* evolved as a key to understanding the development of Western cultures[19] at the point that the artistic avant-garde movement during the 20th century was motivated to a greater or lesser extent by a desire to contravene such an aesthetic canon. Abstract paintings and Dadaist poetry both reject the role of arts as representations of the natural world.

In that regard, literary criticist Earl Miner (1927-2004) proposed a different term for examining Japanese cultural production, particularly in literature. According to him, being either mimetic or anti-mimetic responds to a debate that is not necessarily adaptable to Asian narrative worlds and, as a result, a more accurate term to define Japanese culture would be "affective-expressive poetics" that, while not necessarily defying a realist perspective, presents different ties with such reality.[20] Affective-expressive aesthetics would be, then,

---

[18] Jan Assmann, *La memoria culturale: Scrittura, ricordo e identità politica nelle grandi civiltà antiche* (Turin: Einaudi, 1997), 44.

[19] Some classic works reviewing the role of mimesis in Western theory and cultural production include Erich Auerbach, *Mimesis: The Representation of Reality in Western Literature* (Princeton, NJ: Princeton University Press, 1953); Walter Benjamin, *The Work of Art in the Age of Mechanical Reproduction* (London: Penguin, 2008); René Girard, *To Double Business Bound: Essays on Literature, Mimesis, and Anthropology* (Baltimore, MD: Johns Hopkins University Press, 1987); Gérard Genette, *Figures II* (Paris: Editions du Seuil, 1969); Ernst H. Gombrich, *Art and Illusion: A Study in the Psychology of Pictorial Representation* (New York: Phaidon Press, 1960); Paul Ricoeur, *Time and Narrative*, vol. 1 (Chicago, IL: Chicago University Press, 1984).

[20] Earl Miner, *Comparative Poetics: An Intercultural Essay on Theories of Literature* (Princeton, NJ: Princeton University Press, 1990), 25.

those that favor changing moods, the display of emotions, and the coexistence of contradicted feelings instead of proportional representations of bodies.

Birth and Evolution of a Global Icon: The Fictional World of Mario

Telling a story through oral traditions, written novels, performing arts, painting, or other techniques that can count on thousands of years of technological, technical, and intertextual developments is not the same as doing the same with syncretic platforms such as video gaming or other device-mediated interactive formats.

The history behind the design of Mario as a character shows us how this style works. Why does Mario wear a cap and a mustache, and why is he stumpy? Following the idea of a character being defined by its biography, we are tempted to say that it is because he was thought of as being an Italian plumber. Many tradesmen wear a cap, and southern Italian immigrants are stereotypically depicted as shorter than the average American with a dense mustache. This was the exact interpretation that audiences had, following the centrifugal model by which characters' bios govern the coherence of the entire narrative world, and then American versions of the storyworld evolved in such a direction.

However, Mario was not originally conceived as such, nor was he called that either. As stated above, his first appearance was in the 1981 arcade game *Donkey Kong*, a title that even excluded Mario from the leading role despite him being the only playable character. Authors like Chris Kohler[21] insist that *Donkey Kong* was a pioneering video game in narrative design because, for the first time, players had to accomplish a series of tasks and challenges while being assisted by a plot whose storyline advanced through cutscenes from one level to the next: Mario (initially called Jumpman) has to rescue his girlfriend Pauline from the monstrous Donkey Kong, who had kidnapped her. This had to be done through a combination of his jumping power and occasional power-ups like a hammer that neutralizes the wooden barrels that the villain threw from above. When Mario reaches the top of the level and the mission is thought to be accomplished, the ape takes Pauline again and climbs to a higher level where the scene is repeated, but where the difficulty is more challenging.

Differently to previous non-plot games limited to mascot characters like *Pac-Man* or proto-narrative ones like *Space Invaders* that posed a conflict without stating further framing, *Donkey Kong* immersed players in a story in which they had to take a position in a given story, they engaged its personal experience in

---

[21] Kohler, *Power Up*, 35-40.

a furnished fictional world, and the players' success can be "translated" into the narrative's happy ending.

Donkey Kong as a game is full of Western influences apart from the obvious resemblance to *King Kong* that brought a lawsuit from DC Universals against Nintendo.[22] Originally, the creator Shigeru Miyamoto wanted to recreate a simplified version of the European folktale *Beauty and the Beast* with the characters of *Popeye the Sailor*: a love triangle between a working-class hero who gets stronger by ingesting a power-up, a passive damsel-in-distress, and a monstrous and clumsy villain,[23] but delays in the negotiations for the rights of use with King Features forced Nintendo to make up a plot and iconography from scratch.

It is interesting to note how technological constraints shaped the creation of this fictional world. A video game based on *Popeye the Sailor* would have provided both Nintendo and players with a known fictional universe but, most importantly, with an easy way to differentiate characters and roles. Beyond who Popeye, Olive, and Bluto might be in popular culture, Nintendo's developers and designers were nonetheless considering their physical appearances and were thinking respectively of an average, a thin and tall, and a large-sized figure. In the early 1980s, shapes were critical for making distinctions among characters, and a three-color palette in an 8-bit design had to be used efficiently.

Thus, the mustache of Mario responds, on a technical level, to the needs for separating nose from mouth but also, on a cultural level, to the tendency in Japanese design to pay attention to facial expressions and movement. Belonging to affective-expressive aesthetics in graphic animation, designers came up with the mustache so as not to have to explain why the character was speaking despite his mouth being closed, a problem that continued to arise in the history of video games for several years.

The hat aimed to solve a similar problem. The hair could theoretically be blue like the mustache, but that did not satisfy a key problem in cinematic design: when the hero falls from a height, how could the hair's movement be represented? A red hat was a suitable solution. Like lip movement, hair movement does not seem to have been a major issue in Western animated design, especially if we consider those technical limitations. Therefore, evaluating whether to prioritize movement or anatomical resemblance can be

---

[22] See Ryan, *How Mario Conquered America*, 33-45 for details.
[23] Sheff, *Game Over*, 47-48.

influenced by a cultural frame. In a culture like the Japanese one that favors movement in design, as happens in manga, it is more likely that those problems are seen as such.

The protagonist was initially called Jumpman because his main functional attribute was to jump, and he was eventually renamed Mario due to funny similarities that Nintendo employees in America found between the character and Mario Segale, the landlord of their local headquarters in Tukwila, Washington.[24] However, Nintendo never promoted its character as being Italian.

In *Donkey Kong*, the character was defined as a carpenter, due to his simple two-colored uniform, and, according to Western patterns, the level was simply known as "Construction site." However, in the 1982 sequel called *Donkey Kong Jr.*, Miyamoto changed the roles around: Mario became the villain, who put the ape in a cage as a punishment for having kidnapped his girlfriend. On this occasion, the playable character is Donkey Kong Junior, and his goal is to free his father. Before securing his own franchise, Mario was presented in a series of occupations, mainly for the rare console Game & Watch: he was a soldier in *Mario's Bomb Away* and a logistics manager in *Mario's Cement Factory*, both released in 1983, and probably a circus manager in the prequel *Donkey Kong Circus*, released in 1984.[25]

Also in 1983, the *Mario Bros.* game was released for arcades as a spin-off of the *Donkey Kong* series. It was not a great success, if we compare it with the subsequent worldwide hit *Super Mario Bros.* that inaugurated platform video games in 1985 with the NES (Nintendo Entertainment System) console. In spite of this, this was the point at which Mario changed his profession from carpenter (or itinerant tradesman, if we consider his less successful appearances) to plumber, because instead of being set on a "construction site," the action from this game onward takes place in an underground scenario where pipelines connect different levels.[26] This account, nonetheless, is never

---

[24] For detailed accounts of Mario's foundational story, see Sheff, *Game Over*, 33-55; Kent, *The Ultimate History*; Ryan, *How Mario Conquered America*, 19-33.

[25] For a careful review of Game & Watch games, see Florent Gorges, *The History of Nintendo*, vol. 2: *1980-1991: The Game & Watch Games, An Amazing Invention* (Madrid: Pixn Love, 2012).

[26] For more discussion on the subject, see Kohler, *Power Up*, 56; Ryan, *How Mario Conquered America*, 48; Sheff, *Game Over*, 50; Bob Chipman, *SMB3: Brick by Brick* (Tucson, AZ: Fangamer, 2013), 15.

clearly stated in cutscenes[27] or external *paratexts*,[28] such as users' manuals or official press releases.

Examining primary sources for this game, the closest reference to a profession I found is in the storyline summary provided in Atari's version of the user manual: "Mario the carpenter and his brother Luigi are hopping mad! The water pipes in their house are blocked with nests of crawling creatures. If the two brothers can't get rid of them, they'll never take a bath again!"[29]

The question of whether Nintendo, Atari, or any other authorized voice is in a better or worse condition to assign or change the profession of a fictional character goes beyond this discussion. From the mid-1990s until 2017, Miyamoto repeatedly insisted that he created Mario as a plumber, but there is no textual evidence in the video games as core works to prove such a characterization. Apart from crossovers that portray Mario playing sports, such as *Mario Tennis* or *Super Mario Kart*, in the following games' descriptions, I found not a single word about Mario's real occupation.

Mario remained in popular culture as a plumber because of a series of implicit markers, all of them related to the scenario in which he performs. He could have remained as a carpenter, as Atari stated, or as a banker who wants to retrieve his coins once they went down the sewer, or as a jobless daydreamer who is in eternal love with a girl who does not return his feelings. Behind this feature of popular culture resides an overt attempt to give the hero the capacity of managing and controlling the place in which he performs. In other words, it is easier for Western audiences to imagine that the character performs underground, for such is his daily routine, rather than imagining that the video

---

[27] In video gaming language, cutscenes are considered the parts of a video game in which the player, instead of controlling the evolution of the plot, is receiving instructions from the game, either operational or narrative. For authors like Rune Klevjer, cutscenes are a key narrative device in video game design because they enable the progression of a story without cutting off gameplay. Rune Klevjer, "In Defense of Cutscenes," in *Proceedings of Computer Games and Digital Cultures Conference*, ed. Frans Mäyrä (Tampere: Tampere University Press, 2002), 192-195.

[28] In Literary Studies, a paratext is "the means by which a text makes a book of itself and proposes itself as such to its readers, and more generally to the public." Clear cases of paratexts are titles, subtitles, descriptions, and any text whose main objective is to clarify the content of another text, considered the main work. Gérard Genette and Mary Maclean "Introduction to the Paratext," *New Literary History* 22, no. 2 (1991): 261.

[29] Atari, *Mario Bros.*, accessed September 2, 2020, https://atariage.com/manual_html_page.php?SoftwareLabelID=1047.

game is proposing a situation that is not representative (thus, mimetic) of his everyday life.

Japanese audiences probably do not demand that fictional characters have a "real" job, nor biographical data prone to be compared with ours. Thus, regardless of the job selected, such a necessity is identified as a Western contribution to the narrative world, while the lack of congruent answers that satisfy that requirement could be related to a Japanese pattern. Indeed, historically, Nintendo has been very careful in "deepening" the fictional world and disclosing biographical data. Mario became the official corporate mascot to the extent of voiding or "hiding" (to the Western eye) mimetic aspects of his characterization. This enabled Mario to narratively perform in a wide series of contexts outside of the *Super Mario* series: he can be hero or antagonist, he can be a race driver, a tennis player, or a doctor, and he can compete with or physically fight against those who help him or whom he has to rescue.

For the 1996 launch of *Super Mario 64* as part of the breakthrough Nintendo 64 console, Nintendo hired actor Charles Martinet to voice Mario. How Mario would effectively sound was a big issue because it was on this occasion that his classic Italian accent was finally imprinted in the character's expression. Following the idea of *mukokuseki* discussed above, this feature reinforced the lack of a Japanese flavor to the character in favor of an Italian one. But despite this suggestive trait, Nintendo never promoted Mario as an icon of Italianness. Indeed, in a 2016 interview, Shigeru Miyamoto stated that aging Mario between 24 and 25 was the only definition they made for the character so he could get older in later versions of the game, a trait that stresses the lack of interest in representing the character mimetically.[30] In 2017, Nintendo officially announced that Mario's occupation was no longer that of a plumber but that he was all-round "sporty, whether it's tennis or baseball, soccer or car racing."[31]

The use of Mario's fictional universe as a wildcard is a constant in Nintendo's recent history, like probably any other multinational would do with such a globalized icon in popular culture. We could believe that this empties the

---

[30] Andrew Griffin, "Mario is Only 24 Years Old, Creator Shigeru Miyamoto Says in Unearthed Interview," *The Independent*, September 30, 2016, https://www.independent.co.uk/life-style/gadgets-and-tech/gaming/mario-super-age-24-25-nintendo-shigeru-miyamoto-game-character-a7338911.html.

[31] Andrew Griffin, "Mario Is No Longer a Plumber, Nintendo Officialy Says," *The Independent*, September 4, 2017, https://www.independent.co.uk/life-style/gadgets-and-tech/gaming/mario-nintendo-super-bros-luigi-japanese-language-profile-character-donkey-kong-a7928486.html.

fictional world of a core of cultural belonging, but I propose to examine some features of the video game in the light of the three patterns discussed above.

Looking for Japanese Influences in Video Game World-Building

The *Super Mario* series presents some references to Japanese folk tradition, particularly in *Super Mario 3*. Independently from discussing if shiitake or maitake inspired red and green mushrooms or Princess Toadstool resembles fairytale princesses, the clearest example of Japanese oral tradition sourced in *Super Mario* can be seen in the Tanooki Suit, an uncommon power-up that appeared exclusively in *Super Mario Bros. 3*. This power-up works once Mario gets a leaf that enables him to shape-shift into a stone statue, and he becomes immune to surrounding enemy creatures. Tanukis, an autochthonous animal similar to raccoons, according to Japanese mythology, have mastered the power of shift-shaping and are a recurrent trait both of local culture as figures in front of houses and of media culture, for example, in the 1994 anime film *Pom Poko* (Dir: Isao Takahata) or the 2005 live-action film *Princess Raccoon* (Dir: Seijun Suzuki.)

Other influences include the presence of mythological *kappa*, which are long-haired water spirits resembling turtles known for drowning people, especially children.[32] Based on how Japanese pictorial traditions envision them, they may have inspired the enemies known as Koopa Troopas in all *Super Mario* games. The main antagonist Koopa and his offspring, the Koopalings, might be sourced from both *kappas* and *onis*, the latter being, according to Buddhist legends, big-mouthed monsters or devils with horns and sharp nails.[33] Despite Koopa's resemblance and the fact it spits fire, bringing it closer to a dragon, Nintendo's official user manual in premiering *Super Mario Bros.* for NES in 1985 identifies the Koopa as "a tribe of turtles famous for their black magic."[34]

In other marginal roles, we can identify minor characters like Thwomp, an animated living stone that debuted as an opponent in *Super Mario Bros. 3* and whose role is to block Mario's route mainly in Koopa's Castles, as a version of Nurikabe, an invisible wall blocking the road of pilgrims and travelers causing them delay in their journeys, according to Japanese legends and folk beliefs.[35] Other creatures in the Castles such as Roto-discs (fireballs), fire-snakes, or

---

[32] Jeremy Roberts, *Japanese Mythology A to Z* (New York: Chelsea House, 2010), 67.
[33] Ibid., 92.
[34] Nintendo, *Super Mario Bros. User Guide for NES* (Tukwila, WA: Nintendo, 1985).
[35] Roberts, *Japanese Mythology*, 90.

ghosts like Boo can be assimilable to mythological figures like *oni-bis* and *hi-no-tamas*, fire demons that emerge at midnight representing suffering spirits.[36]

In brief, Japanese folklore has made its way into and plays a modest role in *Super Mario*'s world-building, but we can affirm that it is not central or constitutive to understanding the narrative. Shigeru Miyamoto himself valued the Tanooki Suit as the main novelty in *Super Mario 3*, although he was fully conscious that it would not make any sense to non-Japanese gamers.[37] That could prove that the rest of its fictional world dispenses greatly with Japanese mythology.

Regarding Japanese popular culture, it is difficult to find icons of contemporary local mediascapes in *Super Mario*'s world-building. The characters' names do not sound Japanese apart from the fact that "Luigi" in Japanese is homonymic with "ruiji," which means "similar." Perhaps Princess Toadstool (called Peach in Japanese and in later versions) would address the importance that this color has in contemporary Japanese pop aesthetics regarding feminine characters like in *Cardcaptor Sakura* or *Sailor Moon* or even in some devices of *kawaii* aesthetics.[38] However, fictional universes developed in the Japanese video game industry like *Pokémon* or *Kirby* provide better displays of *kawaii* and, besides, the reference to 'Peach' for the Princess could also have been motivated by other mythological accounts such as that of Momotarō, a hero who comes to Earth as a baby inside a giant peach to become the son of a childless couple.

What the *Super Mario* series and Japanese popular culture might share is a trait that goes beyond iconography. Regarding J-pop idols, Hiroshi Aoyagi affirms that Japanese audiences tend to look for *toshindai* ("life-sized") heroes, unlike Western idols who highlight their differences with their fans. He supports his thesis in a study that points out that

---

[36] See Lafcadio Hearn, *Kwaidan: Ghost Stories* (Mineola, NY: Dover, 2006), 3-15 and 19-24 for folk stories, and Laurence C. Bush, *Asian Horror Encyclopedia: Asian Horror Culture in Literature, Manga, and Folklore* (New York: Writers Club Press, 2001), 36 and 69 for descriptions.

[37] Shigeru Miyamoto, Koji Kondo and Takashi Tezuka, *Super Mario History: 25th Anniversary Booklet* (Tukwila, WA: Nintendo, 2010), 13.

[38] For a better understanding about the importance of kawaii aesthetics in contemporary Japan, see Sharon Kinsella, "Cuties in Japan," in *Women, Media and Consumption in Japan*, ed. Lise Skov and Brian Moeran (Surrey: Curzon, 1995), 220-254.

most stars in Western countries are popular because of their outstanding physical or personal attributes. Japanese idols, on the other hand, typically depict images that are "fairly standard." Their appearance and ability are above average, yet not so much so as to alienate or offend the audience – just enough to provide their fans with the sense that they too can be stars if they try hard enough.[39]

Belonging to a fictional world, it is not easy to assert that Mario properly fits into the category of "idol," but he at least follows this pattern. Nothing extraordinary is present in his biography; he is thought of as being an *ossan*,[40] a regular middle-aged man, and the emptiness that Nintendo left in his characterization is probably aimed to make him usable in different contexts. Some voices, both from video game studies[41] and from industry,[42] even argue that the main role in *Super Mario's* narrative has to be ascribed to the player, not to the character, which is secondary. And we all know that Western tradition has also historically emphasized the role of "mesocratic" or low-profiled heroes/idols, from King David to the American Dream. But in this case, Mario does not even have a moral virtue that justifies his goals because there are no psychological ties between Mario's characterization and the assigned mission. In the guidelines to *Super Mario Bros.* (1985), it is stated that "Mario, the hero of the story (maybe) hears about the Mushroom's Kingdom plight and sets out on a quest to free the Mushroom Princess."[43] In *Super Mario Bros. 2* (1988), Mario is surprised by a strange nightmare becoming real during a picnic with friends. In *Super Mario Bros. 3* (1990), Mario and Luigi must recover the royal magic wands stolen by Koopa's offspring.[44]

Mario, as *toshindai*, may respond to the fact that video games portray the protagonist following a centripetal hierarchy, that is, he is being governed by the environment instead of him being the one who rules and manages it. None of the power-ups nor the Mushroom Kingdom or the Mushroom World or

---

[39] Hiroshi Aoyagi, "Pop Idols and the Asian Identity," in *Japan Pop! Inside the World of Japanese Pop Culture*, ed. Timothy J. Craig (Armonk: M. E. Sharpe, 2000), 311.

[40] Ryan affirms that, before the character became known as Mario, one of the possibilities discussed was Ossan because he represented an average middle-aged man. Ryan, *How Mario Conquered America*, 24.

[41] Newman, "In Search of the Video Game Player," 412-414.

[42] Gonzalo Frasca, "Play the Message: Play, Game and Videogame Rhetoric" (PhD diss., IT Copenhagen University, 2007), 95.

[43] Nintendo, *Super Mario Bros*, 2.

[44] Nintendo, *Super Mario Bros. 3: User Guide for NES* (Tukwila, WA: Nintendo, 1990), 5.

several other scenarios are thematically related to his biography. On the contrary, the video game profits from what media scholar Henry Jenkins, among others, conceived as the more important aspect of video game design: the design of spaces.[45] Indeed, the author pointed out that *Super Mario* games were fundamentally a series that aimed the player to project their experiences as if they were a traveler.[46]

The player has a limited capacity to manage and store power-ups because they are mainly located in levels that are thematically associated with the hidden power-up. The clearest case is the Frog Suit, placed in underwater levels in order to swim faster, but also in *Super Mario World* (1990), flying feathers are frequent in air scenarios. In *Super Mario Bros. 3*, the Tanooki Suit appears in instances in which evading opponents is harder. The architecture and gameplay of the space define a series of relevant power-ups, the ones that, at the same time, mecha-transform Mario from the outside. Mario becomes Fire Mario when using a fire flower, Frog Mario, when dressed in the Frog Suit, Tanooki Mario when using this suit, and so on. Power-ups are not presented in the video games as mere auxiliary devices but as magic elements capable of changing the character both in his appearance and functionality. In other words, the hero is not an independent agent who controls his superpowers, but the result of what those superpowers have provoked in him.

Complementarily, this brings Mario's fictional universe closer to the Japanese tradition: characters do not act alone but are presented as part of larger collectivities mainly grouped according to family ties. Mario and Luigi are brothers, Koopa is the father of the Koopalings, the King of Mushroom Kingdom is the father of Princess Peach, and many other minor opponents or enemies along the way are also presented as members of a specified family: brothers include Hammers, Boomerangs, and Sledges, while Bloober, an underwater jellyfish, is always escorted by its offspring. Personal identity seems to be relieved by collective identity.

An interesting fact to observe is how Mario connects to the main conflict of the storytelling. Western world-building tends to present an initial situation in which the hero's daily routine is mimetic to ours. They have a job, a residence,

---

[45] For a general argumentation on this topic, see Henry Jenkins, "Games as Gendered Playspace," in *From Barbie to Mortal Kombat: Gender and Computer Games*, ed. Justine Cassell and Henry Jenkins (Cambridge, MA: MIT Press, 1998), 262-297.

[46] Fuller and Jenkins, "Nintendo(R)," 60; Henry Jenkins "Game Design as Architecture," in *First Person: New Media as Story, Performance and Games*, ed. Noah Wardruip-Fuin and Pat Harrigan (Cambridge, MA: MIT Press, 2004), 121.

a series of motivations, an entire lifestyle before becoming heroes, and the way in which those characters become the protagonist is narratively told through different modes to connect to the main conflict of the plot, that is, a narrative shackle that links their pre-heroic life with the aftermath: as mentioned before, Peter Parker gets bitten by a spider and then becomes Spiderman, but also Bruce Wayne is traumatized after the death of his parents and then becomes Batman to fight against crime occurring during the night, and so on. This is missing in *Super Mario*, at least in the core works such as the video games. We do not really know what calls him into the action, and that is a typical display of affective-expressive aesthetics because, on the other hand, the video games show us he feels pain, excitement, suffering, illusion, and delusion (the iconic phrase after conquering an intermediate castle sums it up perfectly: "Thank you Mario! But our Princess is in another castle!"). It would seem that Nintendo never really cared about anatomically proportionated sizes or other mimetic representations: Mario and Luigi's sketches were identical except for their color until *Super Mario 64* (1996), although technological progress enabled the company to differentiate both characters long before.

Contributions from Transmedia Outputs:
Japanese and American Animated Versions

Video gaming was a limited platform to freely develop storylines and expand fictional universes when *Super Mario* was born as a successful franchise in the mid-1980s. Consoles and video games were mainly targeted at child audiences, a reason why several other media, licensed or not, used the fictional universe of *Super Mario* and, logically, made their contributions. By watching TV series, films, animated fiction, comic books, and even puppet performances based on the universe, audiences were told different angles of the story in ways that video games could not.[47] Some media producers and particularly distributors understood perfectly that they needed to create such products to get children engaged with the universe so that gaming could become a more pleasant experience for them.

How these "empty spaces" were filled is a matter of higher cultural variability because their consumption was more limited to local audiences and, in this direction, I will explore some contrasts that a Japanese and an American version present. They belong to the same expressive language (animated

---

[47] For a careful review of this topic, see Marsha Kinder, *Playing with Power in Movies, Television and Video Games* (Los Angeles, CA: University of California Press, 1991).

fiction) and were released at a similar time (1986 and 1990), although the former is a feature film and the latter a television series.

Super Mario Bros.: The Great Mission to Rescue Princess Peach!, an animated film, greatly mirrors the plot from the original video game: both Mario and Luigi have to rescue the kidnapped Princess Peach, who is trapped in the heights of a castle by Koopa, and doing so implies a long journey through different lands, as shown in the video game. The film tries to respect, then, the main task presented in the game: a spatial challenge endured in the remote location where the kidnapped Princess is placed. It also follows the centripetal model in which the environment is the main priority in the process of design and world-building. Accordingly, power-ups are "hidden" in different locations, and its action is functionally the same as in the video games. In the animated film, when Mario ingests a red mushroom, he grows to a disproportionate size, echoing what happens in the video games but breaking any Western aspiration of anatomical representation.

In this animated film, mythological accounts fit better with visual representations. Villain assistants, identified as turtle-like Koopa Troopas in the game, are drawn as *kappas* with monk-style haircuts. On the other hand, the storyline enables a transformation that is not suggested in the video game: Mario and Luigi are escorted by a light blue dog called Kibidango (named after a Japanese snack) along the way, and when they have accomplished their mission and rescued the Princess, the dog turned out to be a prince destined to marry her. The Princess's father is called Kinoko, like a common figure in Japanese mythology, and is depicted as a hermit whose magic gifts the characters with valuable resources, mirroring video game power-ups like the mushrooms, the fire flower, the star, and the coins. The latter are narratively introduced as economic rewards for Mario and Luigi in case they free the Princess.

Feelings play a huge role in the storyline at the expense of mimetic or realistic representations, and the affective-expressive perspective distinguishes Mario and Luigi: while Mario, in love with the Princess, follows a sentimental motivation, Luigi is enthusiastic about the economic reward. The villain also shows strong affective motivations: Koopa kidnapped the Princess because he wants to marry her and is apparently truly in love, which is why he wants to gain her affection, a characterization that radically differs from the tyrant mood with which he is usually depicted.

On the other hand, relations with the "real world" are blurred and disconnected. As in the game, pipelines serve as the entrance gate to the Mushroom Kingdom, but they are reached not as a result of Mario or Luigi's professional mastery (their skills are irrelevant to the assigned task since they actually manage a grocery store) but by following Kibidango to the outskirts of the city.

The selected American animated fiction, *The Adventures of Super Mario Bros. 3*, is a 26-episode television series whose average duration is 22 minutes each. It explores worlds and scenarios from the eponymous video game and displays the same characters and resources. However, it is noticeable that the most recurrent power-ups were almost displaced by other resources absent in the video game. Mario and Luigi are basically depicted as skilled plumbers whose preferred tools are plungers and wrenches. It is their professional expertise and their ease with warp tunnels that enable them to solve the conflicts in different episodes. They even have a meta-narrative hero called "The Mighty Plumber." The series offers different pathways by which the heroes engage with the Mushroom Kingdom, such as the one that is told in Episode 8 ("Toddler Terrors of Time Travel"): Mario and Luigi, then living in New York, were called to fix a blocked pipe in a domestic bathtub and, after accidentally falling in it, they ended up in the Mushroom Kingdom.

Ties between the fantasy world and the "real world" in fiction are stronger in the American version than in the Japanese one. The "real world" is frequently referred to as such, and many of its features are faithfully represented in the fictional universe. Apart from previously having lived in Brooklyn, the Mario brothers discovered in Episode 25 ("The Venice Menace") that their ancestors were the "Mario Polo" brothers who brought plumbing to Venice from China, among other clichés on Italianness. In Episode 22 ("7 Continents for 7 Koopas"), the main antagonist plans to conquer the so-called real world by assigning the conquest of each continent to a different son or daughter. While asking them to do so, he commissioned each of them with a special task related to the continent ascribed to them: "you're going to East Asia, bring me chop suey," "you're going to Australia ..., bring me a kangaroo" or "be wild in Africa." In Episode 7 ("Stormy Reign"), Mario and Luigi are in charge of the Mushroom Kingdom as Princess Toadstool is on vacation in Hawaii. In Episode 9 ("Dadzilla"), two sons of Koopa get to know about Godzilla and go to Hollywood to meet their "authentic" father.

These relations show a series of requirements for verisimilitude that are typical of Western narrative worlds. No matter how unreal and surrealist a fictional world might sound, creators need to insert a double-degreed movement by which characters connect with the fictional world as if their previous life were like ours. This mimetic pattern is enacted in *Super Mario*'s

American series like in *Alice in Wonderland*: through a warp tunnel that connects both worlds.

A remarkable innovation of this series is in the characters' motivations. If the Japanese version offered a sentimental Mario who accepts the challenge because he is in love with the Princess, this time, the characters are fueled by a sense of justice and political legitimacy. Naturally, Mario and Luigi are kind and hold friendly relations with the Princess and Toad but, most importantly, their interest is institutional: they protect the Princess because she is the fairest ruler of the Mushroom Kingdom. The main conflict does not mirror the storyline of the video game because the logic of episodic narrative arcs demands new plots and dramatic events. But, differently to what can be expected, the villain's evil is focused on the democratic system rather than on actual subjects, both in the fantasy world and in the real world. Episode 5 ("Princess Toadstool for President") is themed on a political campaign where Koopa tries to get power in the Kingdom through suffrage while Episode 2 ("Reptiles in the Rose Garden") unfolds the story of Koopa stealing the White House in order to crown his daughter as Empress of America. The mission of the Mario brothers this time is to rescue the Presidential couple who incidentally resemble Barbara and George H. W. Bush. This kind of mimetic representation differs greatly from the affective-expressive poetics shown in the Japanese version.

Conclusions

In this chapter, I crossed two perspectives of *Super Mario*'s narrative universe in order to catch its complexity in different domains. On the one hand, it was shown how the world-building from the video game was adapted in other media and how this process of intersemiotic translation, on the other hand, was done following some cultural insights.

It was expected that each transmedia extension would reinforce aspects from the cultural background to which it belonged. What is interesting to note in this case study is how a technical language such as video game design that was creatively restricted in its first years imprinted patterns from Japanese culture and how this universe was enriched differently in two different media cultures. Firstly, the design of the subsequent video games itself contained some traits of aesthetic-expressive poetics, like the display of emotions over the demand for representing anatomically correct characters. Secondly, *Super Mario*'s universe presents metaphors and a degree of ambiguity that are central to the world-building, which therefore have to be assimilated and explained via other narrative devices when adapted to other storytelling platforms like animated film. Thirdly, the presence of Japanese folk tradition is present, albeit slightly, in some isolated power-ups and characters and, most importantly, it could be reinforced when adapted to other media, like the case of *kappas* in the Japanese animated film.

The strategies implemented by the Japanese and the American animated versions on how to adapt the relations between characters, resources, and levels in the fictional world varied significantly, and they could be taken as proof of how each culture understands the hierarchy of those elements. Considering the video game initially respected a hierarchy ruled by the scenario, the Japanese anime reinforces the structuring role of the space while the American TV series stresses the agency of the characters.

As a final remark, I hope this essay will contribute to the development of further methodologies to combine intercultural studies and transmedia theory, considering that no media should be taken apart from its cultural context of creation and reception.

Works Cited

Aoyagi, Hiroshi. "Pop Idols and the Asian Identity." In *Japan Pop! Inside the World of Japanese Pop Culture*, edited by Timothy J. Craig, 309-326. Armonk: M. E. Sharpe, 2000.

Assmann, Jan. *La memoria culturale: Scrittura, ricordo e identità politica nelle grandi civiltà antiche.* Turin: Einaudi, 1997.

Atari. *Mario Bros.* Accessed September 2, 2020. https://atariage.com/manual_html_page.php?SoftwareLabelID=1047.

Auerbach, Erich. *Mimesis: The Representation of Reality in Western Literature.* Princeton, NJ: Princeton University Press, 1953.

Befu, Harumi. *Hegemony of Homogeneity: An Anthropological Analysis of Nihonjinron.* Melbourne: Trans Pacific Press, 2001.

Benjamin, Walter. *The Work of Art in the Age of Mechanical Reproduction.* London: Penguin, 2008.

Boronat, Manuel Garín. *El gag visual: De Buster Keaton a Super Mario.* Madrid: Cátedra, 2014.

Bush, Laurence C. *Asian Horror Encyclopedia: Asian Horror Culture in Literature, Manga, and Folklore.* New York: Writers Club Press, 2001.

Chipman, Bob. *SMB3: Brick by Brick.* Tucson, AZ: Fangamer, 2013.

Eco, Umberto. *The Role of the Reader: Explorations in the Semiotics of Texts.* Bloomington, IN: Indiana University Press, 1981.

Frasca, Gonzalo. "Play the Message: Play, Game and Videogame Rhetoric." PhD diss., IT Copenhagen University, 2007.

Fuller, Mary and Henry Jenkins. "Nintendo(R) and New World Travel Writing: A Dialogue." In *Cybersociety: Computer-Mediated Communication and Community*, edited by Steven G. Jones, 57-72. Thousand Oaks, CA: Sage, 1995.

Genette, Gérard, *Figures II.* Paris: Editions du Seuil, 1969.

Genette, Gérard, and Mary Maclean, "Introduction to the Paratext." *New Literary History* 22, no. 2 (1991): 261-271.

Gill, Tom. "Transformational Magic: Some Japanese Super-Heroes and Monsters." In *The Worlds of Japanese Popular Culture: Gender, Shifting Boundaries and Global Cultures,* edited by Dolores P. Martinez, 33-55. Cambridge: Cambridge University Press, 1998.

Girard, René. *To Double Business Bound: Essays on Literature, Mimesis, and Anthropology.* Baltimore, MD: Johns Hopkins University Press, 1987.

Gombrich, Ernst H. *Art and Illusion: A Study in the Psychology of Pictorial Representation.* New York: Phaidon Press, 1960.

Gorges, Florent. *The History of Nintendo,* vol. 2: *1980-1991: The Game & Watch Games, An Amazing Invention.* Madrid: Pixn Love, 2012.

Griffin, Andrew. "Mario is Only 24 Years Old, Creator Shigeru Miyamoto Says in Unearthed Interview." *The Independent,* September 30, 2016. https://www.independent.co.uk/life-style/gadgets-and-tech/gaming/mario -super-age-24-25-nintendo-shigeru-miyamoto-game-character- a7338911.html.

———. "Mario Is No Longer a Plumber, Nintendo Officially Says." *The Independent,* September 4, 2017. https://www.independent.co.uk/life-style/gadgets-and-tech/gaming/mario -nintendo-super-bros-luigi-japanese-language-profile-character-donkey- kong-a7928486.html.

Hall, Edward T. *Beyond Culture.* New York: Anchor Books, 1989.

Hansen, Dustin. *Game On! Video Game History from Pong and Pac-Man to Mario, Minecraft, and More.* New York: Feiwel and Friends, 2016.

Hearn, Lafcadio. *Kwaidan: Ghost Stories.* Mineola, NY: Dover, 2006.

Hofstede, Geert H. *Culture's Consequences: Comparing Values, Behaviors, Institutions and Organizations Across Nations.* Thousand Oaks, CA: Sage, 2001.

Iwabuchi, Koichi. *Recentering Globalization: Popular Culture and Japanese Transnationalism,* Durham, NC: Duke University Press, 2002.

———. "How Japanese is Pikachu?" In *Pikachu's Global Adventure,* edited by Joseph Tobin, 53-79. Durham, NC: Duke University Press, 2010.

Jenkins, Henry. "Games as Gendered Playspace." In *From Barbie to Mortal Kombat: Gender and Computer Games,* edited by Justine Cassell and Henry Jenkins, 262-297. Cambridge, MA: MIT Press, 1998.

———. "Game Design as Architecture." In *First Person: New Media as Story, Performance and Games,* edited by Noah Wardruip-Fuin and Pat Harrigan, 118-130. Cambridge, MA: MIT Press, 2004.

Juul, Jesper. *Half-Real: Video Games between Real Rules and Fictional Worlds.* Cambridge, MA: MIT Press, 2005.

Kent, Steven L. *The Ultimate History of Video Games: From Pong to Pokémon and Beyond.* New York: Three Rivers Press, 2001.

Kinder, Marsha. *Playing with Power in Movies, Television and Video Games*. Los Angeles, CA: University of California Press, 1991.

Kinsella, Sharon. "Cuties in Japan." In *Women, Media and Consumption in Japan*, edited by Lise Skov and Brian Moeran, 220-254. Surrey: Curzon, 1995.

Klevjer, Rune. "In Defense of Cutscenes." In *Proceedings of Computer Games and Digital Cultures Conference*, edited by Frans Mäyrä, 191-202. Tampere: Tampere University Press, 2002.

Kohler, Chris. *Power Up: How Japanese Video Games Gave the World an Extra Life*. Indianapolis, IN: Brady Games, 2005.

Loguidice, Bill, and Matt Barton. *Vintage Games: An Insider Look at the History of Grand Theft Auto, Super Mario, and the Most Influential Games of All Time*, Oxford: Focal Press, 2009.

Lotman, Juri. *La Semiosfera I. Semiótica de la cultura y del texto*. Valencia: Frónesis, 1996.

Miner, Earl. *Comparative Poetics: An Intercultural Essay on Theories of Literature*. Princeton, NJ: Princeton University Press, 1990.

Miyamoto, Shigeru, Koji Kondo, and Takashi Tezuka. *Super Mario History: 25th Anniversary Booklet*. Tukwila, WA: Nintendo, 2010.

Newman, James. "In Search of the Video Game Player: The Lives of Mario." *New Media & Society* 4, no. 3 (2002): 405-422.

Nintendo. *Super Mario Bros. User Guide for NES*. Tukwila, WA: Nintendo, 1985.

———. *Super Mario Bros. 3: User Guide for NES*. Tukwila, WA: Nintendo, 1990.

Nisbett, Richard E. *The Geography of Thought: How Asians and Westerners Think and Why*. New York: The Free Press, 2003.

Picard, Martin. "Video Games and Their Relationship with Other Media." In *The Video Game Explosion: A History from PONG to PlayStation and Beyond*, edited by Mark J. P. Wolf, 293-301. Westport, CT: Greenwood Press, 2008.

Ricoeur, Paul. *Time and Narrative*, vol. 1. Chicago, IL: Chicago University Press, 1984.

Roberts, Jeremy. *Japanese Mythology A to Z*. New York: Chelsea House, 2010.

Ryan, Jeff. *How Mario Conquered America*. London: Portfolio/Penguin, 2011.

Sheff, David. *Game Over: Press Start to Continue – The Maturing of Mario*. Wilton, CT: Games Press, 1999.

Stanton, Richard. *A Brief History of Video Games: From Atari to Virtual Reality*. London: Robinson, 2015.

Trompenaars, Fons, and Charles Hampden-Turner. *Riding the Waves of Culture: Understanding Cultural Diversity in Business*. London: N. Brealy, 1997.

Yoshino, Kosaku. *Cultural Nationalism in Contemporary Japan*. London: Routledge, 1992.

Contributors

Giacomo Calorio is adjunct professor at the universities of Turin and Bergamo, Italy.

Gianmarco Thierry Giuliana is a PhD student at the University of Turin, Italy.

Remo Gramigna is a Post-Doc reseracher at the University of Turin, Italy.

Frank Jacob is Professor of Global History at Nord University, Norway.

Juan Manuel Montoro studied at the Catholic University of Uruguay and is currently pursuing a Master's Degree in Semiotics at the University of Bologna, Italy.

Bruno Surace is a Post-Doc researcher at the University of Turin, Italy.

Mattia Thibault is a Post-Doc researcher at Tampere University, Finland.

Index